MAKING DAY CARE BETTER
Training, Evaluation, and the Process of Change

MAKING DAY CARE BETTER

Training, Evaluation, and the Process of Change

201738936

Edited by

JAMES T. GREENMAN

Glendale Child Development Center

ROBERT W. FUQUA

Iowa State University

TEACHERS COLLEGE PRESS

Teachers College, Columbia University
New York and London 1984

Published by Teachers College Press, 1234 Amsterdam Avenue,
New York, N.Y. 10027

Library of Congress Cataloging in Publication Data

Main entry under title:

Making day care better.

  (Early childhood education series)
  Bibliography: p.
  Includes index.
  1. Day care centers — Addresses, essays, lectures.
2. Day care centers — Evaluation — Addresses, essays,
lectures. I. Greenman, James T., 1949–
II. Fuqua, Robert W., 1942–   III. Series.
HV851.M34 1984   362.7'12   83-18261

ISBN 0-8077-2750-4 (pbk.)

Manufactured in the United States of America

89 88 87 86 85 84   1 2 3 4 5 6

CONTENTS

PREFACE

The irony of change is that it increases the importance
of understanding the status quo (Lortie 1973, 478).

Daily, hundreds of thousands of women and a small number of men
struggle with the responsibility of caring for millions of children in
day care homes and centers. Many wrestle alone with minimal resources, precarious funding, inadequate training, and the feelings that
accompany low pay and lack of recognition for a job that is complex
and demanding. Children experience the outcomes of these lonely
struggles. Many children are in settings providing excellent care. Many
are not. In the last decade the rapid growth of day care services has
given rise to an increase in day care training, regulation, and support services. As the vision of a nationally coordinated comprehensive child care system fades, supporting institutions will need to assume
an increasingly important role helping child care providers obtain
greater expertise and more resources to perform their jobs. However,
it is probable that day care providers themselves (directors, board
members, owners, caregivers, and provider associations), using whatever resources they can beg or borrow, will still bear the main burden
of putting together their own staff and program development efforts.
This volume is intended for change agents in any of the aforemen-
tioned roles. *Making Day Care Better: Training, Evaluation, and the Process of Change* is for advocates, professionals, and students interested
in improving day care.

THE COMPLEXITY OF CHANGE

This book was prompted by our involvement with day care training, consultation, research, and teacher preparation. It dawned on
us (surprisingly slowly) that actually producing positive change is very
difficult. Offering courses or workshops, developing manuals, spon-

vii

soring conferences, or even providing additional equipment to homes and centers does not necessarily change the actual experiences of the children and parents in day care, however well received these efforts might be. The hardest-learned lesson is that change rarely occurs by simply providing new knowledge or good ideas. This problem is certainly not limited to day care. The profusion of self-help books and programs testifies to the widespread belief that dramatic change of all kinds is largely a matter of discovering the right knowledge or formula. Knowing how we should change, even wanting to change and knowing that change will ultimately make our lives easier, does not automatically result in change. This is not always a consequence of weakness, or laziness, or a lack of intelligence. We behave the way we do in response to a complex interweaving of internal and external forces. Institutions, naturally enough, are even more complex. The status quo is the status quo for compelling — if not sensible — reasons.

Professionals and advocates in key roles can be effective agents of change but should be under no illusion about the ease of the process. In day care, as in other social institutions, despite our best efforts, the more things change, the more they stay the same. Impatience, fueled by pressure for early tangible results from funding sources or our own eagerness to prove the effectiveness of our "new, improved" theory or training model, often leads to disappointment and a reinforced status quo.

Due to the complexity of the organizational processes in day care and their varied influences upon the children and adults, we believe an ecological perspective (cf. Bronfenbrenner 1979) is necessary to an understanding of how to improve day care. This perspective requires that we not only examine day care today, but that we also look at where it has come from and the prospects for the future. In addition to the children in day care, the influences and effects upon adults need to be considered. For example, What does the job of doing day care involve? What demands are placed upon caregivers? What demands are placed upon parents? What sorts of relationship are fostered among staff, the children that they care for, and parents?

To properly understand the processes of day care, we must go beyond examining the people within day care and the particular setting within which they work. We need to also explore the influences of individuals, agencies, and institutions outside of a particular program. Day care programs do not exist as isolated entities within our society. Rather, they are part of a network of settings that form interdependent relationships. An ecological perspective requires that we not only examine day care today but that we look at where it has come from and its prospects for the future.

DAY CARE IN ITS OWN RIGHT

Day care has an identity problem. Misconceptions about day care arise because of the similarities between day care and purely educational programs for children, between day care and other human services, and between day care and child care in the home. The similarities mask important differences, differences often undetected or slighted by professionals trained in early childhood education, child development, or social work. Day care is an early education program, but child education is only one of its purposes. Day care may be a social service, but it is no longer only a service for children from broken homes or needy families. And day care is similar to child care in the family, yet caring for children in groups, especially other people's children, presents some very different problems. Providers, trainers, and others in supporting roles, lacking clear conceptual models of day care, often confuse or impede the change effort by attempting to refashion day care into the model most familiar to them — the nursery school, kindergarten, or social service. As a result, many changes may never take hold, and other "improvements" may not necessarily be in the best interest of children or parents. For example, a day care home or center may not benefit from adopting the notion of curriculum derived from a half-day nursery or kindergarten program (Greenman 1978). The result may be an actual decrease in learning opportunities through a failure to recognize the value of the home environment on the one hand, or, on the other, the opportunities for learning present throughout the course of an eight to ten hour day of child care. An ostensible improvement for some programs, for instance the obtainment of a social worker, might be a serious mistake for another program if the position is viewed by parents as unnecessary or even insulting. Day care is neither school nor social welfare, although it may serve both purposes.

THE IMPORTANCE OF EVALUATION

Central to improving day care, or any institution, is the ability and the willingness to observe and assess what is actually happening and the real effects of what we do. This sounds rather obvious. However, at all levels — that of regulators, directors, caregivers, trainers, and, we confess, university professors — there is an understandable but dangerous tendency to assume that the intended good effects are resulting from established practices — that teaching equals learning, a certified staff equals good caregiving, or that parent involvement equals positive parent outcomes. Any endeavor intended to change people or institutions has inherent uncertainties. Results are difficult to measure. It is easier (and often necessary) to place our faith in the means— the practices with which we are familiar—and to view success in terms of whether the teaching or other practices went well. "Went well" is usually an assessment of the immediate consequences—short-term learning, satisfaction of the participants, and the feelings of the practitioner. The danger lies in the fact that the means to improvement become ends in themselves. Whether real change takes place is unknown.

We believe that monitoring and evaluating, knowing the real outcomes experienced by children, parents, and caregivers, is important for real improvement of day care. But those involved in day care must be convinced that some form of systematic study, however informal, is beneficial. This is understandably difficult when just the doing of day care under existing conditions is an overwhelming task.

THE PURPOSE OF THE BOOK

The purpose of *Making Day Care Better* is to bring together day care professionals to discuss the workings of day care, the nature of the change process, the methodology available to evaluate the experience of children, parents, and caregivers, and to explore the advantages and limitations of various training models and improvement strategies. We do not attempt to develop a conceptual model of day care—only to raise issues and provide ideas to further that effort. Nor do we intend to extend the readers' knowledge of child development, early education, or the art of doing day care. There are numerous good materials on these topics, and our purpose is different. We hope to provide information, raise questions, and challenge assumptions that will enable professionals and would-be professionals to apply their knowledge and skills to greater effect. Further, the book is intended to direct the reader toward material not widely disseminated and to identify areas where more study is needed.

We strongly believe that day care can be improved by maximizing the use of existing resources. It would be a great injustice, however, not to stress that the vast majority of providers struggle with resources and support barely adequate for survival. They deserve better, and so do the millions of children in their care. Ultimately, providing high-quality day care on a wide scale depends on an increase of societal support.

Part 1, "The Ecology of Day Care," describes and analyzes the real world of day care: the people, the settings, the working relationships, the conflict, and the "feel" of day care to those involved. In chapter 1, "Perspectives on Quality Day Care," James Greenman briefly sketches the rise of day care in the last two decades and the development of the current delivery "system," as background for discussing some of the key issues involved with deciding what "better" day care might be. Chapter 2, by June Sale, explores the world of family day care, combining analysis with case studies. The physical aspects of day care environments and their relationship to the behavior of adults and children is analyzed by Elizabeth Prescott in chapter 3, "The Physical Setting in Day Care." In chapter 4, "Caring for Children as Work," Marcy Whitebook describes the working conditions that child care employees experience and the actual work involved in doing day care. Pettygrove and Greenman examine "The Adult World of Day Care" in chapter 5, looking at both characteristics of parents and teachers and the relationships that develop among staff and between staff and parents. The final chapter in part 1 is Roger Neugebauer's analysis of the necessary relationship between day care centers and the external setting.

We have stressed the importance of being able to accurately assess the actual experiences of the children and parents served, to separate out what really occurred from what was intended to happen. This is important at all levels, from the caregiver on the floor with children to the researcher funded by Washington. Part 2, "Unraveling Outcomes: Observing, Recording, and Evaluating Day Care," examines the different needs for data of day care providers, support professionals, and researchers; analyzes the available methodology; and explores the issues concerning the usefulness of monitoring and evaluation in day care. In chapter 7, Robert Fuqua and Dorothy Pinsky help caregivers to understand the value of studying children in relation to improving the experiences children and adults share together. Robert Fuqua, in chapter 8, "Improving Program Evaluation in Day Care," discusses some issues involved in evaluation and some ways of examining programs.

Part 3, "Changing Day Care," explores the advantages and limitations of the varied efforts to improve day care, the potential positive or negative side effects, and the potential long-range implications of using different training strategies. Chapter 9, "Change Through Regulation," is Gwen Morgan's analysis of how regulation, past and present, has effected the development of quality day care. In chapter 10, "Training Individuals: In the Classroom and Out," Elizabeth Jones looks at teaching and training and discusses how effective training builds on the best instincts of the student. The following chapter, "Program Development and Models of Consultation," by James Greenman, explores the growth of programs as opposed to individual development. Greenman considers how programs change and looks at consultation models designed to facilitate program improvement. The final chapter, "Information, Referral, and Resource Centers," by Patricia Siegel and Merle Lawrence, examines the potential of resource and referral agencies to improve day care services.

ACKNOWLEDGMENTS

We are grateful to many people who, either directly or indirectly, made this book possible. We would particularly like to thank Gerri Bugg for helping us edit part of the manuscript. Her expertise in day care administration and regulation was most valuable. We are also indebted to Tanya Stouffer and Sandra Shranklen for typing various versions of the manuscript and for their thoughtful editorial suggestions.

PART I

The Ecology of Day Care

Chapter 1

PERSPECTIVES ON QUALITY DAY CARE

James T. Greenman

Although day care has been around for quite a long time, it is really a
new social form in the sense that those who use day care aren't only problem families that social workers are trying to save from a dreadful fate.
It has become a fact of life for virtually all American families. The problem with a new social form, however, is that most of us did not grow
up being children in day care so we don't have very clear models in our
heads about what day care is like, how it is to be used, or how you share
the child's experience with the parents (Prescott 1979).

Only two decades ago, day care, the care of children outside the home
by a nonrelative, existed on the margins of society. A minor social
welfare program for broken families or needy children, day care centers
rarely attracted the attention or interest of anyone other than the families involved and social work professionals. Family day care homes
were virtually invisible, the "women down the block who care for kids."

No longer. Day care has become a visible, tangible facet of American family life. Families from nearly all economic strata, in all kinds
of communities, are using day care homes and centers to help raise
their children. La Petite Acadamie, Oak St. Community Day Care,
Maple Grove Nursery School Extended Day Program, Child Welfare Society Day Care, and thousands of similar programs all over
the country open their doors at 6:30 or 7:00 A.M. to the over nine
hundred thousand children of working or student parents. Many more
children arrive at the homes of their family day care provider. Other
families who are not now using day care are recognizing that day care
is an option often chosen by people much like themselves. This is an
important break with the past. Only in times of war or during the

Depression did day care extend far beyond the social welfare field (Steinfels 1973).

Day care's newfound acceptability is evidenced in other ways. It is acknowledged by building developers who include child care facilities along with swimming pools and playgrounds in new developments and by Chambers of Commerce that include information about the community child care programs when seeking new industry or skilled personnel. Long-established nursery schools now offering extended days, schools offering latchkey programs, and hospital-sponsored day care designed to attract and keep nurses are all evidence of the new legitimacy of day care.

However, the break with the past is far from complete. This emergent social form, day care for all kinds of families, exists amid the old. For over a century, day care has served families in distress caused by poverty, divorce, death, and other sources of family instability. Much of day care today is embedded in this social welfare context, including nearly all day care receiving direct public support.

Day care is apparently here to stay. The question, as Margaret O'Brien Steinfels points out, is not "Shall America have day care? We already have day care. The question is what kind of day care shall we have? Excellent, good or bad?" (Steinfels 1973, p. 216). The purpose of this chapter is to consider what quality day care might be, to attempt to present a view of good day care that encompasses both the new and old social form. To do that requires a sense of what day care is like today and how it got that way.

DAY CARE TODAY

Day Care in the Public Eye

"The history of child care in the United States is a history of diverse programs, offered under different auspices, to different populations, for different reasons" (Joffe 1977, p. 15). It is convenient, if not entirely accurate, to consider day care today as a child of the 1960s. During a period when social institutions were seen to possess great potential to cure many of society's difficulties, day care lay at the junction of numerous social concerns: eliminating poverty and inequality, welfare reform, the liberation of women, and the maximization of human potential through the recognition of the importance of early childhood (Greenblatt 1977; Steinfels 1973; Steiner 1976). The growth of day care was intermeshed with the rise of Head Start and

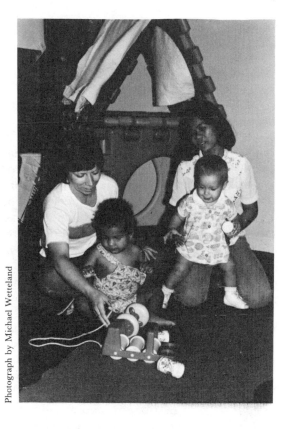

Photograph by Michael Wetteland

similar early childhood programs and with the growing belief in the ability of government, primarily the federal government, to engineer a "Great Society" through social welfare programs. The public and professional consciousness of day care was shaped by the debate over the appropriateness, size, and form of public support. In one vision, day care was to be similar to public schooling, an alternative available for all families at reasonable cost, a logical marriage of the need for all-day programs for working parents and the desire for all children to benefit from enriched early experience. A very different scenario limited publicly supported day care to the poor; the issue was whether programs should be comprehensive and educational or a more basic service achieving the same primary goal: allowing, or coercing, welfare recipients to work. Day care was proposed as a service to children, to parents, as a means to organize communities, as a first step to the dawning of a new age. Quality day care, more often than not, was conceived as active and comprehensive, in the sense of striving to positively affect all aspects of the child's development and many aspects of family life. Prior to 1971, the direction seemed clear and inevitable; day care would be recognized and publicly supported to some degree as a service to families at all economic levels (Lazar and Rosenberg 1971; Struer 1973).

President Nixon's veto of the Comprehensive Child Development Act and President Ford's subsequent veto of a similar bill abruptly shattered the confident vision of the steady expansion of publicly supported comprehensive child care, a vision encouraged by Nixon himself. It was his Family Assistance Plan that proposed "greatly expanded child care facilities for the children of welfare mothers who chose to work. . . . Day care centers devoted to the development of young minds and bodies" (Naughton 1969). The Nixon veto had a devastating effect because it was based on the belief that day care would weaken families and "replace family centered child rearing with community centered child rearing" by "commiting the vast moral authority of the national government to the side of communal approaches to child rearing over against the family centered approach" (Rosenthal 1971).

Nixon's willingness to support, even require, day care centers for low-income women and challenge day care for other families illustrated a pervasive inconsistency in American social attitudes. As Carol Joffe (1977) points out in her study, "There is a deep cultural ambivalence about the very idea of childcare — an ambivalence especially about the tampering with the functioning of 'normal' families. . . . Although we may hestitate to tamper with some families, it is clearly wrong *not* to intervene in others; families with parents who have been designated in some way 'unfit' or poor" (p. 3).

Since 1971, efforts to pass similar day care legislation have met increasingly staunch opposition by conservative groups on the grounds of both cost and the fears about interfering with the family. However, in 1971, the year of the Nixon veto, federal financial support was authorized for child care for the nonpoor for the first time through legislation authorizing extending the benefits of the child care tax deduction to middle-income families (Levitan and Alderman 1975).

A decline in the feeling of economic prosperity and diminished faith in federal intervention for social betterment have derailed the day care visions of the 1960s and early 1970s. Yet even without those visions, public support for child care has grown enormously in the last two decades. In 1967, the federal government spent under $100 million on day care; by 1977, the figure had reached $2.5 billion (Malone 1977). Support for moderate and middle-income families through the child care tax credit established in 1976 was expected to only reach

$483 million by 1981. However, over one billion dollars of credit was actually claimed, and the Office of Management and the Budget expects the figure to reach $1.5 billion by 1985 (Senator David Duvenburger, personal communication, 1982). During the same period, support from local and state programs, the United Way, and other charitable sources has also increased significantly. Since 1980, government support for social programs has declined. Funding to subsidize child care for low-income families and jobs programs such as CETA that reduced the cost of staffing day care programs have been sharply reduced or eliminated. Yet in dollar amounts, public support for child care has remained relatively constant, due to the tax credit. If projections are fulfilled, support for child care for nonpoor families through the tax credit will dwarf support for low-income families. While there is little unanimity about the appropriate extent and the nature of the public support, the idea of public support for day care has gained considerable acceptance.

The Growth of Day Care

Another picture emerges if we shift our attention from day care in the public arena to the private sector. From this vantage point, the growth of day care paralleled the rise of fast-food restaurants, nursing homes, even massage parlors — institutions arising to provide for the needs of modern life once met within the family.

Although day care was being proposed and debated as a solution to problems ranging from rising welfare costs to declining reading scores, the primary reason for its dramatic growth was the phenomenal increase in mothers going to work. Between 1940 and 1976, the number of working mothers increased tenfold. In 1965, 20 percent of mothers with children under six years of age were in the labor force (Johnson 1979). By 1981, the percentage had grown to 49 percent (U.S. Department of Labor 1982).

The need for day care as a service to "normal" families with working parents, with no stigma of family inadequacy or any vision of bettering society attached, is likely to continue. The entry of women with children into the labor force is not slowing; quite the opposite. At the same time, the number of young children in the population is likely to rise steadily in the 1980s (Hofferth 1979).

It is important to note that the majority of parents needing child care do not choose out-of-home group day care. Most care (63 percent) is provided by a friend or relative in the child's home or the home of a relative (Hofferth 1982). Whether this will continue to be the case

Photograph by Michael Wetteland

is unclear. Smaller families, continued mobility, and the decreasing supply of informal caregivers appear to be resulting in a steady increase in the demand for group day care (Hofferth 1982), although this view is not unanimous (Woolsey 1977).

In response to the tremendous growth in interest and demand, day care services grew rapidly. In 1951, there were about fifteen hundred licensed day care centers; in 1964, sixty-three hundred. In 1978, Coelen, Glants, and Calore (1978) reported that there were more than eighteen thousand licensed centers. There are over 1.3 million day care homes (Divine-Hawkins 1981).

Day care exists in nearly every conceivable setting. Organized by women's groups, community organizations, churches, "mom-and-pop" entrepreneurs, government agencies, and desperate parents, day care centers opened up wherever space was available: in homes, storefronts, warehouses, garages, schools, offices, hospitals, and often churches, particularly the ubiquitous church basement. Day nurseries, open for decades, suddenly had company. Nursing schools began to extend their operations to include all-day care. Day care homes are located in nearly all kinds of neighborhoods, in all sorts of dwellings: high-rise apartments, tract housing, stately Victorian homes, and tenements.

Centers today range in size from those caring for hundreds of children to those with under a dozen. Most centers are independent units, some are units in for-profit chains or in large nonprofit organizations. Because most states have relatively minimal requirements for staff qualifications, the easy entry into child care results in wide variations in the background, experience, training, and future ambitions of caregivers. The women, and sometimes families, who provide family day care may simply be seeking income while tending to their own children or grandchildren, or may be committed to it as their chosen work.

The Delivery of Day Care

Part cottage industry, part small business enterprise, and part social welfare concern, day care has been subject to little planning or coordination. Although the boundary lines are hazy, one can distinguish three day care communities, defined by their funding and self-perceived missions. There are the largely nonprofit, predominantly center-based programs, with a sprinkling of licensed homes and home systems, that receive public support beyond parent fees, from local, state, or federal programs, the United Way, or other charities. Support is usually predicated on the desire to enable "needy" low-income families to afford day care or to enroll the children in day care that offers services beyond basic child care. This group has received the lion's share of the public and professional attention and resources. The second community consists of private proprietary centers wholly dependent on parent fees. Family day care homes, the great majority unlicensed or unregistered, and probably for the most part unaware that they are family day care homes and not simply babysitters, make up the third community. For these latter two groups, day care has more in common with private schools, babysitters, housekeeping services, and other services a family may purchase than with social service agencies. There usually is no stigma of need or inadequacy attached to the families, no eligibility requirements beyond ability to pay.

This distinction is not absolutely clear-cut, however. Many of the programs in the first category refuse to accept the notion that inability to pay full costs signifies the family pathology associated with being needy. Some homes and private centers behave a great deal like social welfare agencies.

Day care homes and centers in all three groups vary in key dimensions, such as the informality and intensity of the relationship between the day care staff and the family. Factors such as size, hiring practices, caregiver characteristics, and location may be more important in determining the relationship between caregivers and parents than program sponsorship or intended mission (particularly in centers) (Powell 1977; Prescott 1972).

The extent to which centers and homes perceive themselves as educational also varies. Education is certainly always a part of care but not always recognized as such. Most centers view themselves as educational enterprises, schools of one sort or another. Many day care homes probably do not take this view, instead seeing their function as being to take good care of, to love, or to help raise, rather than to educate children. As support systems grow, it is increasingly likely that family day care providers' conceptions of themselves as teachers will continue to grow. Whether this leads to day care homes becoming more schoollike is an important question. Whether education eclipses care as the perceived major characteristic of centers is an important question.

Although the present delivery "nonsystem" clashes with the vision of coordinated, comprehensive child care mentioned earlier, since the early 1970s the attitude of many people toward large institutions and coordinated systems has changed. There is an undercurrent of anxiety that child care could result in greater uniformity or end up in the wrong hands, such as (depending on one's views) the public schools, the social workers, government bureaucrats, or community activists. The diversity of the delivery of day care today is viewed as a virtue by many advocates, although one born of necessity. The range of child care providers today nearly matches that of the families served in terms of race, class, beliefs, and values. Homes and centers, with some exceptions, are not imprisoned within large bureaucracies and are of a much smaller scale than the schools and other institutions that parents relate to. Parents, at least theoretically, have choices that allow them to retain some control over the rearing of their children. However, choice evaporates in the localities where demand exceeds supply and waiting lists and high costs reduce parents' concerns to the question of availability and price. The concept of choice is also meaningless if quality is low or if parents are unaware of all the homes and centers available, a real problem in a nonsystem.

The Quality of Day Care Today

A natural conclusion to this section would be an analysis of the quality of today's day care. No analysis is possible, because the data are simply not available and because attempts to precisely define quality across the range of programs have been unsuccessful. This is curious, given the attention paid to day care and other early childhood programs in the last several years. Why this gap?

At the policy level, much attention has been directed toward defining the basic nature and the parameters of the service. The plethora of rationales and purposes has made it difficult to resolve issues of quality. Does quality day care simply fill in for Mom or Dad, make families better, prepare kids for schools, improve I.Q.'s, provide health services, or do all of these things?

Secondly, during the rapid expansion of day care, the struggle for quantity generally has taken precedence over the struggle for quality. The energies of organizers, advocates, and providers have been directed toward getting programs started, expanding services, obtaining new resources, and (recently) holding on to old. Opportunities to hold back, to consolidate, to direct resources to improvement are few when survival is in doubt, waiting lists are long, and the pressure to keep parent fees low is ever-present. Attempts to substantially raise regulatory standards have been opposed on the realistic grounds that higher standards, in the absence of increased financial support, would cause many programs to close, drive other programs, particularly day care homes, underground, and result in rising costs to parents.

A by-product of this struggle is relatively little self-examination by day care professionals. It is not accidental that more has been written about the need for quality and how quality might be regulated than about the kind of care that existing homes and centers offer. It is not easy for professionals, working hard to establish the validity of day care as an alternative for normal families while supporting providers who work hard for few rewards, to at the same time make critical public assessments of the current state of the art. Criticism of current quality gives ammunition to critics of day care and of working mothers, creates anxiety and increases guilt among parents, and lowers the morale of day care providers.

While the reasons for avoiding a critical analysis are understandable, without such an assessment we run the risk of permanently accepting low standards and mediocre care as the norm. Worse, there is a danger that we may lose the capacity to even distinguish between

second-rate and good-quality care. Much of today's day care undoubtedly differs little from the dreary picture reported in Keyserling's 1972
Windows on Day Care. The heroic efforts of many home and center providers to achieve the level of quality that does exist does not change
that fact.

Concluding that present day care quality is at best adequate is in
no sense an argument against day care, which is necessary and probably would be utilized in modern society regardless of quality. Without being dishonest in our public front, day care can be portrayed in
the most positive light. Yet high standards among professionals and
advocates, a clear understanding of what quality is, and an equally
clear sense of the distance homes and centers are from the idea are important.

THE NATURE OF DAY CARE QUALITY

We come to day care as parents, caregivers, or professionals with
images of experiences we assume to be similar: nursery school, babysitting, kindergarten, or sometimes social services that assist families.
Out of these we fashion a sense of what we think day care should be
like — perhaps a scaled-down version of an elementary school, or an
all-day nursery school, or a child-filled home. One vision may be dom-
inated by laps and hugs, another by teachers and books, another by
social workers, and most often by a combination of these elements.
For quality to be achieved, day care needs to be considered in its own
right and in light of its own purposes and operational imperatives. New
social forms are charged with uncertainty. There is no guarantee that
they will develop in a manner beneficial to society.

The Basic Purpose of Day Care

All day care shares one common purpose: to provide care for the
children of absent parents. Beyond that, a day care program, depending on its clientele and secondary purposes, may provide other services to parents, special programs for children, or serve as a vehicle
for providing a range of services to families and the community. These
services should not be taken as an indication of quality or lack of quality — only of the range of services. In other words, comprehensive programs are not necessarily better day care, only more comprehensive.
This seemingly obvious point is important because too often attention is focused on the range of services rather than on the quality of
the essential service — daily care for children.

Quality in terms of the basic purpose, however, involves more than looking at the effect on children. Day care has important effects on parents, the family, and society (Belsky and Steinberg 1978). Does the day care home or center, through its policies, procedures, and staff–parent interactions, strengthen families? Do parents feel in control and positive about their children, themselves, and their day care arrangement? Not all parents need or want parent education or counseling, but all parents need to feel competent and secure.

Defining Quality

Everyone wants quality. Parents seek it, caregivers try to provide it, licensing agencies hope to regulate it, and people in all sorts of roles are trying to improve it. Quality is an elusive concept. Is everyone talking about the same thing? To a large extent yes, but like the blind men and the elephant, it all depends on your vantage point.

Quality can be viewed in terms of program ingredients or characteristics, the right kinds of facilities, teachers with certain qualifications, the staff–child ratio, and the presence of certain program features such as a social worker, a parent education component, or a particular educational component for the children. Quality can also be discussed in terms of identifiable program outcomes—what the children and parents actually experienced, as opposed to what they were intended to experience. Such outcomes include the type of interactions between caregivers and children and parents, the warmth or safety of the physical environment, and the learning experiences available to the child. Or, quality can be considered in terms of another set of outcomes—the achievement, behavior, or feelings of the child or parent. The satisfaction of the parent, a happy, busy child, or the attainment of certain skills or knowledge may be taken as indices of quality.

Parents are concerned about whether the home or center meets their particular needs and standards. They may select a program because of characteristics they associate with quality, but they will ultimately evaluate the care on the basis of their experiences. If the other children are thriving and their child is miserable, then that day care program is not likely to be acceptable to them, no matter what anyone else thinks. Those charged with regulating day care obviously have a different perspective. Their concern is specifying certain ingredients or program characteristics whose presence or absence are likely to result in an acceptable quality (G. Morgan 1979; Class 1980).

In this volume, we are primarily concerned with quality viewed from the standpoint of providers, trainers, and others in supporting roles. Because assessing outcomes is complex and time-consuming, quality is all too often viewed in terms of ingredients and program characteristics. If the center can manage to acquire certified teachers, a detailed curriculum, and a parent advisory board, then (we tend to think) it must be pretty good. If a home provider is connected to a toy lending library, has years of experience, and has recently received some training, he or she must offer quality child care. These propositions may or may not be true, but we commonly act as if they are, as if characteristics are not means of achieving quality, but quality itself. In the struggle to secure the ingredients to improve a program, such as good training materials or certified staff, we make these things into ends in themselves. We forget the original assumption that these things are only worthwhile if they produce the desired outcomes; they are no guarantee of quality.

The potential drawbacks to a misplaced faith in ingredients are threefold. First, it is easy to lose touch with the basic goals and to produce "help that hurts" (Ryan 1971). A second danger is that once all the assembled ingredients are obtained and all is still not well, the faith in the ingredients commonly leads us to "blame the victim" (Ryan 1971). If the child is not happy or learning, then the problem must lie with the child, perhaps as a result of something happening at home. If the training program for paraprofessionals resulted in little change, then something must be wrong with the aides themselves. A third drawback that is of particular concern to change agents is that a focus on program ingredients or characteristics drastically limits our perspective. It atrophies our capacity to generate alternative ways of seeing and doing things. As Sarason (1971) pointed out, there is a tendency to forget that there is a universe of alternatives to the way we think and do things. There are diverse routes to quality. In day care, the way the time and space are structured, the curriculum, how staff are assigned, the planned interactions with parents, all include choices, alternatives selected at one point in time to reflect existing beliefs and conditions. All too often, once chosen, policies and procedures become cast in stone. An emphasis on certain forms or means limits our strategies. For instance, if parent–caregiver partnership is the goal, a dependence on parent conferences and a newsletter as the means toward the end unnecessarily limits alternatives. In our misplaced faith in those means, we may fail to recognize that no one reads the newsletter or that conferences are teacher-controlled and one-sided. Instead, one might begin with the desired end—joint decision making and a feeling of mutual trust and respect—and from there explore all possible means. This might include enlarging the staff to increase teacher availability to parents and thus maximize daily parent–caregiver contact, increased use of the telephone, polling parents, staff training, or a host of other options. When faith is placed in program characteristics, the inevitable result is a severe narrowing of the universe of creative solutions to the many difficult problems intrinsic to day care.

Agreement on Quality Care

Can any consensus be reached as to what constitutes quality care, particularly if we foreswear a reliance on program characteristics as automatic indices of quality? Yes, probably — *if,* and this is a critical *if,* there is a recognition that good day care comes in different forms and that a key aspect of quality is a congruence with the beliefs and values of the families served. People differ in their views of child rearing and what makes up a good environment for children.

The following observations on quality day care are presented not as a definitive analysis but as a starting point for discussion and de-

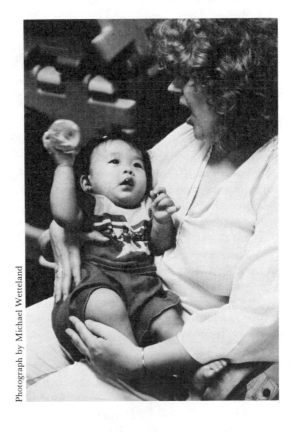

Photograph by Michael Wetteland

bate. Quality will be characterized here largely in terms of outcomes for programs, parents, and children. The term *environment* is used to include both the human and material environment, the totality of the actions or inactions of the people, the presence or absence of materials, and the structuring of time and space. For example, in saying that good day care provides a healthy environment, we would be referring to such things as the practices the caregivers follow (obtaining tuberculosis tests, washing hands, not smoking around children), the cleanliness of the surroundings, the amount of fresh air children get daily, and how well the physical space and daily schedule are planned to reduce undue stress or fatigue.

Guidelines for Quality

SUPPORT FOR PARENTS. The more the program accommodates the concerns and desires of individual families, the more partnership engendered, the higher quality the day care. The more opportunity for parent involvement in the lives of their children, the better the home or center.

A SAFE, HEALTHY ENVIRONMENT. What characterizes a safe, healthy environment of acceptable quality is a decision that the providers, parents, and licensing officials should all be party to, with an awareness of the necessary trade-offs between safety and health and other program goals.

A COMFORTABLE ENVIRONMENT. Young children need a soft, warm environment, opportunity for privacy and quiet, and freedom from coercion. Because cultures differ in their view of what is comfortable, a reasonable standard is the sort of surroundings that the families served would view as comfortable.

A NURTURING ENVIRONMENT. What is nurturing is certainly open to some interpretation depending on the age of the child, cultural background, and individual differences among children and adults. Again, one must refer to one's conception of a good home and the relationship a child should have with adults who care about the child. To what degree nurturing is a matter of laps, hugs, smiles, soothing, or quiet presence is subjective.

A SECURE ENVIRONMENT. In good day care, the child must feel secure. How much stability in the environment and continuity between home and day care are necessary depends on the individual child.

AN ENVIRONMENT THAT PROMOTES FULL DEVELOPMENT. This area is certainly subject to much interpretation in terms of how much variety is necessary, which areas of development should receive more attention, and what is developmentally appropriate. What does seem to be unequivocally accepted today is that day care should be committed to development in a wide sense.

AN ENVIRONMENT THAT PROMOTES VALUES AND BEHAVIORS IMPORTANT TO PARENTS AND CAREGIVERS. Parents need to feel comfortable with the way that the child is being socialized at the home or center. When disagreements occur, parents should feel that their values and beliefs are considered and respected.

AN OPEN COVENANT. A high-quality day care home or center makes evident to parents the philosophy, values, and assumptions that underpin the care that the children receive. Only if caregivers have a sense of what they are doing, and why, can a partnership with parents that includes a give-and-take be possible.

A REASONABLE ENVIRONMENT FOR CAREGIVERS. The day care environment should be comfortable for adults as well as children. Caregivers should be treated with respect and consideration.

It should be evident that these guidelines are based on a particular set of premises about the nature of childhood and the proper relationship between parents and professionals. Inherent in the guidelines is the belief that above all else children should feel comfortable, secure, prized as individuals, and experience an interesting and challenging environment. Training to achieve some future state is secondary in day care. Equally important is the assumption that child care is of necessity a shared enterprise between parents and professionals and that primary control and responsibility for the child should rest with the parents.

Day Care Tomorrow

This is not a good time to make predictions about the future course of child-rearing institutions. It is a time when opposing beliefs continue to gain strength.

Day care seems destined to have a permanent role in American society. Any major structural changes in the present delivery system seem unlikely. The mixture of public and private, nonprofit and proprietary homes and centers is likely to continue, although any proportionate share of the child care demand met by each type of program may well change. A major determinant of that change will be the amount and nature of public subsidy. A new, large infusion of public funding appears unlikely, and any private-sector initiative will be gradual and tentative. What will have a great bearing on the delivery of day care is the extent to which the available subsidy is channeled directly to the consumer through tax credits, an AFDC disregard, or instead to the provider of day care. Reliance on the former (which appears likely) has the effect of reducing the market share of costlier public and private nonprofit centers and increasing the use of family day care homes and lower-cost centers. This might result in a great increase in franchise day care.

Subsidy through the tax credit has the least direct impact on program revenues. Although it pumps a large amount of dollars into the day care market, those dollars are often viewed as a way to reduce a too high tax bill, not as a child care subsidy justifying higher costs such as improved salaries or lower staff–child ratios.

If current trends are an indication, public support for day care in a zero-sum economy (Thurow 1980), aside from the tax credit, will once again be limited to day care as a social welfare program for the very poor and will be provided on a modest scale. Low- and moderate-income families for whom the tax credit served as too small and too partial a subsidy will find it difficult to make adequate child care arrangements.

The Relationship Between Day Care Programs and Families

Currently the range of the relationship between homes or centers and families is wide: some relationships are analogous to the intimate, personal sharing of children in an extended family, others to the distant partnership between families and schools or to the one-sided influence and control that some social welfare programs have over their clientele. Will day care programs in time coalesce into a similar stance and be perceived as analogous to the school, babysitters, or grandmothers? Will quality day care be seen as the province of skilled professionals who are experts in child rearing and education, or perhaps of families, or of trusted amateurs? Answers to these questions hinge on assumptions made about the importance of early education, parental control, and the importance of technique versus personal relationship in caring for others (Lasch 1977, 1979).

The growing presence of infants and toddlers in group care may have the effect of muting the tendencies toward relationships between staff and parents that reproduce the distance and formality often found between school teachers and parents. Sharing care, rather than handing over the child to be educated, is clearly primary in infant/toddler day care. On the other hand, the growth of family day care systems may have the opposite effect and heighten tendencies toward more formal relationships with parents.

An important question is whether in fact the new and old social forms of day care will merge into one. This might occur if the assumption becomes general that low-income families are normal and differ from other families primarily only because they have insufficient income to pay for the goods and services other families are able to purchase. All would be viewed as consumers instead of clients. Given the pervasiveness of the "myth of the self-sufficient family" described by Kenneth Kenniston in *All Our Children: The American Family Under Pressure* (1978) and the current resurrection of the expression "truly needy," this is unlikely. However, the opposite is also possible and perhaps more likely: an acceptance of the notion that all families are generally "needy" in the sense that they require the support of trained professionals. This might result in day care programs assuming a broader responsibility for family well-being. The rapid growth of the helping professions that minister to the large and small needs of individuals and families makes this direction entirely plausible. Whether this would lead to greater family health or an unhealthy dependence is a matter of considerable controversy (Lasch 1977, 1979).

The Prognosis for Quality

The availability of decent or excellent day care depends on a societal recognition of the importance of early childhood experience and a concern for the well-being of all children. The state of the economy will undoubtedly have a good deal to do with society's commitment. It was only during one of the most affluent periods in the history of the United States, the 1960s, that the idea that government had a responsibility to maximize opportunities for each child took hold. It remains to be seen whether this notion will survive bleaker economic periods. At present, there seems little reason for optimism.

Programs that achieve high levels of quality usually have resources beyond parent fees: some type of financial subsidy, volunteer labor, or free occupancy. Since the late 1970s, the outlook for these resources to continue at the same level or grow does not look bright. When programs are solely dependent on parent fees, the pressure to keep prices low results in practices antithetical to quality: minimum space and resources, little time to involve parents, and personnel practices that exploit child care workers, such as low wages, minimal benefits, and layoffs based on low daily attendance. The appearance of quality — space that is inadequate but appears good to parents — and educational gimmicks are less costly than the substance: thoughtful, well-treated caregivers who remain with the program. Profit programs, particularly large chains of centers, seem susceptible to promoting appearances over substance (for example, supplying a computer for child use and an impressive facility, but utilizing a poorly trained staff with a high turnover rate). They are not alone, however, as many nonprofit programs faced with limited resources behave in a similar fashion.

Quality day care, by the standards outlined earlier, depends on the recognition by professionals of the limits of their authority (and wisdom) and of the distinction between the roles of parents and professionals. Looming behind the desire to help or support is the dark shadow of temptation to control, for experts to make the family "better" according to their own standards or to rescue the child and make the child over according to the professional's image of what he or she should be or become.

Achieving quality day care will require a struggle. The degree of success of the struggle will help to determine the nature of family life for generations to come.

Chapter 2

FAMILY DAY CARE HOMES

June Solnit Sale

WHAT IS FAMILY DAY CARE?

The most widely used and least understood form of child care in the
United States is family day care. Nearly half of all children who receive out-of-home care for ten hours a week or more may be found
in the home of a neighbor or friend, a family day care provider who
cares for nonrelated children in his or her own home for less than
twenty-four hours a day (Fosburg 1981). It has been estimated that
94 percent of family day care is unregulated and remains an informal
neighborhood system providing support for the increasing number of
working parents in the United States.

A profile of a typical family day care provider might well reflect
a description of a particular neighborhood. The National Day Care
Home Study (Fosburg 1981) is the most extensive exploration of family
day care conducted to date. Family day care was studied over a four-
year period from 1976 to 1980 in three sites: Los Angeles (pilot site),
Philadelphia, and San Antonio. Three groups of caregivers were described:

Young White mothers in their late twenties and thirties with their
own young children at home; women in their forties and fifties with
at least one relative's child (often a grandchild) in care; and women
in their thirties to fifties who care for the children of friends, neighbors, and others in the community but are not caring for their own
or a relative's child. Whereas the first two groups tend to provide
unregulated care, the last group of providers constitutes a large
proportion of the regulated and agency-sponsored caregivers (p.
46).

Other findings of the study that help fill in the family day care profile are interesting to note:

- The white providers who generally start out by staying at home to care for their own children are slightly over thirty years of age on the average; black and Hispanic providers are older (an average of forty-five years of age) and may be caring for grand-children as well as unrelated children.
- White caregivers are more likely to be married (80 percent), have a higher family income than other groups, and have finished eighth grade (95 percent). Fifty percent of black providers are married, have a median income of ten thousand dollars, and 90 percent have completed eighth grade, while 80 percent of the Hispanic groups are married, have a low income, and only half have attended school above the elementary level.
- Across all groups, 25 percent of the providers surveyed had been doing family day care for less than a year, while the majority (50 percent) had been involved for one to seven years and 25 percent had been providing care for from seven to thirty-six years (37–49).

The statistics hardly convey the depth of commitment or the characteristic differences and similarities of the providers. In most center programs, the observer finds a similarity of equipment, curriculum materials, and layout. Somehow, no matter how varied the program and the personnel, there is a familiar ambience, with sounds and smells that are typical of a center program. But in home day care, each caregiver brings a flavor and quality that is unique, and the differences among family day care environments are fascinating.

Each family day care provider brings his or her culture, values, housekeeping skills, and personal ideas and moods to the home he or she shares with other people's children. An invitation to a family day care home may be an invitation for tea and scones, wine and cheese, strudel and coffee, or rice cakes and herbal tea. The home may be located in a small walk-up apartment in a densely populated urban area, a house with limited outdoor space in the inner city, or a house with enough outdoor space for the children to romp freely. The program may vary from being very informal with no scheduled activities, to being highly structured with a lesson plan for each week. A television soap opera may be constantly droning in the background, or the television may be turned on at regular times for *Sesame Street* or cartoons, or there may be no television set at all.

In short, it is difficult to categorize or paint one picture of family day care. Family day care, like most services, ranges in quality from excellent to very poor, with most care falling in the middle range. It does, however, represent the best of the United States in its heterogeneity and its goal of helping and assisting others. It presents us with a range of services and walks a fine line between being classified as educational, developmental, or custodial, whatever those classifications may mean to the many professional groups examining this phenomenon we call family care.

CASE STUDY

Mrs. Arriego slipped into providing family day care when her daughter Consuelo had her first child. Mrs. Arriego was very willing and able to provide care for her granddaughter. This would help fill the nest in a home that had once had five active children, now all grown and departed.

The Arriego home is located on a quiet, tree-lined suburban street near a main thoroughfare. A small garage is attached to the home and serves as a workshop. A small, fenced-in yard has a bed of colorful flowers, a pear tree, and a lawn that ranges from looking like dried wheat to resembling a yellowish green outdoor carpet. A swing set and sandbox are randomly placed, with a couple of tricycles and sand toys scattered about willy-nilly.

Consuelo found it very convenient to drop off Teresa at Grandma's house. She would arrive at 6:30 A.M. with the baby still half asleep in her nightclothes and then would complete the hour-long drive on the jam-packed freeway to her work.

Consuelo's neighbor and car pool companion, Audrey Williams, had a two-year-old son, Jonathan, who was being cared for at home by a housekeeper. The day that the housekeeper did not report for work and called to say that she had a sick aunt whom she must visit in another state was the turning point for Mrs. Arriego's career. It was a natural. Since Mrs. Arriego was already caring for Teresa, why not Jonathan? Ms. Williams persuasively offered to pay the going rate of care, which would give Mrs. Arriego some pin money without a good deal of extra effort.

Before long, a neighbor of the Arriegos noticed that there were small children present on a regular basis, and word spread that Mrs. Arriego was "watching" children. Within a six-month period there were five children from eight months to four years of age in the Arriego home, which was operating without benefit of a license.

Mr. Arriego was happy to have his granddaughter around but was a little skeptical about taking care of other people's children. It was not long, though, before he was looking forward to the children's arrival and had given each child a special Spanish nickname. He can often be found in the morning showing one of the older children how to use some of the equipment in his workshop.

Mrs. Arriego sees herself as a confidant and family counselor for several of the families who look to her for help. Her years of experience in caring for children make her especially knowledgeable in how to handle everything from biting to toilet training, as well as in preparing the children for kindergarten. She is available on a few weekends to care for the children, since she recommends that the parents need some time alone.

The Arriegos are proud of their Mexican background and teach the children Spanish phrases and customs. Grandma does not especially enjoy cooking, but she read some books about nutrition to be sure that the children have balanced meals. The children help with housekeeping chores, including washing the dishes, cleaning the bathtub after a bath, vacuuming, and dusting. The house is never completely in order except for the day when the licensor comes. This happened for the first time a good five years after Mrs. Arriego began caring for her granddaughter.

When the children nap after lunch, so does Mrs. Arriego. She has learned to pace herself so that she is not completely exhausted at the end of the day. She has strict rules that are usually obeyed and are authoritatively enforced. These include "No going outside of the fenced area," "No going into Grandma's and Grandpa's bedroom," "No hitting, biting, kicking, or using bad words." Older children who forget the rules are helped with "time out" for a short while; younger infants and toddlers are picked up and told gently, "No."

Mrs. Arriego joined a family day care organization when it was developed in her community. She attended meetings that seemed to be of interest and even held a minor office at one time but has no overwhelming interest in being in the leadership. She attended classes relating to family day care given by a local community college but quickly learned that she could probably have taught the classes—although she did enjoy the camaraderie of the other providers.

When she began doing family day care fifteen years ago, Mrs. Arriego charged twenty-five dollars a week per child. She now charges sixty-five dollars. Where this used to be a minor supplement to her husband's income, with inflation and the rising cost of living, it has become a necessary complement.

Photograph by Michael Wetteland

WHO DOES FAMILY DAY CARE SERVE?

Family day care is a neighborhood phenomenon. It reflects the mores of the community, including the housing patterns, prejudices, and the way in which children are valued. In densely urban downtown areas, family day care is usually segregated and may be found in low-income, run-down rental housing. If it is not agency-sponsored, it tends to be unlicensed, because most housing in those areas would not pass licensing health and safety standards. Agency-sponsored family day care networks are an exception to this rule. Since the purpose of this subsidized system is to serve the poor, the location of the programs is in low-income areas, and the funding source requires some form of regulation, whether it be licensing or registration. In higher-income areas, where the population is less dense, the programs become more integrated, and more licensed programs may be found. Family day care also tends to be more segregated in upper middle class neighborhoods among women who have made the decision to work within the home rather than seek jobs or open a business outside the home.

In the Community Family Day Care Project (Sale et al. 1971) in Pasadena it was interesting to note that many of the family day care homes were integrated. Despite a hugh outcry in this community of 125,000 people against busing for integration, there was racial and socioeconomic integration of the consumer families. In a survey of the literature, Emlen has concluded: "All socio-economic levels was represented. Family day care is widely used by those who can afford it and by welfare recipients whose care is subsidized" (Emlen 1980).

HOW DO PARENTS FIND
FAMILY DAY CARE HOMES?

Finding an adequate, stable child care arrangement can be one of the most stressful situations facing working parents. Making a good match in child care between a provider and a family can dramatically improve the chances of parents being effective workers, parents, lovers, and friends. Preferences in child care arrangements are dependent upon the age of the child(ren), past experience of the parents, location, financial considerations, program expectations, and ethnicity.

In the National Day Care Home Study, parent respondents preferred care in the child's own home for children under a year of age, family day care for children from one to three years of age, and a more structured arrangement such as center care for the children above three (Fosburg 1981). A common concern voiced by many family day care providers is that when children reach the age of three, parents want a day care environment where "children will learn"—in other words, they prefer a more structured program in a day care center. This also coincides with the supply side of the child care economy: numerous types of center care are available in the private, nonprofit, and subsidized sectors for children who are three and toilet-trained. Many centers sell their programs as being more schoollike and as "kindergarten preparation academies."

Ethnic differences in making child care arrangements surfaced from the National Day Care Home Study. There was apparently a strong preference for center care among the black families interviewed.

It has been interesting to note that working parents who are new to the work force or new to making child care arrangements tend to choose more experienced providers, while parents with two or more years in the work force and with knowledge of how to make a child care arrangement tend to choose caregivers with little experience (Emlen 1980). But the factors of greatest importance to parents in many surveys that have replicated a 1973 study conducted in Massachusetts continue to be (1) affordable child care, (2) located near the parents' home, (3) at convenient hours, and (4) the "right kind with respect to sponsorship, facilities, program, and personnel" (R. Rowe 1972, p. 16).

Although advertisements in newspapers and in the yellow pages of the phone book as well as signs posted in laundromats or local stores provide some sources of child care information for parents, most family day care arrangements are made through word of mouth passed along by friends, neighbors, or relatives. This important network may know little more than the parent about home care providers beyond its own immediate neighborhood. The distraught parent may take the first arrangement he or she can find, when it is possible that one block farther away is a more suitable provider who needs children for his or her program. Very often, parents either do not have or do not take the time to find the "right" place for their child, or lack the slightest notion of how to find that place.

Zigler and Hunsinger pointed out in 1977 that "a major problem with day care is the lack of centralized information to help parents locate existing day care services" (Zigler 1977, p. 8). In the past ten years, however, information and referral programs (I&R's) have sprung up to fulfill this great need of bringing caregivers and parents together to make a good child care match; chapter 12 discusses these new programs in detail.

CASE STUDY

Emily Jenkins is thirty-two years old and has two children: Sarah is seven and John is four. Sam Jenkins is an actor and likes the idea of providing child care in his home, as long as Emily takes the responsibility of keeping the finances in order.

When the Jenkinses started caring for children four years ago, they were faced with child care problems of their own. Emily had been working as a teacher in a large, urban school district before the birth of her second child. Her mother and husband had managed to put together a patchwork schedule of caring for Sarah until she was three years old, but when John was born the burden and responsibility of caring for two children put too much of a strain on the informal arrangement. Because Emily did not like the idea of a stranger caring for her baby and her financial needs were becoming more pressing, she decided to look into family day care before John's birth. Through various inquiries, she learned that she was in a good position to open a licensed family day care home; her large first-floor apartment was located in a fenced complex, there would be no problem with a safety inspection of the interior, and fingerprint clearances for her husband and herself had been obtained in previous jobs. Emily went ahead with the licensing process so that she was ready to start her "child care business" by the time John was four months old. Her location was ideal, and in two months' time she was caring for six nonrelated children, one child under two and the rest of preschool age.

Emily and Sam decided that this venture had to be profitable in order to continue and went to their accountant for assistance in setting up procedures to keep track of income and expenses. A formal contract was developed, and a list of rules and regulations were reproduced for all clients. They also agreed that they could easily care for more children then the licensor had determined, because of Emily's past teaching experience. The age mix was important, since they wanted youngsters near the ages of their own children in order to provide suitable playmates and permit appropriate programming.

Emily drew heavily upon her school teaching experience in planning the program for the children and in her approach to the parents. A formal schedule was posted each week for the parents to see. A specific time was planned for the preschoolers for story time, musical activities, crafts, lunch, naps, visits to the public library, outings to local places of interest, and free playtime. The infants and toddlers also had set schedules that were nicely integrated with those of the older children. Parents were presented with these plans during an initial interview and asked for their approval; if major questions were raised, the family was not accepted into the Jenkins's program.

Policies relating to fees, pickup and delivery times, vacations, and other matters relating to parental responsibilities were clearly spelled out in the contract and thoroughly discussed in the initial interview. Two weeks' notice was required if either party wanted to terminate the arrangement. The fee in 1983 was seventy-five dollars per week for infants and toddlers and sixty dollars for preschoolers.

Emily views her program as one that prepares children for school. "All of my children can write their names, read simple primers, speak well, and behave themselves when they've been with me. We have fun, we do things together, but there's no nonsense when it comes to learning. If the children can't behave and their parents don't care enough to help them, then they need to find another home." This philosophy is also carried out by Emily's mother, who is available for occasional assistance when needed.

The parents who live near the Jenkins are great supporters of this family day care home. They too are concerned with preparing children for school, and they appreciate the time and effort Emily and Sam put into their program. If parents have a developmental, social, or emotional question about a child, Emily can be counted upon for a clear, concise, and authoritative answer. If the solution is not practical or acceptable for a parent, then the problem lies with the recipient of the sage's advice—not the sage.

Emily Jenkins runs an efficient and prosperous business that serves the needs of the community. When a good match is made—that is, when parents find this a comfortable arrangement—children do well. A good deal of thoughtful effort has been put into this program, and it has served the children and families of this community well.

FAMILY DAY CARE: 1971–1983

Family day care has been with us for a very long time. Those of you who know about Mel Brooks's "Two Thousand-Year-Old Man" might wonder why family day care was not mentioned in that recording. The dialogue might have gone something like this:

Interviewer: What was it called when a man and a woman got married and had children?

Two-thousand-year-old Man: I remember it well; when Melvin and Sophie got married and had children, we called it a *fam*. Some public relations guy got ahold of it and said it didn't have the right ring—so he called it *family*. It does have a better sound.

Interviewer: Who took care of the kids when the father was hunting and the mother was tending the crops?

Two-thousand-year-old Man: Well, if there was a grandmother around she would. But I remember that Melvin hated his mother-in-law, so he asked the lady in the next cave if she would take care of the kids. We worked out things like that.

As long as family day care has existed, it has suffered from lack of an adequate name. In the short period from 1971 to 1981, those who have provided this kind of child care have been called *babysitters, family day care mothers, family day care givers, family day care operators, family*

day care providers, home child care providers, and *family child care providers.*
The change in names has reflected the change in status. Collins and
Watson comment,

> The word "babysitter" . . . which to a semanticist might be a fas-
> cinating subject . . . is a thorn to anyone interested in day care. As
> a term it is defined in the 1971 *Webster's Unabridged Dictionary* as "a
> person engaged usually for pay . . . to take care of a child or chil-
> dren while parents are away from home." One English dictionary
> explains that this term was originally applied to teenagers but is now
> in general use. Certainly, it is not its definition that has given the
> term what most people would agree is a poor reputation even while
> almost everyone, including babysitters, makes use of it — from the
> beginning of the project we struggled to find a word that would de-
> scribe central characters in the work which would make it clear that
> they had a special role and performed a particular task which was
> somewhere between a profession, an occupation and a craft. It was
> decided that family day care user and family day care giver were
> the terms used. Babysitter was ruled out, since [the term] was ap-
> parently seen by many as denoting an inferior person performing
> a menial task (1976, pp. 16–17).

As recently as May 1982, Alleas Baldwin said in a speech to the Third
Western Regional Family Day Care Conference in Seattle, Washington:

> By now I would hope that we've all learned to deal with our jealous
> friends who want to know, "how can we stand *just staying at home* with
> all those little grungy kids, *just Baby Sitting*," when you should get
> a real job in the real world of nonfree thinkers, punchin' somebody
> else's clock (p. 8).

She concluded her talk with these words:

> At sometime in this conference, can another name for "Baby Sit-
> ting" be invented? — Why, I've never sat on a baby in my life (pp.
> 8–9).

While the babysitter tag still remains an annoying description of family
day care, in the last ten years a good deal has happened to change
its name and its status. In the early 1970s, few studies of family day
care had anything positive to say about it as a service (Grotberg 1971;
Keyserling 1972; Willner 1970). The studies that raised the question

of the positive potential of family day care were found in Portland, Oregon (The Field Study of the Neighborhood Family Day Care System) and in Pasadena, California (The Community Family Day Care Project). The negative aspects of family care were highlighted in broad surveys that looked at the service from the outside in (outside observers examined and questioned a large number of providers in one-time meetings). The highlighting of positive aspects resulted from studies that examined family day care from the inside out (through two- and three-year interactions, observations, discussions, and ongoing contact with a smaller number of representative providers).

The sudden interest in family day care in the 1970s was not an accident. The need for a cheap form of care was vital for working parents and for the federal government, which did not want to pay for the continually rising cost of center care for AFDC parents. The need for infant care was also a factor, and group care of infants was frowned upon up to that point.

The "discovery" of family day care was a mixed blessing. While providers were no longer called babysitters and were accorded the verbal respect they deserved by many early childhood professional groups, the family day care territory was open to the missionary zeal of professionals who wanted to change the service in their image. Just as Henry Higgins wanted Eliza to be more like a man, so unknowing child development professionals and government policymakers wanted family day care providers to be more like center providers — this kind of care is so much neater, so much more controllable, and so much more accountable.

Training

The discovery of family day care has had other effects, both positive and negative. There is no doubt that there has been a great increase in educational opportunities for providers (see chaps. 10 and 12). However, with the erosion of financial subsidies for family day care training programs, the future of such projects is bleak. With the increase in status and income of providers, more sophisticated courses at higher fees are being offered, and it will be interesting to see how they will be received.

Regulation

It has often been assumed that the licensing of family day care ensures the quality of the program. Nothing could be further from the truth (see chap. 9). Licensing of family day care is not an effective

regulating tool. At its best, it assures minimal health and safety standards, and at its worst it is a deceptive device that promises parents
more than it can deliver. The National Day Care Home Study reported in 1980 that

> most of the fifty states have laws governing the regulation of family
> day care homes. However, by its very nature, family day care is
> very costly for the states to supervise. A typical licensed home may
> have only three children. On a per-child basis, the cost of licensing
> and monitoring a home is, therefore, burdensome in comparison
> with the costs of monitoring and licensing a day care center where
> the average enrollment may be fifty or more (p. 27).

An expert in the field of child development would generally have
a hard time understanding, let alone enforcing, the family day care
regulations written in most states, although in all fairness one can say
that there has been a trend toward simplifying the language.

It is easy to understand the resistance to family day care licensing. "It reflects the attitudes of most families about outside interference
in personal matters. Like a family, there is great reluctance to give
a government body the right to come into the place we call home and
tell us how to raise our children, how many children we may have,
how we should feed them, teach them, etc. And this is how many,
probably most, family day care providers feel" (Sale 1980, p. 10).

The parents who bring their children to a family day care home
daily could be the most effective regulators. They are able to see what
is happening more realistically than the licensor who may drop in once
a year or once every three years. However, most parents do not understand or exercise the power they have as regulators to make complaints
to the providers and, if that fails, to the regulating agency. Withdraw-
ing their child from the program is another form of control. These
options are not exercised because parents feel that there is little or no
choice in arrangements, or they are afraid that somehow their complaints will result in mistreatment of the children.

From a parental perspective, licensing is often deceptive. Parents
erroneously believe that the license hanging in the living room gives
some guarantee that the home is regularly inspected and supervised
by a local agency for all kinds of things, including healthfulness, safety, cleanliness, programming, and quality. Of course this view is a
long way from fact. The only assurance of regular home visits is after
complaints have been filed against a provider.

Despite the ineffectiveness of licensing, those providers who are licensed are usually great advocates of that form of regulation. They will fight to retain this form of licensure because of the public validation it provides, while acknowledging that the license does not guarantee much more than compliance in terms of filing the necessary papers.

Another form of regulation in operation in several states and being considered in others is registration.

> Registration generally requires providers to register with a government agency and attest to the health and safety of the environment in the family day care setting. Fingerprint checks and TB clearances are also required. A complaint system is clearly established and all complaints are routinely investigated. The regulatory and support functions are separated under this form of regulation. There is no lengthy wait to discourage prospective providers from entering the field, and home visits are made of a random sample of providers to check for compliance (Sale 1980, p. 12).

There is little debate over whether or not family day care should be regulated. The disagreement arises over the form that regulation should take. Given the trend toward deregulation on the part of federal, state, and local governments (for financial and philosophical reasons), registration is the option being chosen by several states. Texas and Michigan have had interesting results after introducing registration laws: an increased number of homes are regulated at decreased cost (Tucker 1980, p. 28).

The major question raised by the controversy over licensing and registration centers on the issue of compliance. The Michigan study showed less compliance with state rules, and the Texas report "revealed that 92 percent of the homes had five or fewer violations of the thirty state standards" (Tucker 1980, p. 28). Child care advocates will probably never resolve their concerns over compliance and the dilemma will continue as to whether the goal of regulation should be to try to keep "undesirables" out of the system through licensing, or to try to include more providers by making less stringent rules and, perhaps, expecting less compliance.

Quality

Quality, like beauty, is in the eyes and hearts of the beholders. The quest for quality is one of the most difficult issues in family day care. While working in the Community Family Day Care Project, child development specialists who were staff members could always agree on the homes that were substandard but could seldom agree on the homes that they would choose for their own children.

As elusive as the search for quality has been, some common indicators have been present in the homes of the providers that I perceive as offering quality day care. These indicators speak to issues over and above such things as a healthy and safe environment; adequate and age-appropriate toys, equipment, and programming; and a provider in good health and interested in his or her work. The quality indicators are

- Informed parental choice
- Support available locally for family day care providers
- Respect for families' life-styles and cultures in children's programming

Photograph by Jean Berlfein, courtesy of Child Care Employee Project

INFORMED PARENTAL CHOICE

The difficulty parents face in making an appropriate child care arrangement has been discussed elsewhere. Suffice it to say, where there are few choices, the chance of making a good arrangement diminishes.

Over and above the need for choice, "It is important for parents and providers to be aware of the kinds of questions they can ask and what their rights and responsibilities are when making day care arrangements. [Both must] recognize that they are colleagues in the shared care of the child" (Sale 1980, p. 12). Assistance in informing parents about their child care choices is provided by information and referral programs (see chap. 12) and community education projects:

Usually regulation through registration includes a community education campaign to raise consumer awareness concerning rights and responsibilities in a family day care arrangement. A simple one-page document, written in English and Spanish, was used in Texas and California and was distributed to each parent using a registered home. This type of education demystifies the child care arrangement and can only help parents in their decision making. More is needed in terms of direct media campaigns to inform parents and the community about family day care.

SUPPORT FOR FAMILY DAY CARE PROVIDERS

With low pay and long hours, a support system for family day care providers is essential. "If an adult is expected to provide a nurturing environment for young children for a seven- to ten-hour day, then that adult must also receive some nurturing; adults cannot always be the dispensers of love and attention without also being the receivers" (Sale 1980, p. 13).

The development and continued growth of provider groups and training programs are examples of this kind of support. Self-help provider groups are growing by leaps and bounds. The goals of such groups are usually lofty, but the more difficult task of reaching their objectives is elusive. More often than they would like to acknowledge, family day care organizations spend a good deal of time in struggling for power, a common characteristic of many emerging organizations. It is not easy to maintain the interest and participation of a group of women and men of diverse socioeconomic, ethnic, and religious backgrounds. The self-help groups are in various developmental stages, yet each has a strong determination to enhance the image of family day care and a commitment to educate the community to the services they provide. It makes a good deal of sense to funnel support services through such groups, especially when there are no existing I&R's.

The training and education offered to family day care providers must be relevant and job-related. Generally the programs that have been developed have required family day care providers to come to the campus in numbers that will justify the class and will meet the rules and regulations of the colleges and adult education schools. After a long day at home with the children, evening and weekend classes located in a formal institution may not attract a large number of providers. The need for more on-the-job, competency-based training is great, and the newly developed Family Day Care Child Development Associate Credential Program is very promising in this regard.

RESPECT FOR FAMILY LIFE-STYLES IN CHILDREN'S PROGRAMMING

Meeting the needs of children and families is paramount in a quality child care program. A good match is essential. Respect for parents' cultures and life-styles results in continuity for children and can be a critical factor in whether or not the arrangement will work. Babies, toddlers, and preschoolers who spend most of their waking day in a place away from home are sensitive to the way routines such as eating, sleeping, toileting, and discipline are handled.

The child whose parent is a vegetarian and is placed in a family day care home where red meat is served each day is put into a conflict-ridden situation. The parents who need their child to go to sleep early and make an arrangement where napping takes place late in the day face some difficult times. In these cases, it is the child who ultimately suffers. If the arrangement does continue, then the child is receiving different messages about value systems; if it does not continue, then the child is put on a merry-go-round of changing providers.

Support systems must be pulled together to ensure that family values are respected and carried into programming for children. I&R's must carry the message to parents and providers; public education programs can help to alert the community; self-help provider organizations should be involved in working with parents so that there can be more mutual communication and understanding; training programs could well emphasize this sensitive area of possible conflict.

CASE STUDY

Josie Johnson had just delivered her second child when her husband died in a car accident. She had always worked, even after Julie, her first child, was born. She had held different jobs, ranging from clerical work to sales, but had never really enjoyed any of them. With the birth of Evan and the premature death of her husband, Josie was determined to stay at home and provide a stable, caring home for her children.

Julie had been cared for by a neighbor when Josie worked outside of the home, and it was clear to her that this type of occupation was hard but very rewarding. Josie lived in a small apartment and found that it was unsuitable for caring for more children than her own. She talked to her sister and brother, Ethel and Jack Ferguson, about using their small home for a joint child care venture. Ethel was childless but looked on this as a good opportunity to use her nursery school certificate from a small college. She had only been able to find work in proprietary centers that paid minimum wages and left her tired, "broke," and unfulfilled.

Josie and Ethel looked forward to following the family pattern of raising a large family. The notion of having a family day care home was second best to having their own large families. It was not long before they were taking care of three children from one family and four from another. There were two school-aged children, including Julie, three infants counting Evan, and the remaining four children were preschoolers.

Josie and Ethel decided not to apply for a license, since they had heard so many stories about the licensor in their area fussing over needless details and dropping in and talking about her own personal problems at inopportune times—like nap or lunch time.

Ethel's house had a large back yard, and the sisters and Jack, with the help of the older children, built a large sandbox, a tree house, a water table, and easels, and put up some small hammocks and swinging chairs for the infants and toddlers.

Even though the house was small, the children had the full run of it. Neatness was not a priority, but the house was clean, and a good deal of emphasis was put on children's health, brushing teeth, washing hands, and personal grooming. Josie and Ethel loved cooking, so food projects were planned with and for the children each day.

The babies set their own schedules, while the preschoolers had a more established program, which could and did change if something more interesting came along. Either Josie or Ethel usually had a baby in her arms or on her hip, and there was seldom any crying; they did not believe one could spoil a child. "If a child cries, she's telling you that she needs something."

Josie and Ethel started caring for children seven years ago. Today Julie is a helper, and Evan is one of the school-aged children in care.

Josie has remarried and is working in a local small business with her husband. Ethel is licensed and caring for six children plus Evan in the same small house, which now also is home to a small dog, a hamster, and a goldfish.

Ethel has strong convictions about child development: children need to be autonomous and try new things and to be able to succeed and fail; they need to have opportunities to be messy; they must have times when they can have privacy; they must feel loved and accepted; and formal reading, writing, and arithmetic will be taught at school— not in her home. Toilet training takes care of itself when the child is ready.

Every week she goes to the library to check out the books she thinks will interest the children. She utilizes the toy loan offered by her local I&R program and participates in the monthly training sessions offered by that agency. She has joined the newly formed providers association and has become the recording secretary. She plans to join Weight Watchers next month.

Both Ethel and Josie have remained close friends of the families whom they have served. There is an annual picnic that is growing in size and occasional camping trips in which some of the families participate.

Ethel now makes a good income from her work. She has a sliding fee schedule and averages seventy-five dollars a week per child. There is a waiting list of families who want to place children in her care. She says that she and her husband have never been happier. "We have all the children around us we could ever want, but we can still take off weekends without a worry. And it sure beats working for the Little Bo Peep Center, making a minimum wage and having nothing to show for it. I'm in charge and can have as much fun as the children. We cuddle a lot, we laugh together, and we're like one big happy family."

IMPLICATIONS FOR CHANGE

Three major trends on the family day care horizon require some thought for the future. They raise concerns that have both positive and negative aspects and raise questions that have no easy answers. The trends are

- The increasing cost of family day care
- The growing number of systems and agency-sponsored family day care homes

• The increasing number of large family day care homes serving up to fifteen children.

Increasing Cost of Family Day Care

The issue of cost is one of those issues that concerns almost everyone who thinks about it. It is not unusual to find family day care providers who work a sixty-hour week and lose money. In essence, many providers are subsidizing the children in their care. On the other hand, there are small but increasing numbers of providers who view themselves as professionals and believe that charging high fees is a measure of that professionalism. These providers charge more than most centers in their areas and make a handsome living but are too expensive for many families to afford. The nonsubsidized working class family that traditionally uses neighborhood family day care may be in the unenviable position of either exploiting a neighbor by paying what the family can afford or not using the service because it is too expensive.

As the number of provider associations grows, the issues of wages and fees (and low status) will always be one of the first topics to be discussed. Like other organizations of human service providers, there is strength in being together and also peer pressure to maintain certain monetary standards. But what happens in a situation where fees are raised and families are not considered? At times these parents are viewed as the enemy.

It is now reasonably clear that there is no such thing as cheap child care. *Someone* has to pay the full cost — and the question of who is going to pay is a serious one. For example, if the provider does not receive enough to reward him or her or take care of his or her family, the *provider* directly contributes to the subsidy. On the other hand, if the provider is adequately reimbursed and earns a decent living, then the chances are that he or she caters to *affluent families* who can afford to pay the total cost of care. And finally, if less affluent parents are unable to pay what is necessary to give them a choice in child care arrangements, it may ultimately be the *children* who pay a price in terms of being placed in an inappropriate situation. These examples are in no way intended to suggest that high-cost programs are necessarily of higher quality. The question is this: Why is it that only the affluent can afford to pay the full cost of child care?

Other countries care enough about their children to make it possible for all families to purchase child care and still pay the providers an adequate living. A federally funded family allowance seems like a workable solution to this problem — giving parents an allowance to purchase the kind of care they wish. Before this can be done, however, we must change our country's attitude about children and shift priorities from weapons and death to children, families, and life.

Systems and Agency-Sponsored Family Day Care

There are a number of advantages to agency-sponsored family day care networks. Providers receive regular salaries and some benefits and training. Being part of a system also adds to the status of the job, as well as providing ongoing adult contact. "The National Day Care Home Study has also found that day care systems play an important role in promoting quality care by maintaining desirable enrollment levels, monitoring regulatory compliance, training caregivers, providing technical assistance to the caregiver and providing a vehicle for parent involvement" (Fosburg 1981, p. 13). In fact, one of the recommendations that came out of this national study was that "the development and expansion of systems be emphasized as one of the principal means of providing subsidized day care in a family day care setting" (p. 125).

The disadvantages of agency-sponsored family day care was not sufficiently described in the National Day Care Home Study. While from the point of view of a government funding agency it certainly is neater and easier to deal with one agency than ten or twenty different providers, there are disadvantages. One of the important pluses of family day care, as opposed to center care, is its adaptability. For example, children may come to a family day care home even if they are mildly ill. Some providers will take children to the doctor, to the barber, on family outings, or on trips to the bank, grocery store, and garage. It is only the most "enlightened" system that will permit these kinds of things to happen, since the need for uniformity, meeting insurance needs of the agency, and the push toward professionalism may mitigate against a more flexible, humane approach in family care homes that are part of systems.

It is also possible that low-income parents who are the users of these systems may have few opportunities to express their parental concerns and exercise their independence. When a child is placed and the bills are paid by an agency, there may be a continuation of the attitude fostered by our welfare system that parents are not competent and are not able to make good child care arrangements, and also a lack of responsiveness to parental needs and concerns on the part of the provider, who, after all, works for and is paid by the agency.

The other major disadvantage facing all subsidized programs is the problem of segregating poor families in one setting. The effect is not only negative on the families, but it also touches the community in which the homes are located. Those homes that are part of a system become "elite" groups because of their access to more training, services, toys, and equipment. Thus the homes serving the subsidized children are more regulated and stand apart, causing resentment and antagonism among parents in communities in desperate need of assistance and support.

Large Family Day Care Homes

Why is it that when we decide to solve a human service problem, we look for some model that works, then apply the principle that big is better and more efficient? We have seen what this has done to hospital care, care of the elderly, and group homes for children at risk. It seems so logical: if family day care can work well for small groups of children, especially infants and toddlers, then why not find larger homes, provide an additional caregiver, and serve many more children in one setting? In California, the trend has been dramatic in the licensed sector: in 1970 there were approximately 130 large family day care homes, each serving from seven to twelve children; today there are estimated to be 3000 such homes (Sale 1982). In the 1970s, those large group homes were not licensed to take care of infants and toddlers; today they are. If this trend has grown among the licensed homes, then it surely has increased among the unlicensed.

In areas where the need for more child care is great and where housing for either center or home care is limited, the logical solution is to increase the number of children served through each family day care program. Also, with increasing inflation providers see this as a way of increasing their incomes. With the trend toward deregulation, there is also a push toward changing and loosening the requirements for the large home care program.

There has been a good deal of research on group size and size of program (Prescott 1970) in center care. When the size of the group or of the program gets beyond a certain point, then the quality of the program often suffers. It takes people with great expertise to develop and maintain high standards in large programs. The same principle may be applied to family day care.

Without benefit of research but on the basis of years of observation, I feel it is safe to say that the large family day care home is a different kind of child care. There seems to be a necessity for more structured activities and more scheduling of those activities. Just keeping track of that number of children makes it necessary for the children and adults (usually a provider and an aide) to have a different kind of interaction. The environment has to be arranged differently. In the early 1970s, large homes were seen as ideal arrangements for school-aged children — and that made a good deal of sense. But now that children can be in care from infancy through school age, it takes an experienced, well-organized, and mature adult to balance the needs of all age groups, as well as to supervise an aide (who, in California, may be anyone over the age of fourteen).

This is not to say that we do not need the large group homes in some areas. We do. However, is this really family day care? The large family day care home is neither small nor intimate. On the other hand, it is not a center but has some of the characteristics of a center. There should be another name that could be applied to this type of care, something that describes it, like "home-based center program." Regulations should be developed that match the program, something between the regulations for a family day care home and those for a small center. Requiring doors that are of a certain width and that open out does not make a lot of sense for this kind of program; requiring some experience on the part of the provider does.

CONCLUSIONS

Family day care has been with us for thousands of years, but only recently has it been considered worthy of study and exploration. In the years since the early 1970s, it has come out of the closet to be examined and judged with all of its positive and negative characteristics. As a service, family day care has much to offer children, parents, providers, and the community; as an occupation, it still suffers lack of status and is not the most financially rewarding job available; as a profession, it has a long way to go.

The future of family day care seems guaranteed. The trend toward larger units, more systems, and growing family day care associations should be carefully observed with an eye to supporting and protecting the people who are being served: the children, parents, and providers. As a long-time advocate of family day care, I believe it is vital that we keep family day care responsive to the needs of all three of these groups and that this can best be done by maintaining the small, comfortable, and intimate service that is so prized in a family. The corporate, institutional model fostered by some is the antithesis of family day care. Alice Rossi says it well: "We must plan and build for the most fundamental root of society in human parenting and not from the shaky superstructure created by men in the fraction of time in which industrial societies have existed" (Rossi 1977, p. 26).

Chapter 3

THE PHYSICAL SETTING
IN DAY CARE

Elizabeth Prescott

One of the easiest ways to make day care better is to improve the physical environment. Behavior does not occur in a vacuum. It happens in a specific place and time frame composed of a particular configuration of objects and people. If this configuration is changed, the cues that elicit behavior and possibilities for responding are altered. Thus the ability to understand physical setting becomes one of the most powerful tools in regulating behavior and in implementing wished-for experiences.

When our research team (Prescott, Jones, and Kritchevsky) first began its studies, we looked at adults on the assumption that it was their interactions with children and their beliefs about these interactions that were important. However, we found over time that we were unconsciously bringing in another variable. After a morning's observations we were saying things like: "I coded her for lots of restricting and directing, but there was hardly anything for children to do — and the shape of that yard was so awkward," or, "I don't think she has had much experience with kids — Why did everything go so well?"

It was in taking these comments seriously that we discovered the importance of the environment. It was the analysis of space that caregivers found most useful. We were learning that the acquisition of a spatial vocabulary seems to help people think more clearly and communicate better about their programs. We also discovered that adults find it easier to analyze and criticize something as concrete and impersonal as spatial arrangements than to address someone's decision-making or teaching style.

The author wishes to thank the Ford Foundation for Grant no. 795-0259, which supported the writing of this and other articles on day care. This research was funded by Grant no. R-219 and its continuations from the Office of Child Development USDHEW.

We often forget that children's early memories take the form of sensory images. Over the years, we have made it a practice to ask older children who were in day care when they were younger what they remember about it. They seldom remember the people. What they do remember are things like "sitting under the big tree in the yard on a hot summer day for a picnic lunch" or "lying forever on that green cot at nap time," or "getting my back rubbed at nap time," or "the string beans, and we had to eat some," or "building a fort with the blocks and hiding behind it."

Adults often are not good judges of the workability of a setting for children. As Peller (1972) observed, "The adults' attitude toward space is usually utilitarian" (p. 225). Adults notice whether an environment is clean or attractive to an adult eye, but neither of these qualities will tell you whether an environment will be a good place for adults and children to live together. Much of what happens in day care appears to have little impact on the child one way or another. A few things may be recalled with negative affect, shutting off possibilities for further exploration. Other experiences open the world for a child and provide positive memories that remain throughout the life cycle. These are the experiences we hope to maximize.

"Quality of life" for the adults in day care, as well as the children, needs much more attention than it has received. The experience of opening the world for a child is incredibly rewarding to an adult, especially if the adult can feel his or her contribution to that moment. All too often, though, day care staff feel that they have little support or power to implement their ideas. Giving maximum control of the physical setting to staff often increases their sense of well-being.

The discussion that follows presents an analytic scheme for examining the physical setting and describes ways in which such an analysis can be used to make day care settings work better. For some this may mean easier and more pleasant ways of getting through the day; others may want more variety and a more stimulating program. Hopefully some will see the possibilities for individualizing the program and giving children more leeway to explore and to make sense of their own experience.

SPATIAL ORGANIZATION

If you look at a day care setting when children are not there, it is easy to identify some key organizing features. These aspects of the setting must be in order if other environmental changes are to work.

Pathways

A pathway defines traffic flow. It is the empty space on the floor or the ground through which people move from one place to another. Pathways are difficult to describe in words, but they are easy to identify, if well defined. Look at a space and ask yourself the question, "How do children get from one place to another?" If you cannot answer this question, then you can be sure that the pathway is ill defined.

Pathways should provide appropriate access to the activity settings that you wish children to use. When pathways are unclear, or when they disperse traffic in inappropriate ways, staff will experience undue fatigue, and children will persist in doing things that do not feel

Photograph by Jean Wambach

comfortable to adults. "Activity setting" describes the place and any objects in the place that must be there in order for the activity to occur (Gump and Sutton-Smith 1955; Gump, Schoggen, and Redl 1957); for example, the block area, the housekeeping corner, and the bathroom. Just as the pathway regulates traffic flow into these settings, the placement and boundaries of these settings will determine the appropriateness of the pathway.

Storage

One defining point for the spatial arrangements just described is the way in which storage is utilized. Storage has not been given enough attention as a key factor in providing good day care. Adequate storage helps to guarantee (1) enough supplies for a good program; (2) safe places to keep things that should not be accessible to children; and (3) basic order (see Waligura 1971). In two of our studies (Prescott and Milich 1974; Prescott et al. 1975), we found that the amount of storage is associated with the richness of the programs. In general, the more the storage, the more there is to do.

Availability can range from closed storage, with nothing ever available to children except the things that are being used at the moment, to totally open storage with everything always available. Osmon (1971) points out that if there is only closed storage, children will have little choice and probably not enough to do. However, too much open storage often prevents the staff from regulating the amount of choice they wish to give.

Peller (1972) also provides an important perspective on the rationale for both open and closed storage:

> For children who are accustomed to find their materials in plain sight, things which have to be taken from a closed cabinet or from behind a curtain have a special attraction. Toys kept in a cabinet locked with a key have a particular appeal. Most young children are fascinated with a key which they can insert in a keyhole and afterwards return to its hook on the wall. Of course, a key which is so freely accessible to a group of youngsters will sometimes get lost, or be taken home by a child. One may argue: why should the teacher add another concern to her full day? There are so many things children like to play with, would not the teacher do better to concentrate her effort on satisfying the children's emotional needs? We do not say that a preschool child who has no chance of handling a key is deprived of an essential experience. Yet he does miss some-

thing. The more all "perishable" items, anything that can be lost, soiled, or pocketed, are removed from the children's reach, the more grows their destructiveness (p. 230).

We also found that organized storage seems to produce more complex and longer-lasting play. It seems that storage can help children to visualize relations and plan future actions. Thus organized storage would appear to support initiative and imagination.

Because day care is so labor-intensive, there is always the temptation to select procedures that appear to simplify the adult's work. For example, Montes and Risley (1975) examined the effect of using shelves versus toy boxes for storage. Toy boxes increased the time in selecting and thereby cut down on playing time, but cleanup was much faster for the toy boxes than for the shelves.

However, Montes and Risley did not take into account other possible outcomes of a more long-range nature. We have often, in our observations, noted a child who sat three to ten feet from an open storage area looking intently, then going over and carefully choosing materials. We have also observed children copying block storage patterns in their building play. Duplicating these patterns seems to have been facilitated by orderly storage and by the experience of putting the blocks back on the shelves at the end of the play.

A storage problem that is seldom discussed is the need for temporary storage of projects that carry over from one day to the next. Day care for school-aged children, for example, often uses facilities that have younger occupants during school hours. If the older children get involved in long-range projects, a very desirable activity, they often have no place to store things safely.

Flexibility

Another important aspect of organization and the control of access is a degree of flexibility in the setting. Permanent shelving, swing supports sunk into the requisite eighteen inches of concrete, and the location of toilet areas are all "fixed-feature" space (Hall 1966). It is important to have some undeveloped areas (potential units) that can be turned into play areas, such as empty tables, a porch, or a corner floor area. When heavy items such as bookcases or storage cabinets are on casters, they are easily moved, and once moved the novelty of old or forgotten equipment is often restored.

The absence of flexibility is often a miserable fact of life for the staff who must live with spatial features that cannot easily be undone.

An example of this is an expensive climbing structure that is underused but ruins visibility for teachers and takes up space that is needed for other purposes. People who work with children are often inexperienced in reading blueprints or in visualizing alterations that are proposed. Therefore, it is not only imperative to discuss proposed changes with those who must live with them, but also to assist them in imagining how the new installation will alter their present behavior.

The presence of flexibility permits staff to respond to individual needs, to changes in development of both children and adults, and to the very human wish for novelty. Some aspects of the indoor and outdoor setting must, of course, be fixed but attention to the importance of enhancing flexibility will encourage active engagement and enliven spirits.

Using Spatial Characteristics for Problem Solving

The goal of good spatial organization is to make traffic flow and access self-regulating so that children are not overburdened by guidance and interruptions and adults can step back and concentrate on giving individual attention.

An example may demonstrate how crucial good organization is to the well-being of both adults and children. At Pacific Oaks, our day care center is located in an old home. The house once had been the college library, and for years everyone entered through the side door. Since we are all creatures of habit and not very conscious of our spatial choices, this door was kept as the main entrance when the building became the day care center. In many ways the program flourished, but there continued to be certain problems that could not be solved: children kept leaving jackets and sweaters and personal possessions lying around instead of putting them in their cubbies; there seemed to be no good place to store the cots; parents persisted in standing around in the narrow entryway, visiting and trying to read the notices on the bulletin board, oblivious to the traffic jam they were creating; children in the bathroom were always being intruded upon by anyone who entered or left the building, because the bathroom was adjacent to the entry; children raced from the entryway into the main rooms; and children disappeared out the door and down Shady Lane without notifying staff.

One day, after a variety of solutions had been tried, the director put her finger on the problem: the pathway was wrong. By reestablishing the original front door as the main entry, she found a solution to every problem on the list. Although they fussed a bit in the beginning, parents soon accepted the longer, slower means of entry. This change in itself provided parent and child with slower, more measured arrivals and departures.

Moving the cubbies so that they faced the front door supported the ritual of parent and child using the cubby together for both arrival and departure and provided a barrier from intrusion for the activity area located behind the cubbies. The old entryway became the place for cot storage. The elimination of traffic in this area established some privacy and made the bathroom a low-key, secluded area. The impulsive entryway dashes also stopped. The parents' bulletin board was placed on the porch, and parents could read it without disrupting the flow of traffic. They could also sit on the wide porch railing and pause or visit for a moment. Note that once this change was agreed upon (and it was simple to implement), the behavior of a large number of adults and children changed immediately. It is for this reason that attention to basic spatial organization is so important.

ACTIVITY SETTINGS

Once the basic spatial organization is in order, it is possible to look more closely at the activity settings. These place/time/task units provide the life of the program. Note the attributes of activity settings: there is a *place* — the sandbox, the swings, the bathroom, the art table. There is a *time*, which may be flexible or fixed. Day care staff become aware of the importance of time when lunch is forty-five minutes late or if the plumber says the bathroom has to be closed from 11:00 to 12:00. On the other hand, the clay table may be provided every morning or not at all. The *task* describes the purpose of a setting and usually — but not always — gives the setting its name. The reason that this seemingly obvious fact is worth noting is that every aspect of the setting should facilitate the purposes for which it exists. If the activity is block play, then the task requires adequate space free from intrusion, plenty of accessible storage for a sufficient supply of blocks and other props. Also, an activity setting may have a purpose that is quite different from its designated name.

Activity settings can be of two types: (1) essential settings, such as those for toileting, lunch, and nap time, and (2) settings for play, considered optional because there is always choice. Curiously, not much attention is paid to essential activity settings.

Dimensions of Activity Settings

In our research (Prescott, Jones, and Kritchevsky 1967; Jones 1973; Prescott and Milich 1974; Prescott et al. 1975; Jones and Prescott 1978), we have identified seven dimensions of activity settings as being particularly useful and important to keep in awareness.

OPEN/CLOSED

Activities that are *open* have no "correct" outcome and do not have an arbitrary stopping point. Examples include painting, playing with sand or play-doh, and tricycle riding. *Closed* activities involve a right answer or a clear ending. Examples include putting puzzles together, playing lotto games, and playing "Simon Says." Some activities—building with legos, for instance—are what we call *semiclosed* because the materials require attention to their constraints even though there is a certain openness of outcome. Open equipment tends to encourage creativity and experimentation and to support social interaction. Closed equipment usually gives "right–wrong" feedback and tends not to support social interaction, although it does give a sense of accomplishment.

SIMPLE/COMPLEX

This classification is based on absorption potential—the extent to which the play unit contains potential for active manipulation and alteration by children (Kritchevsky, Prescott, and Walling 1969).

The *simple unit* has one obvious use and does not have subparts or a juxtaposition of materials that enable a child to manipulate or improvise. Examples include playing on a swing, jungle gym, rocking horse, or tricycle.

The *complex unit* has subparts or a juxtaposition of two essentially different play materials that enable the child to manipulate or improvise. Examples include a sand pile with digging equipment, a doll bed with dolls, and single play materials and objects that encourage substantial improvisation or have a considerable element of unpredictability, such as play-doh or paints, a table with books to look at, or an area with animals such as guinea pigs or rabbits.

The *super unit* is a complex unit that has three or more play materials juxtaposed. Examples include a sand pile with digging equipment and water, a jungle gym with movable climbing boards and a blanket, and a play-doh table with tools and pieces of cardboard of varying shapes and sizes.

HIGH/LOW MOBILITY

Activities differ in their requirements for body movement. Running, climbing, and tricycle riding all specify much mobility, utilizing large muscles. Doing puzzles and listening to a story require sitting still with very limited mobility. Stringing beads requires low mobility and high fine-muscle and eye–hand coordination. Some activities require what we have called moderate mobility in that some movement is either permitted or required. Examples would include indoor block building or quiet dramatic play.

Children differ greatly in their need for high mobility and their comfort in activities that restrict mobility. Adults sometimes forget how difficult it is for children to mold their bodies to the demands of some settings.

SOCIAL STRUCTURE: LARGE GROUP/INDIVIDUAL

Activities also differ in social structure. Listening to a story at group time is quite different from having a story read only to oneself. Playing with a best friend in a sand pile is very different from playing alone or sharing the play with six other children.

Children differ greatly in their skill in handling different kinds of social structure. An awareness of these varying skill levels is of great help in facilitating children's social problem solving.

SOFT/HARD

The dimension of "softness" was so named because it appeared to indicate a responsive quality of the environment to the child, especially on a sensual/tactile level. It was based on the presence or absence of eleven components: (1) malleable materals, such as ooblek, clay, or Play-doh; (2) sand that children can be in, either in a box or play area; (3) "laps" — teachers holding children; (4) single-sling swings; (5) grass that children can be on; (6) a large rug or carpeting indoors; (7) water as an activity; (8) very messy materials, such as finger paint, clay, or mud; (9) child/adult cozy furniture, such as rockers, couches, or lawn swings; (10) dirt to dig in; (11) and animals that can be held, such as guinea pigs, dogs, and cats. The softest activity settings are also the most perennially appealing.

INTRUSION/SECLUSION

A high possibility of intrusion is appropriate for some activity settings and ruinous to others. For example, high-energy, fast-moving dramatic play sometimes thrives on intrusion. Making social contact

Photograph by Jean Wambach

and getting something started often requires an opportunity for some intrusion. Climbing structures from which a child at the top can call, "See me! See me!" are appropriately planned for intrusion.

Seclusion, on the other hand, is created by providing places where a child can play privately or in a more deliberate, intimate way. In homes, one of the important ways in which the adult regulates children's experiences is through the judicious use of private or protected boundaried areas. Children also intuitively self-select such areas. The fact that a child at home can crawl into a big easy chair, settle under the dining room table, or take a soothing bath in a smooth, boundaried tub before nap time, contributes to the well-being of everyone involved. These are ways in which children can have privacy to pursue their own ideas and regulate their own needs for active and quiet time. In group care, private corners are often strikingly absent, and their creation takes thought and ingenuity.

RISK/SAFETY

Everyone in day care understands the importance of safety, but the importance of opportunities for risk often are overlooked. Children are fascinated by height, speed, moving objects, fire, and other situations that involve an element of risk. So often in day care, rules of prohibition (frequently passed down from administrative levels far removed from the daily life of the center) surround the child. "Don't run fast," "Don't swing sideways," "Don't jump off the barrel." Risky things are interesting and exciting, and contact with them gives a child a sense of power.

Children love to experiment with their bodies in space. The provision of an environment with loose parts means that children will experiment and try unusual ways of doing things. For example, if swings have seats that can be unhooked and placed very high, very low, or crooked, children will try out these possibilities with great interest. There are always adults who will say that swinging crooked is not safe. Safety is clearly an important issue in day care, but there is a difference between caring for safety by teaching children how to do interesting and challenging things safely and forbidding any kind of risk or innovation because it is unsafe. Typical of safety rules are those proposed by the National Safety Council (n.d.):

> Children should not be allowed to stand up or kneel on swings, or to jump from moving swings. Children should be discouraged from holding smaller children in their laps while swinging. . . . Crawling or running up the slide, sliding down backwards and sliding in wet bathing suits should not be allowed (p. 1).

The problem with these rules is that these are things that children will do. Any adult reading these rules can conjure up a vision of an accident that would explain their origin. Conversely, as adults most of us can remember our ease and delight as children in doing all these things. If these things are strictly forbidden when an adult is watching they will be tried when no adult is around. Figuring out the consequences and possibilities of actions is an especially effective way of encouraging children to think ahead and to see the usefulness of words to map bodily action. If equipment is located on soft ground cover and children have facilitative supervision, they will more quickly learn how to take care of themselves. It is essential to build in safe design features, but, in our opinion, it is also stifling to prohibit experimentation. Accidents can be minimized by eliminating booby traps such as sharp concrete edges that are covered up by sand, broken equipment, and poor placement of activities.

Using the Dimensions for Problem Solving

The dimensions just described can be used in a variety of combinations for the purpose of problem solving. Suppose, for example, that a group of fast tricycle riders persists in playing "crash," despite constant admonitions and occasional benching. An analysis using the dimensions might run as follows.

Tricycle riding is a very open activity. The addition of props such as stop signs, gas pumps, and roads designated by chalk would serve to introduce constraints. However, the introduction of props also makes the activity more complex. If tricycles are of different types (i.e., one with a rumble seat that carries one or two children, or a pickup with room to carry things), the quality of the play and the holding power of the activity will be increased.

Undoubtedly, one of the attractions of tricycle riding is the high mobility; risk taking is also involved here. Perhaps an occasional game of "crash" is permissible, or perhaps there could be a "hot wheels day" when children bring these vehicles and race them.

Another attraction is the possibility of intrusion. Adding props supports the development of initiative, described by Erikson (1950). Bumping and pushing interruptions are precursors of later interactions that are more sophisticated.

The soft/hard dimension is only indirectly applicable to this situation. Children who are confined to hard settings often respond with an insistent need for release of tension. Ample chances for sand and water play, for lounging on soft rugs and pillows often help high-energy children to find a better balance in the types of activity they need and seek out.

Dimensions in Essential Activity Settings

The dimensions just described do not apply only to optional settings but also to essential settings, such as those for eating, toileting, sleeping, and separating. In programs that serve the function of a "school," often attention is given to educational settings, and needs for care are only tolerated as unavoidable. In day care, we suggest that the caring function should be given a major priority. Lifelong patterns of body experience are at stake here. Therefore the creation of these settings so that they are as comfortable and pleasurable as possible is of high priority.

Photograph by Jean Wambach

Entryways

These are the places where children separate from and reunite with
parents and the day care staff. It is in these places that the intrusion/
seclusion dimension needs to be delicately balanced. Separation and
reunion seem to work best when the entry area provides a predictable
and nonabrupt transition from "out there" to "here" and a certainty
of being greeted on arrival. If the space permits a way of slowly eas-
ing into activities, the transition becomes smoother for many children.
We have often watched a newly arrived child select a swing or tricycle
or a seat at a table and then intently scan all the places and the people in them before moving into active play.

Parents, too, seem to thrive on spaces that provide a place to watch
after the goodbye or before the greeting, and parents also benefit from
smooth transitions. At the moment when parent and caregiver are together, authority can become ambiguous. Again, a predictable entryway can help to clarify for both parent and child (and caregiver)
that a transition is occurring and that it is time to end one series of
relationships and begin another.

BATHROOMS

The lack of attention given to this crucial area is surprising. Bettleheim (1974) has described the importance of making the bathroom a comfortable and pleasing place for both children and staff. Economy of construction tends to dictate the location of the bathrooms in one central area instead of dispersed facilities located in separate group areas. When toilets are poorly located, without very careful planning, teachers will be handed toilet schedules, and children ordinarily will not be free to come and go according to individual need.

Bathrooms are often planned to be small and efficient. As a result, much of the teacher's energy will be directed toward "keeping the show on the road" and snuffing out any illicit water play or questions about anatomical differences.

Bathrooms that are comfortable and pleasant for both adults and children can encourage quiet, intimate times. It is during these times that children may raise those important questions about body differences. Of all the settings in which one would wish to generate good feelings, this is one of the most important.

SLEEPING AREAS

The important dimensions for nap time seem to be seclusion and softness. These are often provided for if some openness or leeway is permitted. Nap time in large rooms with strict rules about body positions (and about not adjusting the position of one's cot) is a hard, closed setting allowing for little seclusion. Children often miss their parents and get close to their fears before falling asleep. It is a time when children need and respond to nurturing.

Nap time rules can permit children to place their cots in their favorite secluded places or behind movable partitions for privacy, to have a blanket and stuffed animal from home, and to select the end of the cot at which head or feet will go. Adding a bit of softness in the form of a moment of lap sitting or a back rub is possible. There might be books for those who are slow to settle down and some option for nonsleepers.

AREAS FOR FOOD PREPARATION AND EATING

Most regulations assume that children will not and should not be in the kitchen area. However, some of the nicest moments that we have seen in day care are those when children could perch in safe places and watch, talk with, or even help the cook. Good kitchen design can keep children safely away from dangerous areas and still not entirely close off contact between the food preparation and the eating of food.

Food and the people who provide it have special meaning for young children. In family day care programs where children are not separated from the preparation of food, we have been struck by the quality of the conversation that occurs in the kitchens. There was an intimacy about these communications that occurred when an adult prepared food with one or two children. Often the talk began about the food and who liked or didn't like it. From there the conversation was often about family members. We did not see much real conversation in day care at other times, yet this seems like a particularly important experience for children.

In some centers, the purpose of lunchtime seems to be to get everyone fed as quickly and efficiently as possible, and every decision about how things are to be handled is judged by these criteria. If lunch is viewed as a social time when "the family," as defined by small groups of children with one or two adults, gets together to share food and good company, then the basis for decision making is different. The placement of tables, the way food is served, the way the transition to and from lunch is handled all clarify for children the adults' true purposes.

ADULT/CHILD PLACES

In homes, there are a number of places where adults can find comfort in doing things that are of interest to them and where children can hover around looking, watching, being close, and engaging in real conversations — for example, when the adult is working at the kitchen table, sitting on the couch in the living room, propped up on the bed, using the sewing machine, or typing. It is in these kinds of settings that much of our child rearing has traditionally occurred.

One of the striking differences between family day care and center care is the difference in furniture. The furniture in homes provides for much greater differentiation of experience; there are kitchen chairs, dining room chairs, easy chairs in the living room, the "fancy chair" that is for guests only, and the patio chairs that are made of tubular aluminum and can be carried and foled.

Little thought seems to have been given to the function of furniture in a broader emotional, educational sense. Couches and easy chairs are seldom seen in day care centers, except possibly in the staff room, away from the children. Day care is not a school; it is a place where adults and children live together for a considerable period of time. This practice of using school furniture seems to have been adopted from half-day nursery schools and public schools on the basis of the unexamined assumption that the function of the adult remains the same across settings. If the function is different, surely the physical setting should support this difference. For example, regulations may require a lounge area for adults, but they do not provide that there will be comfortable places for adults to sit with children. Most adults in day care spend little time in the adult lounge. They need comfort out where the action is — with the children. However, if group care were to move more in the direction of providing a more homelike environment, this step would certainly be resisted by many maintenance and purchasing authorities, departments geared to uniformity and efficiency.

PROGRAM FORMAT AND THE PHYSICAL SETTING

If you enter a day care home or center at any given time and observe what is going on (exclusive of lunchtime or nap time), you will find that you could classify the arrangement of people-doing-things-in-places in one of five ways:

Teacher-directed group activity: the teacher leads an activity in which the children engage as a group, such as story time, music, or rhythm games. Children are expected or required to participate.

Teacher-directed individual activity: the teacher has planned an activity in which all children are again expected to participate but that is carried out individually by each child, such as pasting, doing puzzles, or drawing.

Free play: children are free to choose among all activities available in the room or yard, such as playing on the swings, climbing equipment, or in the sand pile. The teacher has not made prior preparations but uses the play area as it exists.

Free choice: children are free to choose among all activities available; however, the teacher has made prior preparation and has set up one or more activities especially for this play period, such as use of a clay table or water play.

Official transitions: these periods provide a spacer between activities required by the adult

Center programs appear to jell around the selection of certain activity formats. In centers where staff feel it is important for children to be engaged in activities of their own choosing, free choice will be the most frequently used format. In centers where adults feel that they should make most of the decisions about how children spend their time, teacher-directed activity formats are frequently used, usually alternating with free play; free choice is seldom used. We have called these alternate types of program structure "open" and "closed." The decision about the use of particular types of activity formats turns out to be a powerful predictor of the use of the physical environment, the behavior of teachers, and the experiences that are made available to children. Centers that use an open program format look very different along a variety of dimensions than centers that use a closed program format. Either format, if thoughtfully developed, can produce a rich experience for children.

The advantages of effective closed structure lie in its clarity of expectations, its opportunities for a child to experience him- or herself as an important part of a group, and the practice involved in attending to adult input. Its hazards stem from the restrictions necessary to maintain the structure: requirements to maintain specific body positions, limits on mobility, absence of opportunities for tactile sensory stimulation, and performance demands that may undermine self-esteem (for example: "All right children, sit up straight, don't wiggle, don't touch your neighbor, and be ready for my question!"). In addition, structured transitions tend to consume large amounts of time.

The advantages of open structure lie in its ability to foster initiative and reward child–child relationships and in the opportunities for mobility and tactile sensory stimulation. Its hazards lie in the difficulty of maintaining focus for individual children, in providing sufficient complexity for meaningful choice, and in the tendency toward diluted adult input.

Since closed-structure settings require much listening, obeying, and imitating, it seems important to build in a high degree of softness. If the program contains at least seven of the components listed above as determining softness, the environment, although closed, provides opportunities for tactile sensory stimulation, permits a range of body positioning, and tends to guarantee some activity settings that are open and have enough props to increase complexity. Also, since the amount of time spent in transitions will be relatively high, it is important to allow for leisurely conversation and some playfulness during periods of waiting.

Open-structure settings can easily become disorganized and boring, both for adults and children. Closed structure is probably easier to handle if the physical setting is inadequately developed and staff are inexperienced. Open settings must have well-developed space and adults who know how to facilitate, problem-solve, and keep track of children. In our experience, it is not easy to produce a switch from one format to another; it is possible, however, to improve the overall functioning within a given format, and this approach is preferable to an attempt to make an immediate and drastic change in program format.

FORCES CONSTRAINING ENVIRONMENTS

Certain decisions affecting the physical setting are made before the center is opened and cannot easily be undone once the location has been chosen and the center is in operation.

Location

The initial decision about location determines once and for all certain aspects of the environment. Unfortunately, restrictive zoning sometimes keeps centers out of pleasant residential neighborhoods and forces them into areas that have commercial zoning. Probably some improvement of sites could be accomplished if the planting of trees and shrubs were undertaken, but once located a center must live with its surroundings.

The building, too, will forever impose its constraints. If it has inflexible features, such as poorly located bathrooms, lack of easy indoor-outdoor access, poor regulation of sun and shade, then these features will continue to haunt the program.

Size of Facility

In our 1967 study (Prescott and Jones), we found that the size of a center stood out as a dependable predictor of program quality. In those centers that served over sixty children, as compared to those enrolling thirty to sixty children, significantly more emphasis was placed on rules and routine guidance. Teacher emphasis on control and restraint was two-and-a-half times higher, and global rating of teacher manner often showed the teacher as neutral or distant, and almost never rated as sensitive. Conversely, in smaller centers, emphasis in these areas was low, but provision of opportunities for pleasure, wonder, and delight was significantly higher.

Large centers almost never offered children the experience of participating in groups in which the age range was wide. (Our data indicated that [settings] programs that have children of mixed ages together for some parts of the day work very well in full-day care, offering many more opportunities for children to serve each other as models and facilitators, as well as greatly enriching the possibilities for play.) Large centers were also found to have play areas that rated low on organization, variety, and amount to do per child. These differences in grouping and in richness of play possibilities within the physical space were associated with a program format that offered fewer opportunities for children to initiate and to choose than the program format most commonly utilized in centers of moderate size.

In large centers, children were seldom observed to be highly interested and enthusiastically involved. These findings on the relationship of size to amount of personal involvement are unique to our study but have been corroborated in other kinds of settings such as schools and factory work groups (Barker 1968). Large centers did have better-trained teachers and an absence of crowding. Although both of these factors typically were predictors of sensitive teacher interaction, this relationship was reversed for large centers.

The Abt Study (1972) also found that although larger centers cost a little less per child, they seem to find it harder to provide quality child care even when they maintain favorable staff–child ratios. Fitzsimmons and Rowe (1971) reported similar findings. Reddy (1980), in an observational study of center size, found that centers caring for 60 to 99 children were of poorer quality, as indicated by on-task behavior and length of time spent in waiting or moving from one activity to another, but that centers caring for over 100 children were of better quality. Some very large centers became more like villages, with smaller self-contained units, and in this way overcame the problem of size.

However, the South Australian Council of the Childhood Services Commission (1975), after extensive visiting of facilities around the world, commented on large buildings designed to serve large numbers of children: "In England and California are examples of elaborate and expensive facilities provided for early childhood care. They are rigid in planning and construction and provide no degree of flexibility to adapt to future requirements" (p. 13). It may be that facilities designed to serve as family centers, hence rather large and complex, are worth considering, but they must be designed so that young children can have a stable, highly individualized experience. As yet, we have found few examples of this possibility.

One finding of the national day care study was that group size was an important predictor of children's experience and that a group size of 12 was associated with more involvement, less wondering, and more interaction with adults than a size of 24 (Ruopp et al. 1979). This finding again supports the relationship of size to quality of experience.

It must be remembered, however, that decisions about size of group are always related to other variables such as availability of qualified staff, size of indoor and outdoor play areas, and decisions about their use. Some of the differences we found between group and family day care are comparable to those found by Ruopp et al. for smaller as opposed to larger groups (Prescott 1973). Questions of scale and their consequences are important to understand as we move toward a more shared rearing of children.

Administrative Locus of Control

As day care centers become more settled into the life of the community, they tend toward more burcaucratic administration. As decision making becomes more organized, it may also become farther removed from the level of action. Children are very perceptive in noting when adults are ambivalent and mechanical in carrying out their authority role. And adults who cannot create their own programs will not be good models for children.

DAY CARE AS A CHILD-REARING ENVIRONMENT

The day care environment provided in a center often looks like and is managed like a school environment, yet day care has a significantly different purpose, as Golan et al. (1976) observe:

> The search for alternative educational techniques and forms has made it essential to consider overall functioning rather than separate bits and pieces of a child's life. Nowhere is this as pointed as in the case of day care. The growing popularity of day care as an institutional form raises serious questions concerning the home–school continuity. The care of very young children for large portions of their days, in a culture that has moved away from the extended family while lacking a clear model for day care, is a serious issue (p. 13).

The model of school always implies that there is a curriculum designed to teach certain skills and that the effectiveness of any school setting, be it Head Start or later schooling, is justified by the achievement of certain outcomes. Adults often prefer to conceptualize day care as "school plus a little more," instead of taking the more radical step of viewing it as a place for living. Many children spend more of their waking time in day care than at home. Children are now enter-

ing care as young as six weeks of age. For infants and toddlers the
inappropriateness of the school model is especially striking.

Regulatory requirements often are stated in terms that reinforce
conformity and eliminate features that are unique, diverse, and novel.
R. Moore (1973) summarizes his convictions about the design of children's environments:

> It is a basic concept of ecology that diverse environments are resilient
> and productive. Kids, too, seem to grow well in rich, choiceful, sup-
> portive surroundings. The more diversity, the more possibilities . . .
> the more likely that each person or group will find their own par-
> ticular "turn on" and the less chance that anyone will start disrupt-
> ing someone else's scene as a result of boredom.
>
> Diversity is a concept that can be applied to everything in the
> child-environment, including the qualities already discussed: place,
> space, time, change, movement, manipulation, openness, scale, in-
> terface, nature, sensory dimensions. All these can be subject to in-
> finite variations (p. 52).

The design of the physical environment of day care also reveals
the expectations for adults who inhabit the setting. The absence of comfortable adult furniture or objects of interest to adults often points to
a total disregard for the needs of adults for stimulation and is indica-
tive of a value structure detrimental to autonomy. We think that an
important principle in child rearing, if it is to provide individualized
care and attention, is that decision making should stay close to the
level of action.

Tizard et al. (1972), in a study of "institutional retardation," found
that "the differences between the way in which nurseries were organized affected all the staff in charge, whether trained or not, in the same
way" (p. 357). It appears that when adult options are low, child options also become limited.

Environmental design cannot be independent of the vision that
caregivers have of the experiences they want for children. As Barker
(1968) has observed, there is an *essential fittingness* between the environment and the behavior of its inhabitants. Golan and his associates
have said,

> although it is very clear that design in and of itself does not have
> universal or direct effect except in situations with limited options,
> children are often in just those low-choice settings. The combina-
> tion of few alternatives and strict enforcement of rules about use,

the reality for children in homes, hospitals and schools, leads to very patterned, stereotyped uses that have limited growth-stimulating qualities. Thus, for most children, almost all supervised settings, in fact, have strong institutional components. When children do take off on a more individual use, they are generally perceived as misbehaving (1976, p. 25).

Day care is certainly a supervised setting. If it is sensibly designed, everyone will get through the day more comfortably. If it were to be designed by caregivers who built in places that resembled those "magic places" of their memories, both adults and children would find more joy and wonder in their time together.

Chapter 4

CARING FOR CHILDREN AS WORK

Marcy Whitebook

The social arrangements that provide for the care of young children have undergone major changes in the last eighty years. Unlike previous generations, most families today contract with people outside of their families to ensure some portion of their children's care. These relationships with child care centers, family day care providers, or babysitters have resulted not only in a major shift in American family life but also in the development of a new occupation. The characteristics of this burgeoning occupation of child care givers will be the focus of this chapter. Because my own broader experience has been with center day care, I will emphasize that type of care and the greater resources available to center care providers. However, much of this information and analysis applies to family day care providers as well.

WHAT DO THEY DO?
A DESCRIPTION OF CHILD CARE WORK

The roles and responsibilities of care givers are numerous and diverse.

> Caring for children, whether in a child care center, a family day care home or other setting, is a job that is difficult to explain to people who are unfamiliar with it. If you are a caregiver, perhaps you have had the experience of having someone ask you what sort of work you do. You reply, "I care for children," and the reaction is, "Oh, that must be fun." You get the distinct impression that the person pictures you frolicking in the park all day with happy, playful, cooperative children. Not quite an accurate picture of a caregiver's day (Stonehouse n.d.).

Tasks and Skills

To those with little direct experience with young children, the work is considered unskilled. Because young children spend much of their time playing, it is assumed that the adults in their midst function in a similar carefree manner. And because the work of caring for children has long been performed by women without pay, it is regarded as something natural and unlearned, an outgrowth of female nurturing, rather than skilled work requiring training and deserving adequate compensation.

In a speech to the National Alliance of Business, President Ronald Reagan stated: "Mothers and grandmothers have been taking care of children for thousands of years without special training. Why is it certain states prohibit anyone without a college degree in early childhood education from operating a day care facility?" (Reagan 1981). To those who actually care for young children or who have occasion to observe those who do, Reagan's remarks are inaccurate as well as insulting. Of course there are similarities between certain aspects of the roles of caregivers and parents. Both must care for, guide, and instruct young children (Almy 1982). These similarities, however, do not render caregiving unskilled. Rather they suggest a pervasive blind spot in the public eye toward the skills of mothers, grandmothers, and attentive fathers.

Some differences between caregivers and parents emerge from the variations in the care-taking environments. Center caregivers are typically responsible for as many as ten children at a time. They must act in concert with several coworkers. Additionally, they relate to each child's parent(s) or guardian(s) when the child arrives at and leaves the center. Caregivers also organize and manage an environment that receives the wear and tear of these many children and adults each day. Finally, caregivers frequently receive mandates such as to prepare children for elementary school and to teach prereading and mathematical concepts.

A wide range of skills is thus required to perform the broad range of functions involved in caring for young children. The image of a jack-of-all-trades replaces that of the unskilled babysitter. Jessie Stanton describes the ideal qualifications of a preschool teacher:

> She (sic) should have a fair education. By this I mean she should have a doctor's degree in psychology and medicine. Sociology is advisable. She should be an experienced carpenter, mason, mechanic, plumber and a thoroughly trained musician and poet (Beyer 1968).

In answer to the question "What is a caregiver?" (and they tend, in her opinion, far too often to be "she's" rather than "he's"), Anne Willis Stonehouse (n.d.) replies:

> a chef and waitress in a restaurant where customers are very demanding, often careless and messy, likely to change their minds, and they never leave a tip;
>
> a translator who can understand and speak not only Greek and Italian but also two-year-old and one-year-old English . . . ;
>
> an architect who designs and regularly rearranges multi-purpose space to meet children's needs;
>
> a removalist who assembles, moves and alters equipment;
>
> a maintenance person, custodian and cleaner, working, often under great pressure and with distractions, to remove paint, clay, water and food hundreds of times a week from walls, floor, furniture and people;
>
> a junk collector . . . ;
>
> a skillful and unashamed beggar;
>
> a dancer and athlete;
>
> a gardener and guardian of overloved animals and insects;
>
> a scientist who understands how the universe works and can answer such questions as "Why do the wind blow? . . . " Who not only knows the answers but can explain them in a way that satisfies a curious four-year-old;
>
> a judge who can make the correct decision about what is fair when she hasn't a clue as to who had the dolly first and both parties say that they did, who settles hundreds of major and minor disputes and also knows when to stay out of the picture;
>
> a magician who can transform active toddlers into sleeping toddlers, who can divide three small biscuits into several equal pieces.

An examination of typical responsibilities included in job descriptions for center personnel sheds more light on the actual tasks child care staff perform: curriculum planning and implementation, parent contacts (meetings and conferences), meal preparation, maintenance, clerical tasks (record keeping), administrative duties (budgeting, fund raising, and supervision), and staff meetings (Whitebook et al. 1981). Listing responsibilities, however, gives only a partial picture of what caregivers actually do. Consider curriculum planning and implemen-

Photograph by Michael Wetteland

tation. In order to perform these tasks, good caregivers must begin by assessing the children and the center environment. They must be keen observers of behavior and must be able to recognize appropriate and inappropriate responses for children of different ages. Additionally, they must ask, What is the range of needs within this population of children? Which activities are appropriate for facilitating the particular skills one is seeking to enhance? Of those activities, which will be most engaging for this particular grouping? Is there sufficient material and staff to implement this activity?

Once these queries are answered, the caregiver must then gather the materials and arrange the space. This may involve taking some toys from a cupboard and setting them on a table, or it may require shopping or scrounging for materials and dragging furniture into new arrangements. Additionally, caregivers must have alternate activities prepared in case of a weather change or other unpredictable occurrence. The time actually spent implementing curriculum constitutes only a small portion of the work; such preparatory functions as thinking and planning consume a large part of the caregiver's day (Almy 1975).

Of course a caregiver's activities are not restricted to creating a rich learning environment. Attending to the physical needs of children over the course of a ten-hour day also consumes a great deal of energy. And the younger the children, the more physically demanding the caregiving (Katz 1977).

In most centers, keeping the program financially afloat is a task that would tax the most experienced corporate executive. Although the burden of activity in this arena falls most heavily on the director or administrative staff, those working directly with children may find themselves embroiled in budgeting, grant writing, fund raising, and scrounging for goods and services in the local community.

Maneuvering among the adults may offer one of the most serious challenges caregivers face. Some facility in training or supervising other adults, whether they are other teachers, aides, or volunteers, and effective communication skills are needed. Staff must also manage relationships with parents, which often involve intense feelings that arise at unscheduled moments.

Negotiating these myriad responsibilities demands flexibility and careful organization. For the work of caring for children, like other household chores, is never done. One cannot prepare a snack, help a child to sleep, comfort a distraught parent or coworker, or change wet clothes and assume that these chores can be permanently crossed off this week's "to do" list. Not only are these demands likely to be repeated frequently, but they are likely to compete with equally compelling pleas, perhaps in the midst of a carefully planned, not easily interrupted project—like cooking corn bread with seven impatient four-year-olds. Although there are moments of calm during the day, they are unpredictable.

ORGANIZATION OF CHILD CARE WORK

To this point, we have looked at the general aspects of caring for children as work. But differences in caregiver experiences emerge when ages of children served, roles within centers, and funding sources are considered.

Ages of Children Served

Most people who care for infants and preschoolers work a seven- to eight-hour paid day. This means that staff within a center are often present at different hours. Negotiating transitions between shifts, as well as arranging staff meetings to accommodate all employees, is a common organizational task. Caregivers working with school-aged children before and after school may face a split-shift workday.

Photograph by Jean Berltein, courtesy of Child Care Employee Project

Besides hours of care, children of different ages demand different responses from caregivers. For example, the pace of a day with infants feels very different from one with older children. In an infant program, workers typically experience several slow times in a day, but seldom is there a time when all children are resting. In an extended-day program, school-aged children may enter the center tired and needing space to wind down (or let go) after a full day in a structured school environment.

Job Titles and Lines of Authority

One's role within a center as aide, teacher, director, or support staff (cook, nurse, social worker, etc.) further shapes the care-giving experience, although job titles seldom clarify exactly how. A San Francisco study found that aides, teachers, and teacher-directors all performed the same range of duties. Job title reflected no differences in paid or unpaid time spent in curriculum planning and implementation, maintenance, and meal or snack preparation but did suggest differences in time spent communicating with parents and performing clerical and administrative chores (Whitebook et al. 1982). The reader should note that the San Francisco sample included a disproportionate number of programs that were part of large bureaucratic structures. Thus on-site directors were often teacher-directors answerable to a higher level of administration.

Job titles indicate differences in power and control over major policy decisions and day-to-day decision making. Major policy decisions deal with hiring and firing, center enrollment, budget, relations with parents and community, administrative structure, and determination of working conditions. Day-to-day decisions include setting-up and cleanup activities, grouping children, determination of appropriate discipline, daily communication with parents, indoor and outdoor supervision, scheduling, and a procedure for division of staff responsibilities.

In the San Francisco study, all staff had significantly less power and control over the former set of decisions than did center administrators. Only 18 percent of the teaching staff were included in major decision making. However, one-third of the head teachers/directors were included in governing bodies, as compared to less than one-quarter of the teachers and fewer than one-fifth of the aides. Most staff found themselves in a hierarchial decision-making structure, and over half said that they were dissatisfied with the arrangement. They found decision makers often ill informed about or insensitive to the ramifications of their decisions.

In contrast to major policy decisions, teachers were more involved in day-to-day decisions. About two-thirds of the teachers and head teacher-directors made these decisions. Although teachers and aides spent equal time with children, only a little more than a third of aides were involved in day-to-day decisions. Aides were dissatisfied with this procedure because their opinions were disregarded, despite their perceived parity in responsibility. Teachers, however, were pleased with their autonomy in this regard (Whitebook 1981).

Some centers chose to eliminate job title distinctions, labeling everyone as teachers and striving toward consensus or collective decision making. At the opposite end of the spectrum, some centers distinguish among aides, assistants, lead teachers, head teachers, and assistant directors. But contradictions arise when the de jure and de facto situations are compared. The so-called collective may actually be controlled by one or two staff members; and the rigid hierarchy may function only on paper. Determination of the real division of labor and lines of authority within a center requires careful observation. Participants within the structure may disagree.

Funding Sources

Working conditions, such as pay and benefits, which affect caregiver satisfaction, turnover, and stress levels, vary in publicly and privately funded centers (Whitebook et al. 1981). Additionally, different funding sources may require different regulations. For example, in California legal ratios of adults to children and training requirements for staff are more stringent for public than private centers (Mayor's Advisory Committee 1976).

CHILD CARE AS AN OCCUPATION

Historical Precedents

Despite the relative youth of nonfamilial child care as an institution, it has a complicated history. Its roots can be traced to three major traditions, each serving different populations with distinct philosophical orientations toward the child and the family. As a result, varied expectations for practitioners emerge from this history.

The *kindergarten tradition* established the importance of a group educational experience for the young child prior to elementary school. Initially for middle class children, by the turn of the century the kindergarten experience touched many working class or immigrant children. The kindergarten teacher's responsibilities include a heavy emphasis on socializing as well as instructing young children, in order to help them prepare for the coming years of schooling (Braun and Edwards 1972). Although this was a secondary function, historically kindergartens have also served as child care institutions, particularly in communities with a high proportion of immigrant working mothers (Whitebook 1976).

Day nurseries are another vital part of child care's legacy. First appearing in the mid-nineteenth century, their heyday was the early part of this century (Steinfels 1973; Kerr 1973). Day nurseries were essentially what are thought of as day care centers today. They were established to provide care for children while their mothers worked. Working mothers, however, were frowned upon even by those who established the nurseries. Only widowed or deserted women were viewed as appropriate day nursery users; working women with husbands were often excluded from service.

The roots of the current debate about whether child care should be custodial or educational can also be located in the day nursery tradition. Despite popular histories that maintain that all nurseries were custodial in nature (Steinfels 1973), some actually did provide educational programs for older preschoolers by employing the services of a kindergarten or Montessori teacher for part of the day (Whitebook 1976). However, the majority of nurseries viewed their primary function as socializing children (into the middle class) or as Americanizing them, rather than as educating them. This emphasis in part reflected the largely immigrant clientele (Kerr 1973).

Most nurseries, consequently, were staffed by a matron, a middle class woman who could create the proper atmosphere for her "wayward" charges, and by helpers, who were usually untrained young women from the local community. A board of directors formulated all policies for the nurseries and was composed of wealthy women who viewed the nurseries as charity work (Steinfels 1973; Kerr 1973; Whitebook 1976).

A third thread in the child care tapestry is the *nursery school,* which became firmly established in the 1920s. The rationale for it grew from the focus within university psychology departments (Braun and Edwards 1972). The programs were established for middle class children in order to enrich their preschool years, rather than to provide child care. Practitioners in nursery schools were and are considered teachers, and many had college degrees in education, psychology, home economics, or child development. Nursery schools were viewed as supports for family life, while day nurseries were seen as necessary evils, a last resort for the needy. Predictably, given these labels, the Works Progress Administration (WPA) nurseries established during the 1930s by the federal government to provide jobs for unemployed teachers were modeled after the nursery schools rather than the day nurseries (Kerr 1973).

Impinging social forces have led to the increasing amalgamation of the day nursery, the nursery school, and even the kindergarten (Almy 1982). World War II gave the impetus to this change when child care centers, staffed by nursery school teachers, were established for women war workers. Head Start and the emphasis on preschool education in the sixties again challenged the autonomous traditions of the nursery school and day nursery. While such programs were exclusively a service for poor children, emphasis was placed on education as well as socialization. Child care, however, was and remains a secondary function of these largely part-day programs. Nursery school teachers swelled the early Head Start payrolls, to be joined by community members and parents who received on the job training through Head Start

(Evans 1975; Hymes 1975). Finally, the growth in the numbers of mothers with young children working outside their homes has particularly contributed to the relative functions of the day nurseries and nursery schools. Many nursery schools now have extended-day programs to meet the needs of the middle class working families. Similarly, many child care centers envision their role as providing a nursery or preschool experience during the day.

The blending of nursery school and day nursery clientele and functions is embodied in the child care or day care center. Yet uneasiness about the partnership continues to surface in debates about the relationship of early childhood education to day care. Perhaps nowhere does the tension produced by the amalgamation of these traditions emerge as clearly as in discussions of the child care practitioner. Is the center worker a teacher? A socializer? A custodian? What kind of training is required to work in child care? Is this professional work?

The nomenclature debate reflects differences of opinion related to philosophical and functional dimensions of the services. Some claim "day care" in their title and reject "teacher" to demonstrate the wide range of services they perform for children (Katz 1977). Some who use "teacher" assume it to include care-giving functions, while others are insulted by being expected to perform tasks that are not strictly educational in nature. More often, the debates about titles reveal differences in opinion relating to strategies for consolidating and upgrading child care work. For example, some argue that only by identifying day care staff as teachers and true professionals will the work be properly compensated and respected (Ade 1982). This position is partially based on an analysis that suggests that child care is a semiprofession rather than a full-fledged profession (Etzioni 1969). Others maintain that identifying themselves as workers who have the right to organize is the strategy that will ameliorate the situation of child care employees. Some argue that the goal should be to agree on any label within the field, no matter which one, in order that a united front can be presented to the larger community. Only with a unified public image will child care work receive its due, according to Hostletler and Klugman (1981). No simple resolution of the nomenclature issue looms nearby.

OCCUPATIONAL SOCIALIZATION

The routes to becoming a child care worker or teacher reflect some of the same contradictory components of child care's historical legacy. Depending on how the function of the service is envisioned, different ideas about preparing practitioners emerge. Credentialing of child care workers and licensing requirements for centers vary considerably from state to state. Some merely require a child care worker to be eighteen years old with no previous criminal record. The informal route of female socialization is thought to provide adequate training for the work.

For those who view the work as skilled and who assume an educational component in the service, a more formal route involving specific education is mapped out. Bachelor degrees in early childhood education, child development, or home economics are frequently required for head teachers in public centers and many nursery schools. More recently, Associate of Arts degrees (two-year college certificates) in early childhood–related fields have gained widespread acceptance as criteria for teaching jobs. Lying between the more formal educational route and the informal path is a third mode of occupational socialization, best embodied in the Child Development Associate (CDA) credential (see chap. 10).

Controversy about training and educational requirements continues. On the one hand, recent research has found child-related training to positively influence the quality of adult–child interactions in day care settings (Prescott, Jones, and Kritchevsky 1972; Roupp et al. 1979; Divine-Hawkins 1981). However, the training judged influential did not exclusively occur in educational institutions. Informal training, such as in workshops and in-service sessions, was also judged effective.

Unfortunately, the current economic realities facing child care support those who favor the completely informal approach to becoming a child care giver. Since salaries are shamefully low and high turnover of staff has been directly linked to low wages, it is argued that to require training for a minimum-wage level job is unethical. Further, training is considered impractical, given employees' short tenure. Thus the financial picture is seen as justifying a fast-food establishment personnel approach: young, primarily female workers will staff the centers for short periods, burn out, and then be replaced by others standing in the wings. Since trained personnel leave the field each year because of the poor working conditions and many in training fail to complete the process when they realize the limited options awaiting them, the revolving door image of occupational socialization seems an ever more likely (and depressing) possibility (Whitebook 1981).

CHILD CARE WORKERS AS EMPLOYEES

Whether child care workers have come to their occupation through formal training or informal experiences, all will discover less than desirable working conditions in terms of pay and benefits. Although over half of all center workers have postsecondary education, most earn close to the minimum wage. While few child care staff earn adequate wages, variations among center caregiver salaries do exist. Those employed in public programs fare better than those in private programs, especially those that operate for profit (Whitebook et al. 1981). Aides and assistants consistently earn less than teachers or directors (Whitebook et al. 1981; Administration for Children, Youth and Families [ACYF] 1981).

But beyond the low pay, the work itself takes a toll on caregivers. Low annual pay is seldom compensated for by a higher hourly rate, a shorter work week, or other nonmonetary benefits. Day care workers not only put in a seven- or eight-hour day with children but frequently log several hours of unpaid overtime as well (Whitebook et al. 1981). Unpaid hours involve curriculum planning, meetings, parent contacts, general maintenance, and fund raising (Whitebook et al. 1982). In the San Francisco study, only half of the sample received medical coverage, sick leave, and vacation pay each year. Teachers and teacher-directors in public day care centers were most likely to be the recipients of these benefits. Aides and those employed in private proprietary programs fared least well (Whitebook et al. 1982).

Working with children demands constant attention. Children cannot be placed "on hold" while adults attend to their personal needs. Consequently, staff frequently work full days without regularly scheduled breaks, even when entitled to them by law (Katz 1977; Whitebook 1981; Whitebook et al. 1981). And because of the nature of the work, staff may not even be able to take personal mental time—just to relax inwardly for a moment—while they are with children (Anderson 1980). Securing relief time is further complicated by the lack of adequate provision for substitutes in many centers (1981). Although staff are theoretically entitled to days off when ill, many continue to work because there is no arrangement for coverage.

Child care employees do not enjoy certain basic rights available to workers in other occupations (Cannon 1979). Many work without contracts outlining their basic responsibilities, wages, and other conditions of employment. Formal grievance procedures seldom exist. In part, limited contracts and agreements reflect the unorganized state of the field; few child care workers enjoy collective bargaining agreements.

All of these factors contribute to chronic instability in centers. Turnover in day care is calculated at 15 to 30 percent annually, as compared to 10 percent in other human service fields (Seiderman 1978). Turnover has been correlated with pay levels, and staff themselves attribute it to low pay and unpaid overtime (Whitebook 1981).

Staff also credit lack of career mobility and the relative insecurity of the field as secondary causes for turnover.

Turnover results in a lack of experienced, trained personnel. Centers must constantly orient new staff members, even though limited budgets allow no resources for such "nonessential" line items. Further, turnover gnaws away at the morale of those left behind. It reflects and fuels stress within the organization. Continual changes in staffing limit efforts to build consistent, creative, and personally responsive environments for children and their families. Turnover is more than an inconvenience; its victim is the quality of care children receive.

Some will argue that turnover is really caused by burnout, that process whereby one gradually loses enthusiasm for one's work. Indeed, many suggest that turnover necessarily occurs in child care because burnout is endemic to the work: the intensive interaction between adult and child is thought to become more draining and less gratifying over time (Freudenberger 1977; Mattingly 1977). Others suggest that those who enter the field have personality types that lead them to burnout: staff members are seen as people with unconscious needs to come to terms with their own troubled childhood experiences who, when unsuccessful in doing this, leave their jobs. A variation of this view suggests that those who engage in this work are idealistic and highly motivated to improve conditions for young children, but they burn out because they do not have a realistic sense of the limits of their own ability to effect change (Freudenberger 1977; M. J. Reed 1977; Sutton 1977).

Causes of burnout are best linked with the structural components of day care centers. Maslach and Pines (1977) found that lower ratios of adults to children, more dependable breaks and substitute policies, and better communication between staff positively affect workers' experience and therefore their ability to perform the job with less stress. When child care staff themselves assess their jobs, they find pleasure in the nature of their work; their complaints center on the structural aspects of the job. In the San Francisco study, over three-quarters of those interviewed reported that direct work with children was what most engaged and pleased them about their jobs. They liked the immediate feedback, the physical contact, the facilitating and observing of children's growth, and the related opportunities for self-reflection. Other sources of job satisfaction included relations with other staff members that involved learning how to communicate and depend on each other; the autonomy and flexibility of the work that resulted in no two days being alike; and the opportunity to learn and grow on the job. Dissatisfaction was again linked primarily to low pay and unpaid hours.

CHILD CARE WORK IN CONTEXT:
A COMPARISON WITH PARENTING
AND SCHOOL TEACHING

Child Care and Parenting

Growing pressures on parents to participate in their children's education through home instruction, and increasing demands on teachers to fulfill more nurturing roles for children, confuse the boundaries between these two social roles (Katz 1981). Although teachers of young children and parents engage in many of the same activities and functions as role models and social reinforcers, major differences can be identified. Teachers have less intensive affective relationships with their charges than parents do. Fein and Clark-Stewart (1973) maintain that teachers, more often than parents, evaluate problems and prescribe treatments for children in their care.

Whatever the overlap in functions, their scope varies for teachers and parents (Katz 1981). Parents have more diffuse and less limited interactions with children. Teachers, after all, only interact with children for a specified number of hours each day. Parents are necessarily partial toward their own children, whereas child care staff must maintain a more detached, generalized concern for all children. Someone working with children is likely to be more intentional in his or her interactions; parents are less likely to plan activities or monitor emotional responses toward children (Conroy 1979).

Teaching in Day Care Versus Teaching in Schools

Although teaching is integral to child care work, the experience of working in a center rather than a school, particularly with older children, varies considerably. Child care workers usually are aided in the classroom by at least one or two other adults; elementary teachers most commonly interact with peers only outside of the classroom. Supervision for elementary teachers tends to be more distant due to the nature of school bureaucracies; principals visit classrooms only occasionally, whereas many directors spend part of the day on the floor with children and staff. Teachers in schools thus experience both more autonomy and more isolation than their child care counterparts (Dreeben 1973).

The greatest distinctions between the two jobs emerge in the arena of pay and status. Consider that the average nine-month contract for a primary grade level teacher in the United States is $14,669, compared to \$9,700 for a twelve-month year for the prekindergarten teacher with a bachelor's degree (U.S. Department of Labor 1980). Differences in the availability of paid vacations, sick leave, and other benefits probably increase this differential. The close connection between status and remuneration in this society suggests the higher, although still limited, respect afforded elementary teachers.

School teachers and child care staff have different relationships to the organizations that represent them. Many teachers are protected by collective bargaining agreements negotiated by either the National Education Association (NEA) or the American Federation of Teachers (AFT). Few early childhood teachers are currently unionized, although interest in union activity appears to be growing. To date, much of the union activity among child care employees has involved those working in public school or other public programs. Several unions represent these workers: AFT; American Federation of State, County and Municipal Employees (AFSCME); Service Employees International Union (SEIU); and District 65 of the United Auto Workers (UAW). The National Association for the Education of Young Children (NAEYC), the largest professional membership group, claims over thirty thousand members with affiliate groups in most states. Although NAEYC awareness of working conditions issues has increased in the last couple of years, it is not organized to represent people at their work places. It remains to be seen whether it will evolve similarly to the National Educational Association (NEA), a professional association that does collective bargaining for its members.

DAY CARE WORK VERSUS OTHER
EARLY CHILDHOOD WORK

Although the overlapping functions and clientele, as well as shared low pay and status of nursery school, Head Start, family day care, and child care personnel have been emphasized in this chapter, distinctions among the nature of the work in the different programs exist. Frequently, nursery school personnel work shorter hours because programs run only half days. Depending on the situation, these staff may be paid for some of their preparation and other duties when the children are not present.

In certain communities a division between preschool and center personnel exists that may be reflected in labels or organizational affiliations. (For example, in some communities NAEYC affiliates have been identified primarily as nursery school or preschool rather than child care organizations.) These divisions reflect tensions regarding the sometimes better working conditions or status of preschool personnel. They also reflect insensitivity, unfortunately often embodied in training programs, toward the particular demands of the child care center, such as with its longer hours and fewer holidays (Anderson 1980).

IMPLICATIONS FOR CHANGING DAY CARE WORK

Current social arrangements require growing numbers of people who will care for children as their paid work. Those who do this job today enjoy the nature of the work; they find it stimulating, challenging, and gratifying. But, as we have seen, many of them will abandon child care as employment because of the long hours, the low pay, the lack of mobility, and the insecurity of the field.

What are the chances for improving working conditions? Some short-term gains are possible within existing resources. For example, limited budgets do not preclude increasing staff input into decision making, clarifying job title distinctions, and restructuring substitute, break, and grievance policies (Whitebook et al. 1982; Whitebook et al. 1981; CCSEP 1982). However, raising salaries, reducing unpaid hours, and providing benefits require increased funds. In the current era of economic recession and shrinking public dollars, this may be an overwhelming challenge.

The issue of increasing salaries is especially knotty. Growing demands for more care, and parents' needs for affordable services, compete with salaries. Public policy debates and private centers' total dependence on fees all fuel a tripartite tug-of-war where nobody can really win. If salaries go up, there is less money for more centers, and parents' fees probably increase. If salaries remain low, both child care workers and the quality of the children's experience suffer (Roupp and Travers 1982). Competition may drive down prices, and thus wages, in areas where child care is abundant. In any case, the workers have no possibility of improving their lot unless they can forcefully make parents aware of the connection between their own salaries and the quality of the service.

The only way out of this dilemma is for parents and workers to join forces. They must first confront their conflicting interests and then acknowledge each other's legitimate needs. In some communities, some parents may be able to afford increased fees. If this is not possible, then parents and staff together must seek additional sources of funds. Of course, the options are limited. Private foundations seldom provide operating funds for ongoing services. Although fund-raising events take a great deal of energy, they can become a dependable income source. The greatest untapped resource for child care, however, is private industry. A great deal of interest in this option has been evidenced by day care professionals in recent numerous conferences and articles. However, most of the activity in this area is still at the discussion level (Whitebook et al. 1982).

Ultimately, obtaining more financial support for child care will require parent and staff involvement in the political arena. Child care advocates must become active in coalitions that challenge the current political priorities of military expenditures over those social services geared toward meeting human needs. If future legislative programs are to address minimal employment standards, child care workers will also have to challenge the view — prevailing even among parents and other social service supporters — that day care is unskilled work.

Effectively arguing for better job conditions further requires workers to grapple with a problem that often divides them within their own ranks: how to meet their responsibilities to the families who receive their services while asserting their own needs for a living wage. Child care workers, by the nature of their work, are encouraged to put their clients' needs ahead of their own, in this case keeping their wages down so that fees remain low. Thus, ironically, child care workers worry that to put forward their own concerns is to undermine the service they provide. But, as has been argued here, when workers sacrifice themselves at the job, they harm not only themselves but also those who depend on the quality of that service.

Encouraging first steps toward addressing all of these problems are being taken. Distinctions are lessening between those looking toward improving the quality of teaching and programs, traditionally associated with professional organizations, and those striving to upgrade salaries and working conditions, generally associated with unions and workers' groups (Almy 1982). For example, the National Association for the Education of Young Children has begun to acknowledge that the status and pay scales of its members are priority issues. On the other hand, groups focused on working conditions issues, like the Madison Area Day Care Workers United (MACWU), the Minneapolis Child Care Workers Alliance (MCCWA), and District 65 of the UAW in Boston (a day care local), hold workshops and participate in conferences centered on classroom issues.

Whether existing professional organizations or developing workers' alliances or unions will be more successful in addressing the needs of child care workers depends on the characteristics of different communities. Certain aspects of the child care delivery system pose obstacles to unionization. Child care workers are located in many different types of programs with diverse funding structures. Some work within a school district that constitutes a large bargaining unit; others are isolated in privately owned centers with one or two employees. Still others find themselves in one of many centers owned by large corporations. Thus it may not be possible for all child care workers in a community to be represented by the same local union. The point now is to nurture workers' abilities to work together in placing their needs on the child care agenda. Like it or not, the quantitative and qualitative future of child care in America will be inextricably linked to the fate of child care workers.

Chapter 5

THE ADULT WORLD
OF DAY CARE

Willa Bowman Pettygrove
James T. Greenman

This chapter will focus on two groups of adults who are associated with day care — the parents who are its consumers and the staff who work in day care. Because children are the whole reason for child care, one might assume that their needs and preferences are the primary concern in the design and conduct of programs. In fact, their concerns are usually represented indirectly through the expectations, desires, and behaviors of other people in child care.

One only has to glance into the adult world of child care to discover that most of the people who depend on child care in order to work, and almost all who work in it, are women. The low value placed on women's labor in the United States, specifically labor seen traditionally as "woman's work," colors all of the adult dimension of day care. "Mothering," viewed as a natural function of women, is given little status or financial worth (Lightfoot 1977), and this fact clouds both staff relationships and relationships between staff and parents.

Beyond this initial glance is another realization: no one quite agrees on the roles that people in day care (including children) are to play. In this chapter, we will bring together a variety of formal and informal observations to attempt to understand why relationships among adults in day care assume the forms they often do.

Issues about parental and staff expectations, needs, and roles will recur in the discussion of families and child care staff. They serve as a meaningful framework in which to place the different statistics and other findings about the adults who use and who work in day care.

84

PARENTS

Before discussing the parents who use day care centers, it is useful to spend a moment considering the social and economic context of parents and families. Increasingly, "the family" has been the focus of weighty social commentary. Characterized as "besieged" by Christoper Lasch (1977), "under pressure" by Kenneth Kenniston (1977), and "breaking down" by Urie Bronfenbrenner (1978), the dramatic rise in the numbers of working mothers, single-parent homes, divorces, and two-income families has been cited variously as symptoms or causes of family change.

Nearly all agree it is a difficult time to be parents. There are few accepted common values to direct parents or to serve as a basis for clear values and standards for children. Few changes have been made in the work place to facilitate the functioning of single-parent and two-paycheck families. Mothers are caught between the low status and declining economic value of homemaking and the continuing expectation that they will seek fulfillment through full-time motherhood. Many men feel that an inability to be the sole provider casts a doubt on their value as husbands and fathers. Many middle income families are troubled by the disparity between the quality of life they have attained and the one they feel entitled to.

Kenneth Kenniston has characterized today's parents as facing society in the position of "weakened executives":

> Parents today have a demanding new role choosing, meeting, talking with, and coordinating the experts, the technology, and the institutions that help bring up their children. The specific work is familiar to any parent: consultations with teachers, finding good health care, trying to monitor television and so on (Kenniston 1977, p. 17).

While the executive of a firm has clear authority and power to influence or determine the decisions of those whose work needs coordination, parents find that they have little or no authority over those who share the task of child rearing.

A preliminary investigation for the National Day Care Study, *Day Care Centers in the United States* (Coelen, Glantz, and Calore 1979), provides a broad view of the families who use day care centers. According to Coelen and associates, three- to five-year-old children form the bulk of enrollment for centers in all categories, or about 73 percent of the enrollment for all programs combined. Minority children are enrolled at a rate higher than that of the population as a whole. This may be due to the higher proportion of minority children in urban areas, where more centers are located; disadvantaged economic status that would qualify minorities for subsidized center care; the historically higher labor force participation of their mothers; or minority families' preference for center care. As one might expect, the nonsubsidized and for-profit programs serve higher proportions of white families and those with higher incomes.

Almost three-quarters of families that use center care have low or moderate incomes. However, there are indications of a shift toward more use of center care by higher-income families. In July 1982, the U.S. Census Bureau reported a shift away from in-home child care for children of full-time working mothers and those with higher income and education. The sharp increase since 1975 in the number of for-profit centers also suggests an increased market among those parents who can pay most of the cost of child care. The number of centers run by the franchise named Kindercare has increased from 173 in 1977 to 717 in 1981 (Perry Mendel [Kindercare President], personal communication 1981).

Most parents who use day care do so to enable themselves to work or receive training. While this may seem obvious, it runs against a not uncommon perception of day care as primarily a means of intervention to help needy families or children. Another characteristic of day care parents, equally obvious but worth keeping in mind, is that they tend to be young, younger than parents of school-aged children. Day care families are often in the initial stages of family development. As the family grows from one to two or more children, center care may become too expensive, so parents using the center are often those with just one child. Thus caregivers can expect to encounter many new parents, adults growing into a new role.

To what extent do families want or need the care provided by day care centers? Most child care seems to come from family day care, care by relatives, and public schools (for older children) (Bane et al. 1979). These statistics have been challenged by Hofferth, who argues that as many as half of all three- to five-year-old children with working parents may now be in centers (Hofferth 1979). She noted that the 10 to 15 percent of children in this age range enrolled in the centers in 1976 represented a dramatic increase from the 5 to 6 percent enrolled in 1965.

Parents choose center care for a variety of reasons. Many parents feel that a center-based program offers educational benefits and important socialization experiences (Steinberg and Green 1978). Single parents may prefer a center program because it is an opportunity for their children to be exposed to more than one adult in a significant role.

Parents may differ, however, on exactly what they define as the benefits of a center's program. For the white middle class parents in some preschool centers in Berkeley, California, the center program was expected to emphasize an "open" environment that would stimulate socioemotional development and creativity. Black parents in the same centers desired an educational curriculum geared toward school readiness (Joffe 1977).

In attempting to find care that meets their expectations for quality, parents may make financial sacrifices or develop complicated work and child care schedules. Sixty percent of the middle and upper income families in Steinberg and Green's (1978) study changed their care arrangements at least once. A major finding in Kamerman's (1980) study was the complexity of care arrangements; almost 75 percent of working parents in the study used two or more kinds of care for their children. Multiple arrangements may reflect the lack of facilities for full-time care, economic necessity, or the decision to use a part-time source (such as a preschool program or relative) that has desired qualities but must be supplemented by other care. Several single mothers in the study made financial sacrifices to enroll their children in center programs that they believed were of better quality. Spouses in two-parent families often worked out complementary work schedules to allow more time at home with the child and to allow for the child to enroll in a preferred program.

PEOPLE WHO WORK IN DAY CARE

Although by definition caregivers (teachers, assistants, or aides) have the main responsibility for care, other adults in a variety of work roles contribute to the center's overall functioning and to the daily experience of individual children. In fact, cooks, bus drivers, administrators, and others may make special contributions to children because of the intrinsic interest of their work and because their relationship to the child is more relaxed. In some centers, the cook's influence rivals the director's.

Describing Day Care Staff

The problem of describing the people who work in day care is not just the variety of work roles within a given center's program. It is also the variety of personal and professional histories that staff bring to a given role. Staff vary in age, attitudes toward child care as work, culture, relevant formal education, experience, and other important variables. It becomes difficult to find observations that will apply with equal accuracy to both the nineteen-year-old who works in a center while waiting for other employment or education opportunities, the grandparent who comes to work in a day care center after fifteen years as a family day care provider in the same neighborhood, and the twenty-two-year-old newly graduated from a college program in early childhood education. Unfortunately, research tends to smooth out or obscure the uniqueness of individuals.

In addition to consisting almost entirely of eighteen to thirty-five-year-old women, the workforce described by the National Day Care Study (Coelen, Glantz, and Calore 1979) includes more minority people than the population as a whole. A majority of the group has had some education beyond high school and almost one-third have had four or more years of college.[1]

The racial distribution of child care workers may be explained in several ways. First, the racial composition of centers tends to match the composition of the community. Secondly, child care has been offered as a career development opportunity for parents of economically disadvantaged children through Head Start and other programs. Finally, the lack of other job opportunities may push minority people into low-paying child care jobs.

Economic factors also contribute to the high representation of both women and minorities in day care employment. As an underfunded and low-status occupation, child care is more likely to employ persons who have experienced educational and occupational discrimination in other parts of the economy and society. Robinson (1979) has observed that men are less likely to enter and do not stay as long in child care work because of other opportunities that pay better. While child care is seen as a job opportunity by many women, for men, who usually have full access to a range of better-paying jobs, it is not. Men in child care usually view their tenure in child care as a rewarding but temporary interlude in their work lives.

---

1. Coelen et al. (1979) noted that these educational levels compare favorably with those for all working women in the United States. The 29 percent who have sixteen or more years of education is twice the percentage for women working in all occupations. While one-fourth of employed women have no high school diploma, only one-tenth of day care workers have not graduated from high school. Thus it appears that day care as an occupation selects for women with higher educational levels or else that day care workers are motivated toward educational achievement.

Photograph by Jean Berlfein, courtesy of Child Care Employee Project

The sex typing of day care occupations reflects the economic and social factors that limit job opportunities for women in other fields. Caregivers may find themselves caught between stereotypic expectations (e.g., that nurturing is feminine, therefore passive) and the practical realities that require assertiveness and instrumental competence for day care work. It is ironic but telling that serious consideration of the androgynous quality of child care work, the need for a combination of so-called male and female qualities in the caregiver, has been discussed only in terms of men's recent entry into the field (e.g., Robinson 1979). Clearly, competence in day care work requires of both women and men a complex mixture of nurturing, assertiveness, autonomy, cooperation, and independence, expressed in both intellectual and emotional characteristics. Staff may find themselves regularly retesting the expectations placed on them and their work, until such time as adrogynous ideas replace sex-typed assumptions about the "right" way to care for young children.

A lengthy career commitment to child care seems an unrealistic expectation, given the staff structure of most day care centers and the low salaries in the field as a whole. The amount of relevant work experience of day care center directors (approximately nine years on average) suggests that some staff have experienced career development within child care. However, the career ladder is short, basically only three steps: (1) various child-related occupations, including volunteering; (2) a position as caregiver in a day care center; and (3) director/administrator of a day care center (Pettygrove 1980). As one moves up, the number of available positions greatly decreases. Thus workers are as likely to move out of child care as up into a new staff role. As their own families grow, child care staff may elect to seek new employment because salaries within the field are inadequate for their needs.

Alice is acting director of a center where she has taught for three years:

> "I never saw myself as a person who could manage finances or tell people what to do. I didn't sleep for two days when I had to fire a teacher. Now I don't lose sleep (much sleep anyway) over audits, or letting someone go, and I can drive the bus. I didn't used to drive at all. All I had ever really done was work with children, but now I'm thinking of going into business."

Alice is an example of a common phenomenon in day care: a woman who "bloomed." Slipping into child care without much thought, having always loved children, she discovered her capacity to perform well in an administrative and supervisory role and has developed ambitions that may carry her out of child care.

This capacity to bloom seems important for long-term success in child care work. Individuals may come to the field because they believe work with children is more rewarding or less demanding than other occupations. However, continued employment in day care requires a transition from a focus on adult–child interactions to broader responsibilities. Even in four-year degree programs, which prepare students to design and administer child care programs, faculty members report difficulty in motivating students to move from roles involving direct interactions with children to supervisory and administrative roles. Successful transition to more responsible roles within the day care center seems to require more than specialized training.

The low economic and social status of child care staff has a direct and adverse impact on job performance, in spite of workers' commitment to work and to serving families and children. Consider the caregiver who is also a single parent and receives only the usual low income of a day care job. Before coming to work, she has probably confronted major management problems (such as starting an unreliable old car) and child care responsibilities (getting her own children to school or looking after their needs). A study of 278 staff members and 50 program directors by Wessen (1981) supports this image. Staff were more likely than their supervisors to mention non–job-related stresses as af-

Photograph by Jean Berlfein, courtesy of Child Care Employee Project

fecting their work performance, and the seriousness of the stresses was directly related to the workers' level of economic disadvantage. Directors reported unexcused and unexpected staff absence as their single most difficult administrative problem. These findings strongly support Whitebook's arguments (this volume, chap. 4) for better pay and benefits for day care workers; most have very limited resources for coping with job and non–job-related stresses.

Staff Attitudes Toward Work

Child care staff confront the demands of their lives and work with many different views. Consider the range of opinions expressed below by caregivers at a workshop on professional development.

Mary Lou, a program coordinator with a degree in child development who plans to return to graduate school to study special education:

> "I consider myself a professional and get very frustrated with people who don't. Training is important. I think a lot of people just babysit, some good babysitting, but they don't really teach and work at providing good learning environments. I'm not a 'caregiver'; I am a *teacher*."

Barbara, a soon-to-be grandmother who teaches in the same program, has a completely different point of view:

> "I have been taking care of kids all this time, teaching them and doing just fine. Most of the courses and workshops I go to are Mickey Mouse, taught by some guy who never has had to take care of kids."

June, a thirty-seven-year-old single parent of three, has worked with children since the early days of Head Start and with the same day care program for the last eight years. After she has completed the courses for a CDA credential, she thinks she may take courses at a community college and receive a degree:

> "I usually like the classes and workshops, if there are other people in them like me. I don't really have the time, though."

Throughout the discussion, clear differences in assumptions about the demands and values of the work emerged. To some, it was just a job, an extension of babysitting or parenting; to others, a chosen profession demanding talent and skill as well as love.

The ambivalent quality of job satisfaction of child care workers reported in the Child Care Staff Education Project (Whitebook et al. 1981) is also evident in another study of caregivers in midwestern states. Although fewer than 7 percent of the participants in this study got a pay raise or promotion during the one-year interval of the research, most named child care as their chosen field of work, their "profession," and tended to see themselves as career women. Consistent with the findings from Whitebook's San Francisco respondents, this midwestern group also referred to the intrinsic values of the work. When asked their reasons for working in child care, extrinsic ("The money is necessary for my family") and intrinsic ("I enjoy what I do") reasons tended to be mentioned with about equal frequency. Thus, while workers experience difficulties in their employment, they also express positive values about themselves and the work they do. Their appreciation of the work seems independent of the financial rewards or ascribed status of the occupation (Pettygrove 1980).

Staff Relationships

The working relationships among the members of day care staffs have been the subject of little study. Day care centers would seem to be fertile arenas for conflict. A number of adults of different rank and status are working closely together, often under trying conditions. There are differences in beliefs about children and child rearing, some deeply rooted in personal experiences. Differences in age, race, and social class are common. Staff members bring quite different assumptions and attitudes about the nature and value of their work. Social complexity increases with increased parent involvement in center and classroom life. At the same time, these social conditions might add richness and function as stimuli for intellectual and personal growth of all involved. The need to work together can result in rewarding collegial relationships, professional dialogue, and creative conflict. In spite of the potential for richness, neither open conflict nor stimulating work environments are found in many centers. Instead, most programs are characterized by routine, circumscribed, and often static relationships. Why? As Whitebook shows in chapter 4 (this volume), there are questions about authority and status; these seem to stand in the way of collegial relationships and may be a source of unresolved conflict for adults in the day care center.

Distribution of Authority and Responsibility

Organizations are given shape by the distribution of authority and responsibilities. Authority is the power to make decisions and to gain compliance, to ensure that certain actions are taken or avoided. It may be based on the power of the employer and specified in the chain-of-command and job descriptions. Conflict, however, is likely if the responsibilities are not clearly divided, the employer's authority is not credible, or the individuals in the roles are not comfortable with supervision.

Authority may also be accorded on the basis of an assumed hierarchy of tasks, the top level requiring a professional with a distinctive knowledge base and expertise to successfully perform the tasks. Professional authority is challenged when there are questions as to the expertise required or the individual's professional competence.

There is also personal authority, independent of role — a function of personal qualities, knowledge, or social position. In a day care center, a low-ranking staff member may have power or influence stemming from ties to the community, parents, or the possession of certain skills.

The best way to understand day care center organization is to view it from the hypothetical starting point of a single caregiver or teacher caring for five to ten children. With increases in the number of children, caregivers must be added, usually lower-paid assistants or aides. Increases in the number of children also result in divisions into separate groups and divisions in the program between teaching and administrative functions. Figure 5.1 is a sample of how such functions and groups might look.

How do day care centers actually work? How is authority divided, decisions made, and the work actually performed? On paper, one would expect relatively autonomous classroom groups planned and directed by a professional — the teacher — with central direction and coordination provided by a director and often overseen by a board of directors. There would be clear divisions between administrative responsibilities and teaching and care-giving responsibilities. Within each classroom one would expect a division between professional and nonprofessional tasks. Is this picture accurate?

Roger Neugebauer's (1975) study supported the central role of the director and the sharp division between teaching and administration. His conclusion "that internal decision-making is substantially controlled by directors in many day care centers" (p. 16) is consistent with the Child Care Staff Education Project study reported on in chapter 4. What is not clear in his findings is the extent to which directors retain control over program issues beyond staff–child ratio, group size, and purchasing. The structure of the curriculum and care routines, the balance between free choice and teacher direction, the kinds of activities and adult–child interactions valued, and the tone that characterizes daily life are areas where a director may exercise control or cede control to center staff. The Child Care Staff Education Project study reported that teachers tended to have much more involvement in day-to-day decisions in matters of curriculum, supervision, scheduling, and division of staff responsibilities.

Within each classroom the reality is often quite different from what one would expect from organizational charts and job descriptions assigning teachers, rather than aides, the professional role. A study by Jacobson and Driije (1969) discovered that in Head Start, teachers and aides expressed a coteacher ideology, stressing that close teamwork is necessary to operate the program. They reported that duties were divided equally, although the teachers handled paperwork and parent conferences. Aides saw themselves as teachers and were viewed as such by parents and children, a source of much satisfaction for aides. Both aides and teachers reported that they relied on informal communication and coordination in making decisions and resolving differences. Solutions were not handed down by teachers but were "worked out."

Figure 5.1. Organizational Chart of Average Day Care Center

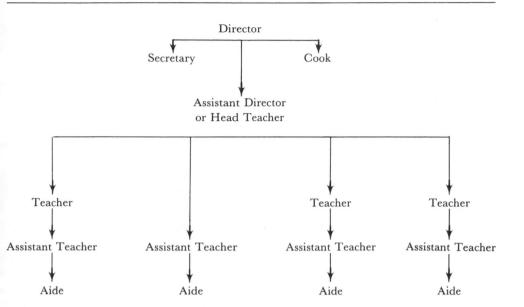

The Child Care Staff Education Project also noted that job titles appear to give very little information about the types of tasks performed by staff of different rank. In dividing classroom responsibilities, a traditional norm of equality commonly operates. Everyone shares in the cleanup, preparation, care routines, and interactions with children.

How does the hierarchy shown in an organizational chart and implied in job descriptions come to be translated into the cooperative ideology observed by Jacobson and Driije? There is in practice little basis for a hierarchy. The distinction between instructional (more important) and noninstructional (less important) activities is not relevant to day care. Further, it is not uncommon for assistant teachers and even aides to have equivalent or superior training to teachers in the same program. Because caregiving staff working in all-day programs share very low levels of pay and status, distinctions among positions are rarely compelling.

There is no clear, shared definition of the meaning of professionalism for work in day care. Day care staff define professionalism in terms of the perceived importance and responsibility associated with the work rather than in terms of possession of a particular body of knowledge and skills, something that all day care workers can share in regardless of externally defined qualifications.

Staff recruited for their ability to care for and meet the needs of young people may find a hierarchy arbitrary or meaningless. It is likely that teachers in centers are rarely suited, either by training or personality, to supervise others in a hierarchical structure. Almy (1975) makes the observation that many teachers of young children may be doing what they do because they perfer interacting with children to interacting with adults.

This discussion of staff relationships opened with the observation that the social complexity of most day care centers seems likely to contribute to conflict. However, neither the complexity nor the challenge to the job hierarchy seems to result in observable conflict. One reason for this may be that the day care staff, most commonly women, have been socialized to avoid conflict that threatens pleasant social relations (Simpson and Simpson 1969). The lack of long-range ambition and the prevalence of high staff turnover may result in conflict reduction because workers are less likely to be involved in controversy if their commitment is short-term.

Jacobson and Driije (1973, p. 174) observed another important reason for the absence of conflict. In spite of what appeared to be close communication between teachers and aides, persons working in the same classroom reported significant differences in beliefs regarding children, child rearing, and education, but *none of the teachers and aides were aware that such differences existed.* Taylor (1975) also reported that communication was limited and was concentrated on coordination of the program routine. Deeper analysis of program goals and children's needs tended to be overlooked. Neugebauer (1975) found that in only 15 percent of the centers studied were staff members in full agreement on the major areas of program emphasis. Staff had never discussed curriculum objectives.

Goodlad and Klein (1974), who directed a study of 201 preschool programs, observed that "certain well established, traditional means initially establish, if not justify, the ends. There are some things that nursery schools just do" (p. 36). Teachers have a much firmer idea of what *to do* than of the goals and choices that underlie curriculum. For example, teachers, when asked about goals, may assert independence as one but few teachers have chosen materials, arranged the room, planned the day's activities, and supervised adult–child interactions with an eye toward independence or most other implicit goals.

A nearly universal desire in day care centers is to achieve a smooth, stable routine that minimizes the chance of confusion and disorder. A routine helps adults and children achieve comfort and easy compliance with the center's activities within a few days of entry into the program. The practical demands of the work leave little time for reflection. The emphasis on routine and activities rather than on goals and outcomes also reduces the need to face areas of potential disagreement. The routine itself has authority as "tradition — the way we do things" — a process of trial and error that has reduced alternatives to the few that are known to "work." It is usually easier to challenge the teacher or director than the routine. To the extent that the routine functions smoothly, it is usually not questioned.

The relationship among classrooms in a center, the way in which decisions are made about common space and scheduling conflicts, the degree of interaction and interdependence among different classes, and the relationships among teachers in different classrooms have not been the subject of study. From our observations in many centers, classrooms seem nearly as self-contained and isolated as in the public schools, despite smaller size and greater informality. The extent of intergroup relationships appears usually to be determined by space requirements, schedules, equipment, or social relationships among staff members.

In short, a trade-off seems to be occurring in staff relationships in day care. The equality norm, the emphasis on routine activities, and the often limited relationships among classroom groups at the center act to reduce the need for communication and coordination and the likelihood of uncertainty and conflict.

This trade-off is at least in part an adaptation to two realities: first, the real lack of time to communicate and coordinate mentioned in chapter 4, and second, the danger that a necessity for extensive adult interaction could lead to a preoccupation with adult needs and adult relationships. A stable environment for children is difficult if adults are at odds or focusing on their own issues.

If there is not an effort to thoughtfully sort out staff roles and relationships, the result is often an underutilization of talent. The knowledge and expertise of exceptional teachers is muted by the equality norm. The opposite also occurs in centers: a commitment to the classroom hierarchy blunts the talents of skilled assistants. And professional growth is stunted when the opportunity for professional dialogue and a collegial relationship requires a personal relationship to germinate.

RELATIONSHIPS BETWEEN PARENTS AND STAFF

A strong sense of clear difference but little observed conflict also characterizes relationships between parents and staff in day care. The confusing range of beliefs, feelings, and concerns that parents bring to the center are met by an equally broad range among staff. Young inexperienced parents, nearly always mothers, somewhat unsure of what "good" parenting and child care is all about, feeling some uneasiness about the idea of day care, not terribly secure about their prerogatives as parents, and struggling to make workable child care arrangements, often face women much like themselves in the role of caregivers. Because there is no set standard, parents and caregivers bring individual idiosyncratic views to bear on what the nature of the relationship should be.

Individual views, however, are tempered by the ideology of the program. "Parent involvement" is an all-purpose term used to describe all manner of parent–program interactions: policymaking, parent education, fund raising, volunteering time, and even the simple exchange of information of various sorts with staff. Under a general goal of continuity of care, the desired end involved may be better parenting, better day care, or both. The parent involvement continuum runs from an expectation of parent control to complete subservience of parents to professionals. Parents may be cast in a variety of roles from experts (on their own children) to students, thus putting staff in positions ranging from servants to savants.

Parental Expectations of Staff

At the heart of parent–staff relationships lies the issue just discussed as key to understanding staff relationships: power and authority. When parents and staff interact, how much weight do parental beliefs based on extended experience with and commitment to their own children carry as opposed to the judgment of child care staff based on training, experience, and professional objectivity? And what are the boundaries of shared concern? How far can parents extend into the classroom and teachers into the home?

Parents do have expectations about the care of their children and will seek ways to influence practices at the day care center. In Powell's (1977) study of staff–parent relationships, 84.9 percent of the parents believed parents and caregivers should discuss goals and general expectations of the center, and a majority (51.3 percent) believed that parental suggestions about caregiver practices were also appropriate. At the same time, there was agreement among parents in the study on the importance of family privacy and autonomy; a majority did not believe in regularly sharing information about the family (61.3 percent) or in discussing family problems with the center staff (51.2 percent).

The Powell study suggested, in addition, that parents may differ in their views on the appropriate relationship between the day care center and the family. Powell described three types of parents who use centers. Some parents see the day care center and the family as *independent* child care systems; in addition to infrequently communicating with center staff, they avoid discussing family matters or child-rearing values. Another group of families sees themselves as *dependent* on the center. While looking to the center for child-rearing information, they communicate little about their families or their expectations for the program. A third group of parents exhibits an *interdependent* pattern of communication; as they receive information from the center, they also openly share family information and feel that family values should be discussed with the center.

Parent Involvement in Day Care

Zigler and Turner (1982) observed that even in a university-sponsored day care program that was specially designed to include parent involvement, parents spent an average of only 7.4 minutes per day in the center. This time included *all types* of involvement — attendance at meetings, informal conversations with staff, and so forth. While many programs probably achieve much higher levels than the Zigler and Turner study, their study demonstrates how difficult it is to achieve parent involvement, even in programs with good intentions. Data from the National Day Care Study (Coelen et al. 1979) present a more positive image of parent involvement in day care. Involvement went beyond the stereotypic bake sale fund raisers for many centers to include decision making, hiring, and volunteering time. The more extensive use of all types of parent involvement in the nonprofit subsidized centers probably reflects the inclusion of Head Start extended-day programs in that category.

The high percentage of centers reporting no parent involvement may reflect both the scarce time resources of day care families and problems in the prevailing concept of parent involvement. Head Start teachers have reported increased difficulty in implementing parent involvement as more Head Start parents take on full-time employment. However, day care parents may influence and participate in their children's day care in ways not usually thought of as parent involvement. For example, Powell's research suggested the importance of informal staff–parent interchanges when the child is dropped off and picked up at the center; 70.8 percent of the parents and 66.5 percent of the caregivers used this form of communication. In addition, informal social networks with other parents were used by a small number of parents (11.3 percent) to discuss the day care center, their children, and other concerns. Future research needs to consider the impact of such informal communication networks on center practices.

Staff Attitudes Toward Parents

In conversations with caregivers, it is clear that they want the same things all teachers want: respect for their knowledge and skills, cooperation with requests seen as essential to performing their jobs (e.g., for information, extra clothes, reinforcement of certain behaviors), and some interest shown in the work that teachers perform.[2] The most frequent complaints heard in centers are that "parents don't care," "they drop off their kid and don't say a word," "they don't show up for conferences."

At the same time, it is also clear to observers that communication with parents is difficult for most teachers. The uncertainty surrounding their status and role, the issue of who in fact is the senior partner and who is the junior member of the partnership result in a hesitancy about engaging in communication on both ends of the relationship. Joffe's study (1977) illustrates this. While teachers wanted contact, they resisted or resented parent demands for changes in practice and saw these as infringing on their (however vaguely defined) professional role. When staff members' formal education and expertise are challenged by parents' common sense approach and knowledge based on child-rearing experience, conflict, rather than shared wisdom, is often the result or, as in the case of staff interactions, non-communication and more distant relations, which reduce the conflict.

Joffe found that parents were encouraged to become involved, yet at the same time staff had difficulty accepting parents who took on

---

2. For a sensitive study of teacher–parent relations, see Sara Lawrence Lightfoot's *Worlds Apart: Relationships Between Families and Schools* (1978).

staff responsibilities for decision making or leadership or who challenged the staff's knowledge of child development in parent education sessions. Staff refused to comply with some parental wishes (e.g., on curriculum content and discipline) on the grounds that they, as professionals, had to determine practice and that some practices appropriate within a family context were inappropriate in the group setting of the center.

Staff-parent distinctions and relationships and the interplay of class and cultural differences are rarely uniform across the center. Consider, for example, the center that wants to recruit staff from within the neighborhood and ethnic group of its clientele. Licensing and certification standards, coupled with unequal educational opportunities, may require that the program recruit city-wide for qualified directors and teachers, while teachers' aides, cooks, and bus drivers can be hired from the local community. In this situation, the teachers will tend to bring into the center values, attitudes, and practices from outside the community; these may become a source of parent–staff misunderstanding and conflict (and intrastaff conflict as well).

The issue of professional authority and competence is more than an abstraction, especially for child care programs serving subcultural groups.

> Over a period of four years we have found that the best workers with families are community residents with similar cultural and linguistic backgrounds. . . . It is far easier to train a community worker to do an appropriate development assessment of an infant than to train a Ph.D. psychologist to appreciate and understand rural Mexican child rearing practices (Charles R. Drew Medical School, n.d.).

It is not only education issues that crystallize staff–parent relations. Issues relating to children's illness, care of clothing, toileting practices, and other socialization issues are equally important. Staff expect parents to understand the limitations of group care, whether it is the difficulty of caring for a child with a cold, keeping track of socks, or the difficulty presented by late pickups of children. Parents expect staff to take into account the other side of the coin — the lack of anyone to care for sick children at home, the cost of clothing, the difficulty of getting to the center by bus before closing time. These issues have the most power to generate tension and conflict. The difficulty of resolving these issues is another pressure toward reduced or more informal communication.

To what extent are staff attitudes toward parents negative? Findings from a recent study (Kontos, Raikes, and Woods 1980) suggest that staff members' expectations of parents may be tempered by their experience in working with parents in the child care center. Staff members in the study tended to give parents in their center negative ratings relative to their concept of the ideal parent. However, the· center parents were rated positively relative to workers' perceptions of "most parents today." This pattern of responses suggests some realism about what parents are like and also some appreciation for what parents can reasonably be expected to do. When attitudes in different types of programs were compared, day care staff tended to give more negative ratings than nursery school staff but were more positive than Head Start staff. The working day care parent may elicit both empathy and criticism, because her situation is perceived to be similar to that of the day care worker. Older staff and staff members with children tended to report more positive attitudes toward parents, again suggesting empathy drawn from an understanding based on common experience. However, differences in income level between parents and staff were also associated with more positive attitudes toward parents.

As might be expected, day care staff gave the lowest rating for center parents on items relating to parental involvement in the center. The day care staff seemed to be reflecting current notions of what parent involvement is and should be, as well as reporting the fact that day care center parents have little time to give for typical involvement activities.

IMPLICATIONS FOR CHANGE

In this chapter, we have suggested that (1) the people in day care are a diverse lot who bring different beliefs, expectations, and concerns to staff and parent roles. Unfortunately, this variability can be a problem when simple solutions are expected and conflict is to be avoided. (2) The parent role and various staff roles are usually vaguely defined and vary across programs. The real roles are often quite different from those envisioned on paper. Questions of authority and responsibility are likely to be unresolved. (3) Nearly all of the adults in child care tend to be victims of sexist attitudes toward the value of "woman's work" and working mothers; that results in low status, low pay, and coping with the day-to-day routines of family and working life that often involve logistical nightmares. What implications can would-be change agents draw from this information?

Improving the Quality of Care

The forces discussed in this chapter often serve to constrain change. New ideas that require much planning, thought, or cooperation to germinate are likely to go nowhere if attention is not given to developing a careful strategy of implementation. Quality can be improved if one can increase the amount and the level of collaboration among day care staff. But where does the time come from that allows this to take place, sufficient time to weather the inevitable conflict that occurs when people try to reconcile differences in views and questions of authority? Staff time spent away from children is the most precious commodity a program possesses. Ironically, finding time becomes more difficult as a program improves and truly considers children as individuals. In infant programs, where individual schedules are necessitated, and in programs for older children that do not mold children into uniform napping schedules, meetings during working hours are hard to manage. Whether through hustling volunteers or parents, structuring mini-meetings, or other means, a change agent's first order of business is usually resolving the issue of scarce time.

Improving Staff–Parent Relationships

A first step is recognizing that parents do not all want the same relationship to their day care program. A second is to realize that parents seem to place limits on the extent and the content of their communication with staff (Powell 1977; Winklestein 1981); this protects their right to privacy and autonomy.

Staff has the responsibility of responding to the diverse needs, personal dispositions, and cultural backgrounds of families in a semipublic context; their behavior cannot be an exact replication of the parents'.

A clearly defined role gives staff the autonomy and privacy needed to protect the confidentiality of individual families while responding to the needs of many. If the adults understand the role differences, the security and latent (and not so latent) competition over the child may be lessened.

"Professionalizing" Day Care

Many of the discussions on the need to professionalize day care to elevate the status of the day care worker have a rather glib quality to them. Because it is work that is important and that requires talent and skill to do well, then professional recognition should follow. But it will not follow unless the questions about the real need for knowledge and training to care for children are answered. Today, any assumed authority derived from day care's presumed status as a profession tends to confuse rather than clarify relationships among staff and between staff and parents. Professional criteria cannot be applied uniformly to all who work in day care, either on the basis of characteristics of the persons or the jobs that they do. Professions, like trade unions, jealously guard the exclusiveness of their area of expertise and create barriers of certification, language, and ritual to ward off the encroachment of lay practitioners. The professionalization of day care certainly would have profound implications for relations among staff, between staff and parents, and between home and center providers. It is difficult to envision how day care teachers can be professionalized as educators without clearly demarcating the lines between the professional and the nonprofessional and assigning many practitioners currently assumed to be more or less equals (family day care providers, teachers with less training, including CDA's) to a lesser rank. And if the professional basis is that of an educator, the risk of elevating the place of education at the expense of good care for children is increased. The increase in day care for babies alone should cast doubt on the desirability of emphasizing teaching over care.

As consumers of day care, parents find themselves in a unique double bind with respect to professionalism in the field. On the one hand, they need assurances that day care staff are worthy of their trust and can help them with their family's most important responsibility. The low status of day care can compound the ambivalence or guilt parents feel in using a service on which society confers little status and assigns little value (Joffe 1977). On the other hand, expressions of professionalism can challenge parents' authority and competence, to say nothing of increasing the cost.

It seems only a slight simplification to boil all the issues down to this: if we decided what day care was, we could know the roles we all were to play: teachers, aides, and parents. If we decide that day care centers, like hospitals or schools, are professional institutions, we could begin to solidify our expectations. Or if we looked to midwives, extended families, or perhaps cooperatives, we could do the same. Or could we? How clearly can we characterize authority relations between women who care for their grandchildren and their daughters? Or between school teachers and parents?

More important than improved definitions is more clarity about the *value* of day care as work and the contribution of staff and parent in making day care successful. There must be ways for staff to see themselves as valuable without resorting to concepts that create misleading and false distinctions among individuals. When questions of status, working conditions, and pay are attacked more directly (see Whitebook's discussion in chap. 4) and more open give-and-take among day care adults is achieved, the problem of professionalism as a word and as a concept may resolve itself.

Chapter 6

THE RELATIONSHIP OF THE DAY CARE CENTER TO ITS EXTERNAL ENVIRONMENT

Roger Neugebauer

Headlines like these are commonplace today:

PERCENTAGE OF WOMEN WITH PRESCHOOL CHILDREN
ENTERING THE WORK FORCE EXPECTED
TO DOUBLE IN NEXT TEN YEARS

UNEMPLOYMENT RATES PREDICTED TO REMAIN
HIGH THROUGH END OF YEAR

FOOD PRICES RISE FOR TWENTIETH CONSECUTIVE MONTH

LOCAL ZONING BOARD TIGHTENS RESTRICTIONS
ON COMMERCIAL PROPERTIES

None of these news items has anything to do with child development or education. Yet all of them have potential impact on day care centers. Whether it be the accelerating return of women to the work force that results in an ever-increasing demand for day care services, or escalating food prices that threaten to burst day care center budgets, the internal operations of a day care center are inevitably affected by events and forces in the center's external environment.

To date, many efforts to improve day care have focused on day care centers as self-contained classrooms. Strategies for bringing about improvement have concentrated on tinkering with internal factors: improving centers' physical environments, shaping up curriculums, upgrading staff skills. The impact of these efforts can be short-lived if a day care center fails to maintain a stable and stimulating relationship with its external environment. In order to survive and thrive, a day care center must adequately respond to changes in and demands from its environment, as well as secure resources, ideas, and stimulation from the environment.

The connection between the health of an organization and its relationship to its environment was the focus of research by Harry Levinson. He concluded that

> the greater the number of attachments [with outside parties], the more secure the organization will feel. The wider the scope of gratification, the greater the likelihood that the organization receives stimulation from many different sources and the more energetic it is likely to be (Levinson 1972).

Applying Levinson's hypothesis to day care, we would conclude that a day care center will benefit from having good relationships with people in its environment such as legislators, bankers, educators, pediatricians, psychologists, doctors, lawyers, bureaucrats, licensing workers, merchants, union leaders, and community leaders. By having such contacts, the center is better able to secure financial support in times of crisis, technical expertise for thorny problems, a rich supply of ideas for the curriculum and the organization, and moral support when spirits are lagging.

Any effort to make day care better, therefore, needs to direct some attention to helping centers develop productive contacts with outside parties. This chapter will explore the specific ways day care centers do relate to their social environments and will assess the effectiveness of centers in maintaining these relationships. Further, some recommendations will be offered on how to make day care better through improving such contacts.

RELATING TO THE OUTSIDE WORLD

Tasks

As the director settled into her chair, she glanced at her schedule for the day ahead. An 8:30 A.M. meeting with the board's Personnel Committee to set up interviewing for the vacant head teacher position. A short meeting would allow her time to review a new article on toddler play in a journal before a prospective client arrived at 10

Photograph by James Greenman

A.M. for a tour of the center. The luncheon meeting of the task force planning activities for the Week of the Young Child would probably eat up two or three hours in the middle of the day. Then back to the office for a final flurry of activity: a quick call to the congressman's assistant to prod her on the child care bill stalled in committee; a call to the building inspector to try to coax him to set up a speedy inspection for the license renewal; and a concerted effort to put the finishing touches on the funding proposal for the new infant program. Finally, her reward for surviving the day would be the monthly dinner meeting of the directors' support group at the new Italian restaurant.

This day would not be atypical for the director of a large day care center; for the director of a small- to medium-sized center, such events might be spread out over a period of one or more weeks. In any case, events like these in the life of a director demonstrate the inevitable need to relate to the "outside world." In fact, in this one day this director was slated to touch on each of the eight forms of exchange between day care centers and their social environments. Let us look at these exchanges.

COMPLYING WITH REGULATORY DEMANDS. Centers must respond to the laws and requirements of funding sources and government agencies. They must comply with local licensing requirements and zoning laws. Periodic reports and audits must be provided for public and private funding sources. Beyond such formal demands, centers are also often required to respond to the unofficial whims and wishes of the bureaucrats administering these requirements. For example, late Thursday a director may receive a call from the state Social Services Department field representative demanding, by close of business on Friday, a complete report on the attendance records of all children receiving state funding. A center has little choice but to comply. Likewise, licensing inspectors often impose requirements, such as adding more outlets or replacing a fire door, which do not specifically appear in the regulations. Centers must respond to these extra requirements either by complying or by filing an appeal.

SECURING FINANCIAL AND IN-KIND RESOURCES. Centers serving families who cannot afford to pay the full cost of care must raise funds to partially or fully subsidize these parents' fees. Funds can be sought from public or private agencies or from private individuals. Resources raised can include grants of money or donations of goods and services. Even centers serving parents who can afford to pay the full cost of care must occasionally seek short-term loans to relieve temporary cash flow crises or long-term financing for capital improvements.

SECURING INFORMATION. Centers should continually be receptive to new ideas, theories, findings, and applications in the areas of child development and education. Such information is needed to provide fresh ideas for the centers' curriculum, to stimulate the rethinking of goals and philosophies, and to prevent the retaining of outmoded, unproductive practices. To remain competitive, attractive, and economically viable, centers must be alert to new developments in the child care profession, in legislation, in demographics, and in social and economic trends. They must keep up to date on new business practices and staff development approaches and opportunities.

SECURING SUPPORT. A much undervalued need of personnel in day care centers is the need for emotional support. Periodically, directors (and teachers) need to be able to turn to someone outside the center to talk, to complain, to cry on a shoulder.

SECURING STAFF. The quality of a center's staff is a major determinant of the quality of care that a center provides. Therefore it is essential for centers to be effective in locating, selecting, and employing qualified staff members.

MARKETING THE CENTER'S SERVICES. A high-quality day care center will be a failure if the people needing its services do not know it exists. Centers need to be effective at attracting the attention and interest of potential consumers.

ADVOCATING FOR DAY CARE. Not only do centers need to be reactive to public rules and requirements, but it is also in their best interest to be proactive — to have a hand in shaping policies and programs. Such advocacy involves efforts to influence public legislation at all levels and to secure the support of charitable organizations and private businesses.

EDUCATING THE GENERAL PUBLIC. In the long run, the profession of day care will benefit most when the general public accepts day care as a normal, natural, and beneficial service for young children. To bring about this positive climate, day care centers need to initiate or participate in efforts to educate the general public locally and nationally about day care.

State of the Art

This list of eight tasks may appear unrealistically demanding for a typical day care center. But in fact, for nearly any other business or profession these tasks are automatically assumed to be necessary and normal components of doing business. An astute entrepreneur opening a television repair shop, for example, would thoroughly investigate all business and zoning regulations and explore all business loan opportunities prior to opening the business. He or she would investigate the potential market area and launch an aggressive marketing campaign; hire trained technicians and keep up to date on new tools, materials, and television innovations; join a neighborhood business association to fight for reasonable ordinances and taxes; and become a member of a national trade association to keep up with relevant national legislation and trends. Day care centers, however, tend not to give high priority to relating to the larger society. As a result, their performance in the eight forms of exchange discussed above is not consistently effective.

In areas where the impact of society on a center's day-to-day operations is most direct, centers have a satisfactory and often outstanding track record. Centers demonstrate resourcefulness, flexibility, and patience in adjusting to burdensome regulatory requirements. In time most centers learn the importance of investing considerable energy in selecting qualified staff. Most important, many centers have displayed ingenuity and boundless energy in raising desperately needed funds. In these areas, the need for relating to the external social environment is obvious, immediate, and urgent, and the response has been solid.

In other areas, where the impact is direct but less immediate, centers' performance has been spotty but is noticeably improving. Marketing is a good example. As recently as five years ago, marketing tended to be viewed as a practice alien to quality day care. Even for-profit "mom-and-pop" day care centers were not particularly aggressive in advertising their services. However, with the advent of Reaganomics and the resulting drop in public funding, many centers are becoming aware of the economic necessity of actively reaching out for fee-paying families to serve. Whereas five years ago national child care conventions would not even consider offering workshops on marketing, no conference today is complete without numerous perspectives on the subject. Five years ago, a center's marketing campaign might consist of a hastily drafted, mimeographed flyer, but today, many centers

Photograph by James Greenman

employ a wide range of promotional tools, from public service announcements to direct mail campaigns.

In areas where the impact of the larger society on the daily life of a center is least direct, centers' performances are least effective. In advocacy and public education, areas where benefits are often not immediate or clearly identifiable, the performance of day care centers has been lackluster. In the 1960s and early 1970s, day care advocacy efforts failed dramatically, on three occasions, to convince Congress to enact comprehensive day care legislation. In the late 1970s, an ad hoc effort to bring a wide spectrum of day care advocates together as part of a "National Day Care Campaign" got off to a promising start but dwindled away due to lack of participation.

Public education efforts by the day care profession have been even less successful. While a few local day care coalitions have developed very effective media materials for their public education efforts, these have been isolated instances.

The inconsistent performance of day care centers in relating to their external environments can be traced to three basic causes: (1) the vast majority of centers are small, independent, resource-poor operations; (2) most day care administrators have been trained in child development, not in organizational management; and (3) the diversity of legal and organizational structures and program philosophies among day care centers tends to work against unity and unified action. A discussion of each of these factors follows.

THE SMALL, INDEPENDENT CENTER

The National Day Care Study (Roupp et al. 1979) made the first detailed examination of the organizational structure of day care. This research revealed that the average day care center had an enrollment of forty-nine children and average annual operating expenditures of $70,300. Fifty-four percent of the more than eighteen thousand centers in the country operated on an independent basis, with less than 6 percent being part of for-profit chains of centers. While the percentage of small, single-center, independent operations has decreased since this study was completed, the industry is no doubt still dominated by small independent organizations.

While small may be beautiful, it is also poorly financed. Small centers typically generate barely enough money to pay for staff, occupancy, food, and supplies. Precious little money is available for marketing, public education, information collection, recruitment, lobbying, or writing grant applications. Whatever staff resources are available are spread thin. A center serving fifty or fewer children typically has only one or two staff members performing nonteaching tasks. Even for these staff members, most of their time and attention is devoted to internal concerns. A recent *Child Care Information Exchange* survey found that the majority of the time of center administrators is consumed by staff management, financial management, and curriculum planning. Relatively little time is available for external tasks. A day care director from Florida commented, "I find that I must work over sixty hours a week just to keep my center going. If I took time away for politics, I'm afraid the quality of my program would suffer" (Neugebauer 1977, p. 16).

TRAINING OF DAY CARE ADMINISTRATORS

Typically, day care administrators are promoted to their positions from the ranks of teachers. Those administrators who have received training in administration have most likely taken a single course that covered everything from staff management to bookkeeping in twelve sessions. Only recently have a few intensive graduate programs in day care administration appeared.

This lack of training in administration lessens administrators' effectiveness in relating to the outside world, in that they often lack the necessary skills to perform many facets of the job. More seriously, they may lack an awareness of the importance of attending to the center's external environment and fostering strong reciprocal relationships with people and groups outside the center.

In a survey of centers in New England performed by Neugebauer (1975), it was found that less than one-third of the centers surveyed had frequent, positive, and constructive contacts with other day care programs, with people in their surrounding neighborhoods, with medical and mental health units, or with colleges and universities. Less than one fifth had such relationships with professional associations, government agencies, news media, other community service organizations, consultants, public schools, and advocacy groups (Neugebauer 1975, p. 25).

LACK OF UNITY

It is often proposed that one strength of the current day care delivery system, as opposed to the delivery system for public education, for example, is the diversity of choices available to parents. One unfortunate by-product of this diversity, however, is that these differences tend to hamper efforts to work together on marketing, advocacy, and public education.

It is inconceivable that representatives of two large oil companies would appear before a congressional hearing and take opposing positions on proposed legislation relating to the oil industry. Yet this occurs routinely when day care legislation is under consideration. Time after time, day care advocates, with an apparent urge toward self-destruction, take opposing or conflicting positions in public hearings.

This proclivity to disunity has several negative effects. Obviously, the effectiveness of providers in influencing legislation is diminished by frequent discord. At the same time, the ability of day care advocates to develop long-term supportive relationships with legislators and public officials is undermined. The attempts of day care advocates to come together to develop long-range advocacy and public education efforts are often short-lived. And finally, the ability of day care advocates to maintain widespread participation of providers in advocacy efforts is continually undercut, since many new participants drop out in frustration over the continual infighting and lack of progress.

STRATEGIES FOR CHANGE

The above discussion may read more like an autopsy than a state of the art report. That is not to say, of course, that the performance of all centers is poor. In fact, many centers demonstrate highly developed skills in interrelating with their social environment. These success stories have been used as the basis for recommending the following strategies.

Strategy 1: Upgrade Administrative Training

Center administrators need many more opportunities to develop their environmental interaction skills. Training needs in this area are quite extensive. Specific attention is particularly needed in helping directors develop specific skills in grantsmanship, fund raising, marketing, staff recruitement, community relations, and advocacy.

Acquiring each of these skills requires many hours of intensive training. Ideally this training would be divided in terms of appropriate subject areas, with enough time between sessions to allow administrators opportunities to try out newly acquired skills on the job. To have the widest impact, this training needs to be offered in a variety of formats. Consideration needs to be given to offering evening courses on an off-campus, noncredit basis. Local day care associations could offer a series of evening workshops on specific skills. Intensive weekend seminars or retreats could be experimented with. Biweekly or monthly "share-a-thons" where directors in a locality informally pool their successful ideas and techniques might be used as a starting point.

Strategy 2: Develop Center-level Action Plans

Especially given the severe demands on time and resources, it is important that interactions with the social environment not be left to chance. In general, activities not budgeted and scheduled do not happen. To ensure that environmental interactions are given appropriate priority, a center should develop an annual environmental interaction plan.

One way to initiate such a plan would be to set a goal for the center in each of the eight task areas. For example, in the area of "complying with regulatory demands," the center may set the goal of establishing positive personal relationships with licensing, regulatory, and contract officials. Once a goal is set, a specific strategy should be established spelling out proposed activities, dates, responsible parties, and funds required to achieve the goal.

To avoid overly ambitious plans, participants need to continually be asking not only questions such as "Is this goal significant?" and "Will its achievement really make a difference?", but also reality testers such as "Can we really marshall the staff time necessary to achieve this goal?" and "Can we afford to commit the necessary resources?"

Once the plan is developed, copies of it should be widely disseminated and dates for specific activities posted as a continual reminder of what should be happening. The director should follow up to be sure that agreed-upon resources are available when needed and that delegated activities are being accomplished on schedule. As the year progresses, the director should also initiate an informal evaluation of whether the goals were realistic and whether they are bringing about the hoped-for results.

Strategy 3: Broaden Involvement of Center Staff

In most small- to medium-sized centers, all responsibility for relating to the world outside the center is dumped in the lap of one person — the administrator. When this person gets overwhelmed, the work does not get done. By delegating tasks to other staff members and volunteers, however, the work can get done without overburdening the administrator. This is particularly true in the area of environmental interaction, where many of the activities are ideally suited for delegation.

The most obvious resource for delegation is the staff. Administrators, however, are often wary of delegating administrative work to teachers for fear that they will resent it or that it will interfere with their teaching. Yet studies have shown that many, though not all, teachers actually welcome involvement in administrative areas. In centers where teachers had been delegated administrative responsibilities, their morale was found to be higher than in centers where no delegation was made (Neugebauer 1975, p. 23). Participation, on a limited basis, in administrative tasks provides teachers with a change of pace from their demanding work with the children and gives them a sense of greater involvement in the life of the center.

A wide variety of tasks could feasibly be delegated to teachers. A teacher could be assigned to periodically review child development literature for ideas and insights applicable to the center. Another teacher could review literature in the fields of business, politics, and economics to search out news and trends relevant to the center. A teacher could be put in charge of hosting the visits to the center of prospective parents or could attend public hearings to state the center's position on issues under consideration. A teacher could be put in charge of drafting a funding proposal.

Delegating responsibility works if the tasks are a significant part of an overall plan that enables people to feel they are making a difference, and if the director provides the support necessary to complete the task.

Strategy 4: Mobilize Community Resource People

Centers' environmental interaction efforts can benefit from attracting the expertise and energy of resource people in the community. Parents, specialists, community leaders, and other volunteers can help a center accomplish many tasks if their contributions are well organized.

Many parents are eager to support a day care center that they are satisfied with, but they often are not offered attractive opportunities for actualizing their interest. Typically parents are called upon to serve on a board of directors or to volunteer to help in the classroom. When parents decline, either because their schedules do not allow such participation or because they feel uncomfortable in these roles, the center's staff then views parents as apathetic or unsupportive. In fact, when parents are given creative opportunities to contribute, many do so.

Many such opportunities exist in helping a center relate to the outside world. While a parent may be reluctant to commit him- or herself to heading up a public relations committee, he or she may be willing to serve as an informal liaison person to the editor of the local newspaper. While another parent may not want to work in the classroom, he or she may be more than willing to spend one hour a week in the local library reviewing magazines and newspapers for articles and ideas of potential relevance to the center.

Other parents may have specific skills they would be willing to put to use for the center. A parent who is a graphics designer might be willing to work with the administrator in redesigning the center's brochure. A psychologist could be recruited to help the administrator organize and facilitate a local administrators' support group.

Other people in the community can also serve as valuable resources to the center. Child development instructors from the local college could be tapped to keep the center informed about new ideas in the fields of child development and education. A local politician could be prevailed upon to drum up support for a local or state day care initiative. A media expert could be tapped to help develop a slide presentation about day care to show to local service clubs and social organizations.

To effectively utilize parents and other community resource persons, three ingredients are required: direction, structure, and rewards. Just as with the delegation of tasks to subordinates, the recruitment of community people to perform tasks should be done as part of an overall environmental interaction plan. Assigning tasks willy-nilly will generate a lot of activity but will not necessarily move the center in any definite direction.

The efforts of community people need to be coordinated by somebody. Contributors need to clearly understand who they take orders from, who they turn to with questions, and who they report their results to. In a small center, where only a handful of people are recruited, they can probably be most efficiently supervised by the administrator. As more recuits become involved, however, the attention of the administrator may become spread too thin. At this point, a specific person or task force should be set up to supervise an overall task and all the staff and community people working on that task.

The third key ingredient to utilizing outside resource people is rewards. People expect to be rewarded for working for an organization. The ego satisfaction of making a worthwhile contribution to a worthy cause will be sufficient reward for many people. If a center is designated as nonprofit, this in itself may seem to give it a seal of approval as a worthy cause (even if the center is not accomplishing anything of worth). However, for-profit centers should not shy away from recruiting volunteers. Most parents and many resource persons from the community are more concerned about the quality and spirit of a center than its legal status.

Other rewards are also available for maximizing outside support. The easiest yet most frequently overlooked reward is positive feedback. Centers should show an interest in the contributions of outside supporters, offer them encouragement and support along the way, shower them with genuine thanks and praise upon completion of a task, and, most important, let them see the results of their efforts — show them how their contribution has made a difference. Also, centers should not overlook the reward value of titles. Rather than simply referring to a helper as a "volunteer," the center could designate him or her a "public relations adviser" or a "coordinator of public education," or a "member of the Advisory Board." Finally, when all else fails, centers should be prepared to reward people with money. If no parent or qualified volunteer can be found to help design a center's brochure, the staff should not try to save money by doing it themselves. Instead, a graphics designer should be hired to do it right.

Strategy 5: Maximize the Effectiveness of the Board

In theory, most nonprofit day care centers are governed by an elected board of directors who serve voluntarily. Ideally the board should serve as a solid link between the center and its social environment. In reality, most boards are not viewed as sources of leadership and support but as liabilities, since the administrator must divert time and energy away from the program into keeping the board functioning.

While many factors contribute to the ineffectiveness of boards, typically their most critical weakness is role confusion. Legally, the boards of publicly supported nonprofit centers are created to assess the needs of the population being served, to establish and periodically review the goals and policies of the agency, and to evaluate the performance of the agency in relation to these goals and policies. The center's board, in effect, employs the staff to implement these goals and policies. As a policy-making body, the board is overstepping its bounds when it becomes involved in day-to-day implementation activities. When the board starts taking on operational responsibilities such as drafting a fund-raising letter, this tends to blur the roles of board and staff. What starts out as a blessing for the administrator (being able to unload some administrative tasks) can become a burden as board members get in the habit of interfering in the day-to-day decision making of the administrator. It can also be a diversion, as board members become distracted from performing their policymaking tasks.

The negative effects of role confusion can be avoided if there is an orientation period in which new board members are briefed on the roles and relationships of the board and staff and, at board meetings, if a clear distinction is made between policymaking and operational tasks.

This is not to say, of course, that board members should be prevented from volunteering for operational tasks. Clearly there are many tasks, especially in the area of environmental interaction, where it would be beneficial to utilize board members' expertise and energies. However, in recruiting board members individually or as a group to perform an operational task, it should be made clear that this work is in addition to their board work — that is, it is not a regular board function. Board members working on such tasks, such as a fund-raising project or an advocacy task force, might even report directly to the administrator of the center rather than to the chairperson of the board.

Finally, in recruiting volunteers to serve on the board, the primary tasks of the board should be kept in mind. An administrator may want to recruit a local politician to serve on the board because of the influence he could bring to bear on licensing problems or advocacy issues; or he or she may want to recruit a woman active in the community because of her fund-raising expertise; or a parent may be eager to help the center with its promotional efforts. These persons may be willing to perform the tasks that the administrator has in mind that are not directly board tasks, but they may not be interested or able to actively participate in center policymaking. In such instances, consideration should be given to recruiting people not to serve on a board but to serve on a more unstructured "administrator's advisory panel." Members of this panel would not meet regularly but would work individually, when the need arose, on specific requests from the administrator, such as to press for a change in a license renewal ruling or to redesign the center's brochure. Another model would be to recruit a team of volunteers to carry out a specific task. For example, "The Friends of Hippity-Hop Day Care" task force could be recruited to promote the center in the community.

Most of the points made here concerning boards of directors apply only to nonprofit centers. However, the last point about additional advisory groups or task forces could apply equally well to for-profit centers. A well-operated for-profit center should be able to attract the expertise and energies of the community as well as a nonprofit center.

Strategy 6: Pool Local Resources

The centers in a community should explore options for pooling their resources to more effectively accomplish common tasks. For example, marketing and public education are functions that could be carried out on a cooperative basis. Individual centers usually lack the resources and expertise to mount an effective media campaign. By pooling resources (both financial and staff), a group of four or more centers could possibly afford to develop an attractive package of public service announcements, display advertisements, and bumper stickers to promote day care in general. A single phone number could be advertised where parents could call to receive descriptions of all participating centers.

One way to facilitate such cooperative efforts would be to organize a local administrative services unit. Such a unit could offer centers a variety of services on a fee basis. For example, in addition to handling marketing and public education, this unit could provide common services such as computerized accounting, staff training, writing grant applications, lobbying, and staff recruitment. The unit could be directed by a board consisting of one representative of each participating center; it could be administered by a third party such as a United Way agency, or it could be operated on a proprietary basis by a former director.

By pooling resources in this manner, day care centers can begin to enjoy some of the clout and expertise of big organizations without sacrificing their much-valued independence. Given the divisiveness that hampered previous advocacy efforts, it is not likely that a large number of centers would readily launch a major mutual venture. More likely, cooperation should start on a small scale among two or three centers that are eager to cooperate. As these centers demonstrate success in their cooperative efforts, other centers may be motivated to join in.

Strategy 7: Build Advocacy on Commonalities

Day care administrators tend to be as independent spiritually as their centers are structurally. Everyone likes to believe his or her center is unique. Not surprisingly, when a group of administrators gets together for the first time, it is their differences that come to the fore and get in the way of unified action.

In studying advocacy organizations in day care that have experienced some success in recent years, one is struck by the fact that these organizations are built around characteristics that participating centers have in common. At the national level, the National Association for Child Care Management (NACCM) has been a most effective day care lobby group. Although participating centers are widely divergent in many ways and even bitter competitors in some cases, they are united by the fact that they all operate on a for-profit basis. All goals of NACCM focus on enhancing the profitability of day care for NACCM members. Unity is maintained by avoiding issues that diverge from this central focus or that would highlight differences among members.

As the details of Reaganomics began to unfold, it became clear that Head Start was one of the very few social programs immune from drastic cuts. The reason Head Start fared so well is certainly not because Reagan admired Head Start. Rather, it was because of the vocal Head Start lobby. Thousands of advocates from Head Start programs across the country became effective by concentrating their attention on saving one program.

Other organizations that have been effective are a number of state-level advocacy groups. Once again, these organizations are united by common interests, even though in some cases they include nonprofit centers, for-profit centers, Head Start centers, Montessori centers, and church-sponsored centers. Operating in the same state, participating centers all confront a common foe — the state bureaucracy — and they all do business in the same economic climate.

It would appear that one way to avoid the divisiveness so typical in day care advocacy efforts is to stress similarities and downplay differences. This means that advocacy organizations may need to start out with a narrow base (only for-profit programs, only Head Start programs, only programs in one state) or with a narrow focus (expanding the tax credit, earmarking state funds for day care). Once advocacy organizations based on commonality of purpose or structure establish themselves and demonstrate some successes, they will be in a position to broaden their influence by working with other advocacy organizations on specific issues where a common end is desired.

One task around which a wide range of advocacy organizations could unite is a much-needed public education effort. One or more well-funded organizations could develop a coordinated series of public service announcements, news releases, slide shows, and other promotional materials. These, along with "how to" public relations kits, could be made widely available to other advocacy organizations. If a public education effort succeeded in significantly improving the public's image of day care, this could have many long-term benefits. All centers could benefit from increased willingness of parents to use day care centers, and all advocacy efforts would be reinforced with greater public support.

In conclusion, what all these strategies basically call for is a reorientation of the way in which centers view themselves. Centers need to begin thinking of themselves not as self-contained units with a life of their own but as integral parts of an ever-changing society. The more effectively they can interchange resources with this environment, the more secure, rich, and vital they will be.

PART II

Unraveling Outcomes: Observing, Recording, and Evaluating Day Care

Chapter 7

IMPROVING DAY CARE
BY STUDYING CHILDREN

Robert Fuqua
Dorothy Pinsky

The notice on the bulletin board in the day care center said, " A training session on *Improving Day Care by Studying Children* will be presented by Robert Fuqua and Dorothy Pinsky. Time: 9:00 to 11:30 A.M.
Date: Saturday, March 23, 1983. Place: Kidsville Day Care Center.
Free registration. Coffee and donuts at 8:30 A.M."

"Say, Chloe, are you going to that session?" Sandy asked.

"I don't know — it's on Saturday morning. And what do they mean
by 'studying children,' anyway?" replied Chloe.

"Well, I'm not sure either," said Sandy. "But I've been to other
training sessions, and they've been pretty good. Besides, they usually give you lots of good handouts that we could bring back and share."

"Oh, I don't know. It sounds like something we've done before,"
speculated Chloe.

"Might be. But remember, now that we have infants in our program, things have changed a lot. And you know we also have different
kinds of families now that Title XX monies are gone. So maybe this
would help us. Let's go!"

"OK, pick me up about ten after eight and we'll get there in time
for coffee. I guess we'll get to see Celest, and Jim, and Stanley from
the Blue Fairy Day Care, and some of the others we don't see very
often."

The doubt expressed in the scenario above is typical, because the
term *studying* sounds imposing and formal. Studying does not have
to be formal. It is simply the process of carefully attending to and thinking about what is happening. At times, studying in day care may be
rather spontaneous and subjective, and at other times it may be care-

125

fully planned and more objective. Caregivers often "study" children without realizing that this is what they are doing. Increasing caregivers' levels of awareness of the value of studying children and improving their skills in studying can result in positive outcomes for children.

This chapter will consider how day care programs can be improved by coming to know and understand the children's experience. The main theme of this chapter, as well as of this book, is to emphasize the importance of viewing day care programs from an ecological perspective. That is, we advocate knowing and studying children across a range of situations and from a variety of personal viewpoints.

Caregivers, as well as parents, other children, and the child who is being studied are all important sources of information to be considered if we are to have a comprehensive picture of each child. For example, different caregivers in the program will often see the same child quite differently because their particular training, experience, and opportunity to interact with the child vary. The sharing of these diverse perspectives can either confirm personal conclusions or provide insights not previously available and can contribute to more meaningful programming for the child. The parents provide a very different perspective of the child, since parents see the child behave in a much wider range of settings and over a much longer time span than caregivers do. Parents can also help caregivers to understand and respond to cultural and family values that influence the child's development. Because children spend more time directly involved with each other than with adults, their views of each other can be not only interesting but enlightening. Last, but in no way least, the child's own perspective can be very valuable. The child's view of things can be learned by a caregiver who can skillfully visit with the child or can be inferred from the conversations children have, from the patterns of behaviors and the cues provided through the activities a child engages in, through the roles she or he adopts, and through the quality of the relationships she or he has with others.

WHY STUDY CHILDREN?

Caregivers who are skillful at studying children focus not just on what is happening at any particular time but also on the outcomes of events. They are not simply concerned with what teaching is taking place or what care is being provided but also with the learning that has taken place or the outcomes of the care. They are not only concerned with smooth functioning, but also with the effects of that func-

tioning on children and adults. For example, some caregivers assume that if teaching is taking place, learning will automatically result, as these examples will show.

Ana, who cares for infants, was observed conducting a "lesson" from a packaged language kit designed for much older children. Not only were the materials inappropriate, but so was the group instructional method she used. The infants quickly became disenchanted with the activity and began to wander away. Much of Ana'a effort during that short time was spent retrieving children and returning them to their original position in the circle. Nevertheless Ana took pride in the fact that she was not simply "babysitting" but was "teaching" children. Sadly, she assumed that because she was providing a structured teaching situation for children on a daily basis, learning was also taking place.

Unless a deliberate and concerted effort is made to study the experiences that are provided for children, outcomes will only be assumed, not seen. The importance of studying children can be seen in the outcomes for both children and caregivers.

Penny, the head caregiver for a group of two- to four-year-olds, knows
that Wade, a two-year-old who often bites other children, usually bites
after some particularly frustrating experience. Experiences such as not
being able to fit all the pieces of a puzzle together or attempting to do
things more appropriate for three- or four-year-olds are particularly frustrating for him. Because she knows this, Penny makes some adjust-
ments in the kinds of activities or materials that Wade will be involved
with. As a result, Wade is happier with himself and his accomplish-
ments, because he is doing the kinds of activities that will facilitate
rather than inhibit his development. Penny now needs to spend less
time "policing" Wade's activities and can be more positively involved
with Wade and other children. She no longer has to explain to the parents of children bitten by Wade how those teeth marks got on their
child's arm.

Penny was able to achieve these outcomes by carefully observing
and recording Wade's behavior at regular intervals. By doing this, she
was able to learn under what circumstances Wade bit and did not bite.
A caregiver skilled at studying children can also learn many other
things about the children she or he cares for and the usefulness of the
activities and the materials that are provided for the children. For example, the caregiver can learn how frequently the block corner is used
and whether some changes need to be made in the kind or amount
of blocks available or their location. Examining the arrangement of
the classroom, the caregiver might determine whether a hidden curriculum exists. For instance, materials and equipment may be stored in
a way that prevents children from having ready access to them, so that
a caregiver always needs to be present to provide what is needed. As
a result, the children's dependence, rather than independence, is being fostered, and the time spent waiting for the caregiver to supply
the needed toys may be filled with unwanted behavior. Caregivers in
this situation may have a sense that what they want to happen for children is not occurring, but they may not clearly understand what is
happening or how to correct it.

Many other valuable lessons can be learned from studying children. For instance, caregivers might learn how much wandering a particular child does and what particularly holds this child's attention.
They might discover why Bart is an outcast, or whether Jill is gradually improving in her small motor skills. They might also find out
whether Michael's swearing varies depending upon the setting and who
he is with, or why Siu Ying seems so lost and withdrawn. Knowing
these kinds of things will not only make the children's and the care-

givers' day more productive and enjoyable but also will increase the caregivers' sense of worth and professionalism, especially when, as a result of their studying, they see that children have grown from the activities that they have provided.

What Is Required?

Simply being aware of the benefits of studying, and learning the skills necessary for effective studying, are not enough. Certain aspects of the day care program can tend to make an ongoing effort at studying children difficult. For example, it is not easy for a caregiver to focus on one or two children while trying to care for six, eight, ten, or more. Also, if one is not consciously and purposefully looking for specific behaviors they may go unnoticed, and so may other important dimensions that define the life of the day care setting and affect the children's behavior.

One of the great disservices done to caregivers is that much of the training taking place is conducted by individuals with backgrounds in laboratory or nursery school settings who fail to take into account the day care context. As a result, caregivers are taught to focus on children in isolated situations and in doing so fail to take into account the system of the setting with all its interdependent parts. Furthermore, these trainers at times teach caregivers to focus on strange or rare behaviors rather than on those that determine the quality of everyday events. As a result, inappropriate and ineffective activities are planned, and because of their failure the confused caregivers become skeptical about the value of studying children. Directors and planners of day care training need to take these factors into consideration.

Increasing a Caregiver's Responsiveness

The process of observing, interpreting, and acting on what occurs in a day care setting is a continual one. Knowing children well results from using a variety of skills, including the more objective and systematic ones as well as those based on our own phenomenological experience. The casual and incidental studying that occurs every day plays an important part in the overall understanding of children. A sensitive director will identify those caregivers who are particularly good at this type of studying and use them as models and teachers of other caregivers. Caregivers should be encouraged to, as Jones (chap. 10) puts it, be in tune with the child within themselves. That is, memories of their own childhood experiences may help them to interpret children's behaviors and plan appropriate responses. Much also can be gleaned from the countless interactions that an experienced caregiver has had with children. Seemingly insignificant nuances of gesture, facial expression, or tone of voice can become very meaningful in certain contexts. Skilled caregivers often are sensitive to these small cues and use them in their communication with children. However, they need to be conscious of these skills so that they can use them even more effectively and share them with others. These are natural ways of communicating that, when developed appropriately, can become effective tools in the process of studying and helping children. Much more attention needs to be paid to these processes, which have too long been cloaked in either mystery or ridicule.

KNOWING CHILDREN THROUGH OBSERVATION

As Almy and Genishi (1979) have said, observation is the basic way to study children; it "is to take notice, to pay attention to what children do and what they say" (p. 21). Observation of children can be conducted and recorded in different ways depending on the needs of the observer and the demands of the situation. It can involve event or time sampling and the use of checklists, anecdotal records, diary descriptions, and narrative records.

The Narrative Record

Almy and Genishi have pointed out that the observations of a skilled observer of children's behavior have three aspects: description, feelings, and inferences. To better understand these aspects of observation, let us look at a caregiver's observational narrative of a child playing with blocks, in which a problem is identified and a solution is suggested.

DESCRIPTION

Jose, a four-year-old who is neatly dressed in a plaid shirt and blue jeans, is in the block corner alone. He has spent the last ten minutes assembling blocks of various sizes and shapes. The structure he is attempting to build resembles a large bridge. As he reaches the top, a tower sways and the blocks fall off with a crash. Jose doesn't speak, but his face shows his frustration and anger. After three attempts, he finally gets the tower to stand. He has similar trouble with another tower

at the other end. However, he finally succeeds in completely building
the entire bridge. This attempt to build a bridge beyond his capability
is typical of several incidents that have happened lately.

FEELINGS

I don't understand why Jose persists at such tasks that obviously are too
difficult for his developmental level. Any success that he makes seems
to occur simply by chance. I become upset and angry with Jose when I
see him persistently punishing himself by attempting tasks much beyond his capabilities.

INFERENCES

Jose seems incapable of selecting activities that are developmentally
appropriate for him. More direction by staff in the selection of activities
and materials will be needed on a regular daily basis.

The *descriptive* portion of the narrative is simply the recording of
how the child appears and what he or she does. In the example above,
the caregiver clearly described Jose's appearance and his efforts at
building a bridge of blocks. This aspect of a narrative is usually written separately from the *inferences,* where some conclusions are drawn
regarding the meaning of the child's behavior. While many observational approaches try to minimize the observer's feelings and attempt
to exclude them from any written record, Almy and Genishi recognize the importance of the observer's *feelings* to his or her understanding of the events, particularly when the observer is a participant. Including the observer's feelings in the report not only allows others to
understand the personal perspective of the observer but also gives the
caregiver who is conducting the observation an opportunity to clarify and evaluate how personal reactions can affect his or her work with
children.

In the case of Jose, for example, the caregiver's feelings of confusion and anger could be clouding the interpretation and recommendations. Another caregiver might interpret Jose's persistence with difficult
tasks differently, viewing it as expressing a need for challenging and
creative activities. While the caregiver may agree that some of the activities that Jose chooses are a little beyond his capability, less, rather
than more direction might be recommended so that Jose's need for
activities that provide a creative, challenging, and developmentally
appropriate task are met. Who is correct, if either, can be judged by

reflection among caregivers and by further observation. The inclusion of the caregiver's feelings in the report can provide clues to the caregiver and to others about the observer's objectivity and can help to prevent an unquestioning acceptance of his or her conclusions and recommendations.

Sampling Procedures

Lidz (1981) has pointed out that there are two basic sampling procedures one can follow in observing children's behaviors. They are *event sampling* and *time sampling*. Event sampling involves the recording of every behavior of the child or children being observed during a particular period of time. Time sampling involves the recording of behavior at regular intervals — for example, every ten minutes.

It is our experience that these sampling procedures rarely are used by caregivers. However, once they realize how their efficiency can be increased by employing these methods, they are more likely to use them. For instance, one child, Donna, seems to shout and fight with her friend Adrian only at snack and meal time. At all other times the two of them get along fine. The caregiver in this situation would probably be able to understand Donna's behavior if she or he intensely focuses on meal and snack situations — that is, uses event sampling. Little information is to be gained by observing Donna's behavior every twenty minutes or so during part or all of the day. In addition, a good deal of efficiency in the use of the caregiver's time would be lost. By comparison, if Donna continually behaved aggressively toward a number of children, in various situations, observing and recording her behavior every few minutes could provide clues by showing when and where the aggressive behavior occurred, how frequently, and with what intensity.

Checklists

Checklists are used to determine whether or not a series of specific behaviors can be performed by a child. Caregivers working together can construct their own lists of developmental skills or use ones developed commercially. Those constructed by staff have some advantages over those commercially available. Constructing them not only brings the staff together, providing a sense of cohesiveness and group identity, but also helps the staff to evaluate the experiences they want children to have. As a result, a program can gain a sense of purpose and direction.

In administering a checklist, a caregiver either observes children in their everyday activities to determine which behaviors they display or, in a more structured situation, simply asks the child to perform certain tasks.

Carlos, an infant caregiver, is interested in assessing eighteen-month-old Annette's language development to help plan some language stimulation activities. A checklist could enable him to observe Annette and determine, for example, whether she speaks five different words, asks for more of something when she wants it, or says "all gone." In addition, he might need to structure a situation where Annette is asked to point to three to five pictures in a book when the objects they represent are named.

Caregivers should be aware of the limitations of checklists. Like all assessment devices, the behaviors included are just samples of behavior. The lists are not meant to be comprehensive lists of behaviors in any developmental area, nor are they necessarily arranged in a developmental sequence. For example, asking for more or saying "all gone" does not necessarily developmentally precede being able to point to three pictures when named, even though the items may appear in that order on the checklist. The caregiver needs to remember that the acquisition of a skill far down on the list is not necessarily dependent upon having acquired the skills needed to perform behaviors listed near the beginning of the list. A whole new set of skills may be required to accomplish a particular task. The checklist simply indicates whether a child can or cannot perform a particular task when tested. When a child is not able to perform the task, the caregiver may have no indication of what skills are required to perform the task or whether the child has any of those skills developed.

Anecdotal Records

This form of recording observations is perhaps the best known and most frequently used one. It simply involves writing down any incidents, interactions, or comments that occur during the day that the caregiver feels are particularly revealing about a child or group of children. Caregivers who use this method usually write their observations in a notebook, log, or loose-leaf binder. Anecdotes need to be recorded promptly to ensure that they accurately and specifically detail a given event. This can be difficult to do during a very busy day. However, brief notes about a particular incident can be jotted on a card or slip of paper and later used to write the complete record. This method permits one to record observations without having to rely totally on memory. It also helps to provide enough detail about what happened and what was said to give the appropriate context and meaning.

Diaries are a form of anecdotal records, but they usually are written daily, dated, and are more extensive, covering longer periods of time. Since caregivers may be caring for the same child daily for two or more years, this particular form of recording observations may be particularly useful in a day care program.

Limitations and Advantages of Observations

One of the major advantages of observing children is that what is learned from the observation is directly related to the day care setting. What the caregiver observes happening in the program during the day may not be applicable to other settings such as the home. The comment by a parent that his or her child does not "behave that way at home" is not necessarily the defensive statement we might think it was. Each child's behavior is related to the demands of a situation. If a parent's expectations are extremely restrictive, for example, a child may behave very well at home but overcompensate in another situation where independent or cooperative behavior is expected.

A limitation of the observational approach to studying children relates to the events occurring outside the day care program that influence a child's behavior. For example, a child's food preferences and eating habits are primarily formed at home, and they can affect how the child responds to food served in the day care setting. Also, a child's sleeping habits can greatly affect how he or she will act during the day.

Sarah, a four-year-old, was increasingly becoming a behavior problem. When she arrived at 6:30 A.M. at Fran's day care home, she appeared as most four-year-olds do at that time—somewhat sleepy and inactive. But shortly after breakfast her behavior changed; she became much more active, behaved impulsively, and moved from one activity to another without completing any. Sarah was aggressive and insulting with others, which led to several accidents and angry confrontations. She ate lunch rapidly and could not be quieted for a nap. The situation escalated daily, and Fran and the children were becoming increasingly frantic. Fran visited with Sarah's mother and learned that Sarah was allowed to stay up until her parents went to bed, usually about midnight. Consequently, Sarah was getting only five to six hours of sleep a day. Fran and Sarah's parents decided to put Sarah down for a nap when she arrived each morning. The first day she slept until 9:45. She awoke refreshed, snacked with the other children, and her behavior was mark-edly different. The overactive and impulsive behavior decreased, and her experiences at Fran's day care home became much more productive and enjoyable for all.

It is not often possible to observe the events that occur at home. Therefore caregivers need to supplement their observational approaches with other means of gathering information from parents and relevant others if a complete understanding of each child is to be gained.

TALKING WITH CHILDREN

Talking with children can be not only enjoyable but can also be an enlightening way of learning about them and the experiences they have. Of course, caregivers talk with children all day long in the process of caring for them. But a caregiver skilled in visiting with children also listens, reflects, and uses what she or he hears to improve the experiences that the children have.

Talking with children should not be confused with interviewing. Adults who interview children tend to ask too many questions and give too much advice. Such caregiver–child "conversations" actually often turn into monologues or lectures by the adult. Furthermore, the topic of conversation is chosen by the caregiver, not by the child, so that little is learned about the child's own concerns or joys. We believe that more is gained from caregivers talking with children than from interviewing them.

While young children vary greatly in their ability to understand and communicate their experiences, a meaningful dialogue between a caregiver and a child can happen when the caregiver is sensitive to and concerned about a child's emotional experiences, aware of the child's level of cognitive and language development, patient enough to listen, and willing to tune in frequently during the day to what a child is saying. Children's attitudes about themselves, others, and past events determine the quality of their experiences. A caregiver sensitive to this fact listens for cues that reflect a child's perceptions and expectations.

Gregory, a kindergartner, repeatedly bothered the group of children in the library corner. After the third disruption that morning, the caregiver calmed the children in the library area, scolded Gregory, and suggested he spend some time thinking about the situation. Gregory seated himself under a climbing frame that was not in use during this activity period and meditated. Shortly afterward, his friend Nicky joined him,

Photograph by Michael Wetteland

and after a couple of minutes of silence Nicky said, "You're a bad boy!"

"I am not! Liz said the kids didn't like me bothering them, but she didn't say I was bad."

"You're bad, you always bug the other kids and you're bad, and when you die you're gonna go to hell and the debil [devil] will get you."

"That's not true; I'm not bad and there's no such thing as a devil and when you die you're just not there any more. My momma told me and she said there's no such thing as heaven and hell."

"Well, my Mom said you gotta be good, 'cuz if you weren't, when you die you go to hell and it's terrible there, and it's hot and the debil keeps you there forever. And you keep bugging those kids and that's bad."

The conversation continued for quite a while with the two boys discussing good and bad, right and wrong as they saw and understood it, interpreting from what they had been told. The caregiver observing this discussion was able to gather useful information about how each of the boys perceived himself, right and wrong, and the consequences of certain acts. She also gained information about the friendship that existed between the two and the support that Nicky was providing for Gregory.

While normal day-to-day interchanges among children and between children and adults usually provide the clues necessary for interpreting attitudes, caregivers may want to further define what they know by structuring opportunities for sharing of feelings and attitudes. These situations cannot only provide greater insight into a child's point of view but can also improve the child's ability to communicate, and enhance his or her self-concept. For example, Canfield and Wells (1976) describe how to provide a group situation for communicating positive feelings. They suggest that the adult, with either a small group or the whole group, have children sit in a circle. A caregiver then asks one child to leave the group and go find an object in the room that makes him or her happy, and then to bring it back to the group and share it. A more personal variation is to have each child share something he or she did that made someone else feel happy. They suggest that the adult start by saying,

> Yesterday I told Jane that I liked the dress she was wearing. I thought the dress was very colorful. She smiled, and I think my comment made her feel good. Would you share with us something you have said or done for someone else that made him or her feel good? How did it make the person feel good? (Canfield and Wells 1976, p. 107).

At other times a more individual approach might be more appropriate. A caregiver skilled at visiting with children will hone in on children's quiet times, rather than pulling them away from a busy activity. If there is a need to ask questions, care should be taken that only very few are used and that the conversation helps the child explore his or her thoughts and feelings about what is happening in his or her life.

In summary, talking with children can provide information about children's thoughts, feelings, and attitudes that cannot always be directly observed. These conversations will heighten observational inferences and allow caregivers to plan more meaningful and pleasant experiences and generally improve the quality of their own experiences.

TALKING WITH PARENTS

As we have seen, caregivers cannot always be aware of the experiences a child has beyond the doors of the day care program and cannot easily know cultural and family values. All of these factors shape a child's development, and the lack of awareness of them can decrease a caregiver's effectiveness. Reciprocally, parents who are not clearly aware of what is happening in the day care program cannot appropriately enhance their children's experiences.

Results from a few studies (e.g., Clark and Fuqua 1982; Powell 1978) suggest some ways of reducing the discontinuity between child care settings. They have shown that more frequent communication happens between homes and day care programs when caregivers use informal means of communication. Specifically, these studies found that talking casually with parents during the transition times when parents drop off and pick up their children is used more frequently than any other form of communication. The traditional and more formal parent–teacher conference is not used by most programs. This is probably because parents and caregivers, in their already busy lives, have little opportunity to schedule such conferences. Combine this reduced opportunity for conferences with the fact that conferences tend to follow a "report card" format, with the caregiver dominating the conversation, and we can see why they rarely occur. While conferences can and should be better handled than this, caregivers will benefit from learning to use informal daily contacts with parents for effective communication. Center-based programs seldom assign a staff person to greet parents as they arrive or make other provisions that invite parents to linger a little longer (cf. Clark 1983; Fuqua and Greenman 1982).

Besides direct contacts with parents, caregivers can also use notes and daily information sheets that provide information to and from parents. Notes need not be long; they can be quickly jotted and placed with other things that a child takes home each day. Typically, notes are used when the child has made some particular accomplishment (e.g., taken his or her first step; tied shoes for the first time) or else when some problem exists. Notes such as these can, in the former case, heighten a parent's sense of guilt for missing out on an important event, and, in the latter, increase his or her defensiveness and create an adversarial feeling toward the caregiver. While it is sometimes unavoidable to write about these things, notes do not have to be used just for this type of message. They can also provide routine information about a child's day. For example, the note might say, "Amos really enjoyed himself in the block corner today. Using blocks and trucks, he and his friend Nate played for over half an hour there." This note tells the parent something of what the child likes doing and who his friends are, information that Amos's parents can use in planning activities at home for Amos and his friends.

Daily information sheets are often used in infant care programs.

One sheet is filled out by the parents for the caregiver upon arrival in the morning, and another is completed by the caregiver for the parents when they return. One center makes mimeographed copies of their information sheet; everyday a new sheet is attached to a clipboard with a pencil tied to it and the clipboard is placed by the child's locker where it is easily accessible to the parents. The parents and caregivers can, for example, provide information to each other about the child's eating behavior: when the child ate, what was eaten, and how much. Similar questions are asked about the child's sleep, while other questions might ask what kind of mood the infant is or was in or whether the child had a bowel movement recently. Caregivers can easily construct their own daily information sheets, including whatever questions they find most helpful for their particular program. No matter what questions are used, space at the bottom for incidental information that can help the parent and the caregiver better understand and care for the child can be quite valuable.

One family whose child had been in a program where daily information sheets were used said at a parent meeting that they missed this form of information sharing now that their child was in the toddler group. Because a caregiver who cares for toddlers looks after more children and cannot easily find the time to fill out the information sheets for six to eight toddlers, as he or she would for three or four infants, a shorter form might be devised that briefly describes a few incidents that might be of interest.

With some creative efforts by parents and caregivers, the benefits derived from good communication between homes and programs can be extended beyond the infant years. What to include on the form could be a topic of a parent meeting or could be a task assigned to an ad hoc committee of parents and caregivers.

Besides the one-to-one contacts that parents have with staff members, group meetings with speakers, or dinners with parents, caregivers, and children can provide a perspective about a child not easily learned by other means. For example,

Gerri, executive director of a nonprofit day care center, has devised a social event that combines fund raising, an opportunity for parents and staff to socialize, and a convenient, inexpensive meal for the families in the center. Two Fridays a month reasonably priced dinners are available at the center for families. These meals generate additional income for the center. Many parents, tired from a long week, appreciate being able to eat out at a reasonable price in an environment that welcomes them and their children. The children enjoy sharing the center with their parents and seeing their friends, their friends' parents, and their teachers interacting. Caregivers, parents, and children get to know each other in a relaxed, informal atmosphere, and all have the opportunity to interact in a variety of ways. These evenings often provide valuable opportunities for caregivers and parents to discuss children without placing difficult constraints on the busy lives of either of them.

GETTING STARTED

If you have begun to be convinced that studying children may be a way of improving the experiences children have in a day care program, here are some practical tips for getting started that may prevent one's becoming overwhelmed by the tasks. Some key points to remember are:

- It cannot all be done right away
- All staff are not going to be convinced of the need "to do one more thing"
- The time to plan and implement studying will be hard to find.

Here is one way that a center we know of began to study children.

Woodland Day Care Center is a program serving about sixty children, infants to six-year-olds, in a large church near the downtown area of a large city. The church provides the program with four classrooms, a central office, and storage area on one floor and a large gymnasium with a stage at one end and the kitchen off the stage on the floor above the classrooms. Meals are served on the stage, rather than in the classrooms.

After receiving some introductory training in different approaches to studying children, Mike, the director of the program, called the staff together to talk about the training and how they might use it.

Martha, an infant caregiver, spoke first. "I really enjoyed the training session. The trainer was really interesting and dynamic, and I'm all fired up to see some of the things she presented. The arrangement of our rooms has been a headache for too long. Perhaps if we used some of the things we've learned in the training, we could finally straighten out that mess."

Marian, another infant caregiver, agreed that something needed to be done but was also concerned about how it was going to get done. "It takes just about every ounce of energy I have to do my job now. I don't know how I can possibly take on another thing. Let's be realistic about this. It sounds nice in the training session, but getting it done is another matter."

Martha replied, "Don't be so negative. Sure, we're all busy. We have more to do than we can handle most days. But maybe if we spent a little more energy on this now, it might make our job easier in the long run."

Marian heaved a sigh, "Boy, I don't know. I just don't know how we're going to do it."

Mike jumped in: "Let's postpone worrying about how it's going to get done just now and first look at what pressing problems we have."

Andy felt that Jamie, a four-year-old whom he had recently started to care for, was having a particularly hard time adjusting to his new situation. Margarita saw the scheduling of large motor activities in the gym as presenting a special problem for everybody. "That place is driving me crazy. The noise level is so high, some days I can't hear myself think. Kids are always getting hurt up there every day. The four- and five-year-olds don't stay where they're supposed to; they drive those tricycles like maniacs into my toddler area. The little ones are always getting hurt. Something's got to be done."

Coralee agreed. "Just try to have an enjoyable meal on the stage while all that racket is going on. The kids race through the meal because they want to get out on the floor to play."

Alice, the assistant director, chimed in, "If you people would just follow the schedule I gave you, things might work out better. But no, everyone drags their kids up there at the same time. Also, a little closer supervision by you teachers might reduce those accidents. By the way, have you seen the pile of broken toys and bikes I have to get fixed? I don't know where the money is coming from. Instead of standing over in the corner chatting away, you might pay more attention to the kids, and we wouldn't have all these problems."

Mike interrupted, "Before this discussion gets out of hand, let's look at where we are now. It sounds like we need to find out why the kids are acting this way. Maybe these are problems that might be helped if we began studying the children—really observing what they're doing. I'm hearing a lot of especially strong feelings about the use of the gym."

"You're right," said Martha. "We all have other problems, but the worst one is the gym. If we start there, we can all be involved, and nobody will need to spend too much time on it. And we can develop some skills we can use later in our own classrooms."

Mike suggested, "So that no one will feel as though he or she is being singled out and evaluated, let's remember that the focus of our studying is the children and the experiences they are having. How should we start?"

Andy volunteered, "If we're going to be studying the kids, why don't we see what we each know now about the kids in our classes? Remember the exercise the trainer had us do to point out that there are some who can go unnoticed unless we observe them? I've been thinking, while the rest of you were talking, and I've sketched out a little pretest we could do right now, kind of like what we did in training, to help us see what we know about how the kids are behaving in the gym—and what we need to know."

Several encouraged Andy to share his idea. "Well, first we list each of the children in our rooms. Then we fill in each of these categories." He wrote four items on the chalkboard:

1. A favorite activity in the gym
2. A problem in the gym
3. The last time I talked with the child in the gym
4. The nature of the discussion

"I like the idea," said Mike. "We still have time left in our staff meeting. Alice, would you pass out some paper and pencils, and let's all give it a try."

Time passed as each person completed the exercise. Near the end, Margarita commented, "I didn't realize how little I know about some of my kids. I even had trouble remembering some names."

Coralee agreed, "It seems I spend most of my time talking to children about what they're doing that I don't like. Wow!"

During the remainder of the meeting, the staff discussed how they were going to observe the children and collect the information they needed. They decided to collect as much information as possible and share it at the next weekly staff meeting. Mike and Alice volunteered to relieve caregivers, when possible, to give them an uninterrupted opportunity to observe and record children's behavior. Notes jotted down at other times would supplement more lengthy recording. By the next staff meeting, caregivers had already seen changes.

"I couldn't believe how much I had been missing," said Andy. "Once I realized that Harold and Mark, the two oldest ones, were bossing around the older kids and then using them to control the younger ones, I gave them some other, more constructive jobs, and things seemed to improve."

"I found I often had to force myself to stop and really look at what was happening," added Marian. "I found it helpful to make up some forms to assess the children's skills and then structure some games in the gym so I could see what each child could do. I organized my materials into folders for each child so I could easily find it when I needed it again."

Others shared their experiences during the past week, along with what they had learned. Possible plans of action were discussed, and a decision was made to make some specific changes and observe the outcomes for children.

Woodland Day Care and its problems may be very different from some readers' situations, but the process the staff went through may have some application for the reader. Woodland did not easily resolve its problem with the use of the gym. Making changes as a result of studying children is a long and difficult process. Woodland did see some early changes that improved the experiences caregivers and children had in the gym. However, after a while financial problems required Mike and Alice to concentrate their individual efforts on fund raising. As a result, they were unable to relieve staff in the gym as often as they had, and the improvements made early on began to crumble. After a very serious reevaluation of what was happening, a renewed commitment led to some gradual changes. It was not easy, but Woodland Day Care found that studying children could lead to improvements in their program.

Chapter 8

IMPROVING PROGRAM EVALUATION IN DAY CARE

Robert Fuqua

Instead of promoting single definitive studies that promise unquestionable guidance on a narrow issue of policy, evaluators should be contributing to the slow, continuous, cumulative understanding of a problem or an intervention (Cronbach et al. 1980, 47).

Despite the many possible benefits of program evaluation, systematic evaluation processes have not been widely used in day care programs. However, there is a growing awareness among day care practitioners of the possible benefits that can come from program evaluation. Unfortunately the inappropriateness of the traditional evaluation methods (such as those mentioned in the quotation from Cronbach et al. that heads this chapter) have often frustrated day care professionals and have led to resistance on the part of staff to evaluation efforts.

The purpose of this chapter is to examine some of the traditional evaluation practices and consider how they have spawned resistance on the part of day care staffs and how this resistance must be dealt with if meaningful change is to take place. In addition, the purposes of day care evaluation will be explored, so that information derived from evaluation efforts can help "everyone" to understand what the program does and does not accomplish. "Everyone" includes more than just policymakers and members of regulatory agencies; it involves day care practitioners and the public that avails itself of the program's services. Finally, this chapter will examine some innovative efforts at evaluating day care programs. While no one of the single efforts to be described provides a comprehensive approach to day care evaluation, together they provide concrete examples of possible ways to improve program evaluation.

TRADITIONAL EVALUATION APPROACHES

Program evaluations in day care typically have not been initiated from within the programs. Rather, regulatory or funding agencies have imposed evaluations on programs, either to periodically determine whether the programs are meeting specified minimum standards or to determine whether the program is satisfactorily meeting community needs and is worthy of continued support. Working within this framework, evaluations have examined in a summary fashion the activities of the program over the past few months or year and their effects upon the children receiving the care. These studies usually are conducted for a short period of time, or they are designed to examine change over time between two relatively discrete and often arbitrarily chosen points. They are not designed to improve ongoing program functioning. Further, they usually attempt to provide definitive and unequivocal answers, often to narrow questions. The assessment procedures have determined what aspects of the program will be examined. Evaluators, having been trained in the classical social science methodology, were faced with the choice of either selecting poorly constructed and nonstandardized instruments that attempted to measure complex program objectives such as promoting warmth and caring, or using instruments such as standardized intelligence and achievement tests that have proven measurement characteristics. These instruments sample a restricted area of development and may be only distantly related to what the children are actually experiencing in the program (D. Rowe 1978).

As a result of this narrow kind of evaluation, a comprehensive view of the life of the day care program and its meaning for the children and adults who participate in it has not been achieved. In summary, what has passed for program evaluation in day care has not been very useful. If positive change is to occur, better evaluations will be needed.

CAREGIVER RESISTANCE

Evaluations have commonly been used as a way of extending power or control over social programs (Cronbach et al. 1980). In day care, this control is exercised through state and federal regulations governing the licensing and operation of local programs, and by various funding agencies and community institutions. Therefore that power has often been limited to a few — that is, to the policymakers, with the notable exception of the formulation of the Federal Inter-agency Day Care Requirements (FIDCR). Fuqua and Greenman (1982) and Fuqua (1981) found that both providers working in centers and providers working in day care homes perceived state and federal regulations as strong influences in their professional lives. However, they also perceived themselves as having little control over these important forces. As a result, caregivers are not always as cooperative as they might be when evaluations are conducted.

Efforts to keep evaluators off balance are not uncommon. Patton (1980) provided examples of staff regularly changing program goals, losing forms, and purposely filling out questionnaires incorrectly. In addition, program staff and directors can be skillful in attacking characteristics of the evaluation design, such as sample size or the reliability and validity of assessment devices. While these individuals may lack the technical jargon that would make their arguments more eloquent, their natural skills are adequate to subvert almost any evaluation project.

Usually resistance to evaluation efforts occurs not because of any single factor but as a result of the interaction of various factors. At times the degree of commitment to a particular program by staff or parents interacts with the kind of evaluation methods being used. Evaluations designed to provide information to improve practice may, in fact, inhibit positive change. Parents do not want to feel that they have placed their child in a program that may not be capable of providing for all their child's needs. Likewise, day care providers working under difficult circumstances need to feel that they are doing all they can do, and they do not want to be targeted for failure as professionals.

Our society, including many professionals as well as the general public, has a tendency to see people — rather than general circumstances — as being ultimately responsible for any particular situation (cf. Caplan and Nelson 1973). This tendency to blame particular persons extends to evaluation efforts in day care. Person-centered variables such as attitudes, intelligence, educational background, personality traits, or motivation receive much more attention than situational influences or ecological factors (cf. Prescott 1975; Bronfenbrenner 1979). As a result, recommendations or proposed solutions are also likely to be person-centered; for example, it might be proposed to train staff in some area of child development. It often happens that providers, administrators, or parents are singled out for blame, rather than the design of the overall program of which the individuals within it are only parts. Yet the resources available, the way the individuals func-

Photograph by Michael Wetteland

tion together as a group, the physical setting, and outside forces are all variables that interact to determine program results.

Caregivers' perceptions about the resources that an evaluation requires also can be important causes of reluctance to participate. This factor may be compounded by the caregivers' feelings of helplessness, which stem from a history of functioning at survival levels. Furthermore, ever-present change or the feeling of constant change can promote the perception on the part of caregivers that a useful study could not possibly be done.

Besides the difficulties arising from these perceptions, resistance to evaluation efforts is also promoted by the fact that most programs have no prior history of planning and implementing a program evaluation. Therefore, as Ingison (1979) has pointed out, "efforts to institutionalize such systems run against the status quo and meet with a great deal of organizational inertia" (p. 26).

If this kind of staff resistance to program evaluation is to be dealt with successfully, some basic changes in evaluation approaches need to be considered. First and foremost, as Cronback et al. have stated, "Evaluators should be contributing to the slow, continuous, cumulative understanding" (p. 47) of a program. Such an ongoing process must become an integral part of the day care program and should reflect an ecological perspective. The information provided should reflect the life of the setting and should be analyzed in terms of its meaning for all of the participants in the program. Any evaluation should acknowledge the interdependence of program components (their relationship to one another and to the overall design of the program) and their cumulative effects over time on the development of the individuals participating in the program. Appropriate emphasis should be given to program activities, families served by the day care, program staff, environmental considerations, community needs, and influences of agencies and individuals outside of the program. In implementing an ongoing evaluation process, staff and administrators, in cooperation with parents, will collect and analyze information using both formal and informal methods.

PURPOSES OF DAY CARE PROGRAM EVALUATION

A basic change in the typical evaluation process would be to realize that information derived from an ongoing evaluation process can be used to meet a variety of needs that periodically arise in day care. Keeping in mind that the basic purpose of any evaluation effort is to gather needed information to use in making program decisions, four more specific reasons why an evaluation may be desired can be identified.[1]

PLANNING FOR SPECIFIC CHANGES. A day care center may need information as to the feasibility of expanding its program to include drop-

---

1. The four categories suggested here are a modification and adaptation to the day care setting of a larger set of purposes outlined by Flaherty (1980) in her discussion of program evaluations for Community Mental Health Centers.

in or school-age care. Programs interested in reorganizing group care from age-segregated care to a mix of age groups would need information regarding a wide variety of factors, such as the ramifications of altering the daily schedule and the demands on the staff's and facility's capabilities that will occur as a result of this change.

CENTER FELT NEED. Occasionally, staff and administrators feel a general dissatisfaction with the way things are going. This is when evaluation information would be helpful in the improvement of operations. This identification process may lead to further evaluaton activity, as in the first category above, if some specific aspect of the program is targeted for change.

MANDATE BY EXTERNAL AGENT. In virtually every state in the Union, state and local government agencies license or regulate the operation of day care programs. At the same time, state and local governments have increased their use of evaluation services (Beckman 1977).

PUBLIC RELATIONS NEEDS. Often information stemming from an evaluation can be useful in advocating a program. In this time of fiscal austerity, when funding agencies are required to make difficult decisions regarding the distribution of a few dollars, programs need to assure their good image in the community. If child care programs assume the responsibility of championing their own programs, they empower themselves, instead of passively permitting the power of the evaluation to remain in the hands of others.

The evaluation studies that will probably result in the most meaningful and useful information will be those that are stimulated by internal factors rather than those that result from an external mandate. Flaherty (1980) found that evaluations mandated by external sources were perceived as useful only when the data were also used for internal center purposes. Studies of cost of operations were chosen by evaluators and program administrators as most useful, while practitioners believed that studies investigating how services were utilized were most important. Finally, another factor associated with useful studies was the evaluator who was interested in helping the staff apply the information so that positive outcomes would result. These evaluators were seen as being sensitive to the program's needs and demands. They did this by functioning with great diplomacy and efficiency to provide information in an understandable form and in timely fashion.

APPLICATIONS AND INNOVATIVE EFFORTS

Evaluation that is an ongoing process and an integral part of a day care program can be used for a variety of purposes. While no single existing evaluation process in day care appears to meet the requirements of what I consider a good comprehensive system, a discussion of a few individual innovative efforts will provide a more concrete illustration of what is possible. The main criterion for judging the worth of an evaluation is its usefulness. To meet this criterion, a variety of methods will need to be employed, both formal and informal.

Formal Approaches

THE EARLY CHILDHOOD ENVIRONMENT RATING SCALE

Since 1977, Harms and Clifford have been perfecting the Early Childhood Environment Rating Scale. This scale examines a component of the day care setting that is often neglected in evaluations: the physical environment (see chap. 3).

Besides providing information about a valuable component of a day care program, the use of the Harms and Clifford environment scale can possibly contribute to a lessening of caregiver resistance. When evaluators include this dimension of the day care program in an evaluation, they are indirectly acknowledging the importance of recognizing the program as an ecological system with more parts than just the individuals within the program. To the program staff, this expansion of the usual evaluation approaches indicates that the evaluator is not, in a simple-minded fashion, going to focus responsibility on them for program weaknesses. Therefore the evaluator is more likely to receive good cooperation from the staff in conducting the evaluation. Staff are likely to perceive this study as being in their own interest.

While Harms and Clifford originally attempted to exclude staff–child interactions from this scale and focus solely on environmental characteristics, they were unable to do so. However, the number of items examining interpersonal relationships is relatively small, and the instrument deals primarily and adequately with the impact of the environment. Included in the scale are items that examine the use of space, materials, and experiences designed to facilitate children's development. The scale also looks at daily scheduling of activities and at the supervision provided.

Several qualities of The Early Childhood Environment Rating Scale suggest that it is a useful tool that could be included as a part of an overall evaluation system. It offers a relatively short (thirty-seven items) but effective way of examining the quality of the environment currently being provided in the day care program, as well as providing a means for planning improvements. It does so in a relatively reliable and valid manner. The authors have not "disdained rigor in preference for relevance" but have built the scale upon their knowledge and expertise in early childhood programs, research literature, and the convergent opinions of colleagues in academia and practitioners in the field. In addition, they have conducted reliability and validity studies (Harms and Clifford 1982) that insure that the information gained from the use of the scale will be relatively consistent and valid.

The scale does not require a psychometrician or a person with a high degree of measurement expertise to administer it. Program staff, parent board members, and community members can learn to rate a child care environment with relatively little training. Again, the participants in a child care center have the opportunity to share in the power stemming from an evaluation. Trainers of caregivers can also use this scale to educate program staff about the importance of the center's environment and how it can be changed. Fuqua and Greenman (1982) found the rating scale not only helpful in training day care providers but also useful in evaluating the impact of training.

Finally, one of the most important strengths of this scale is its inclusion of a separate subscale addressing adult needs, both of the teachers and the parents. Harms and Clifford (1980) contend that unless "the personal comfort needs and professional needs" of the caregiver are met, they will have difficulty in meeting the requirements of their role with children (p. 1). Furthermore, Harms and Clifford contend that parents need to be reassured and included in the program, and that the early childhood program can be a resource to help parents in their parenting role.

ECOLOGICAL APPROACHES

Two other approaches that also recognize the importance of a broad perspective in evaluating early childhood programs are Prescott's (1975) ecological approach in the assessment of childrearing environments and Day's (1979) naturalistic evaluation for program improvement. While Prescott's approach was originally designed for research purposes, it has several qualities that also make it valuable for the evaluation of individual programs. Both approaches are somewhat more formal and elaborate in nature than the rating scale developed by Harms and Clifford and probably would require outside assistance and training to implement. However, this formality does not exclude staff participation. Indeed, Day recommends that ideally his evaluation process should be completed by an early childhood practitioner in cooperation with an evaluation consultant, and a trained caregiver could profitably contribute to Prescott's evaluation process. While both approaches share similar theoretical perspectives regarding the importance of the environment (derived from Barker's [1968] ecological theory of behavior settings), only Prescott references a developmental theoretical perspective. Specifically, she cites the developmental stages defined by Erikson (1950) and Cumming and Cumming's (1967) conceptualization of ego sets.

Prescott has developed an environmental inventory that includes an observational recording system for collecting information about children's behavior and an observation schedule for physical space. The child behavior schedule provides a comprehensive description of a child's experiences within the framework of the larger setting of the center. The schedule permits a description of activity segments and allows for the recording of children's behavior and adult behavioral input if it happens during the observation period. The activity segment descriptions include (1) the program structure: for example, whether the activity was within a free-choice structure or various teacher-directed structures; (2) the physical setting in which the activity took place and whether equipment or props were involved and their particular nature; (3) the degree of mobility; (4) the people with whom the activity occurred; and (5) the kind of teacher influence. In addition, the segment descriptions specify what the child was doing, his or her relation to the kind of play structure, and the effect of the structure on the child.

With the help of an evaluation consultant, a day care program using this procedure can begin to examine the relationship of children's behavior to the structure of the center. This would not only provide a description of the center and its effect upon children but would allow caregivers to determine whether what they saw happening was what they wanted for children. If not, the information could be used as a basis for planning and monitoring change. For several reasons, an evaluation consultant is essential for the successful implementation of this procedure. First, the inventory and its administration is fairly sophisticated, requiring trained observers. In addition, several children would need to be observed for various periods of time under different situations, and the kinds and amounts of data collected would necessitate computer analysis. For these reasons, this process would be used only occasionally. Probably it should be used only when no specific changes are being considered but the center's staff has a general feeling of dissatisfaction with the organization and delivery of care to the children. It could also be used, however, as part of an advocacy effort to either seek external funding or to improve the program's community image.

The naturalistic evaluation process for program improvement designed by Day and his colleagues is very similar in theoretical orientation and design but is not as complex or elaborate in its methodology. It is therefore more readily available for use by programs, even though an evaluation consultant might be required. In designing his naturalistic evaluation process, Day built upon research that he and Sheehan (1974) had conducted earlier. From this research they concluded that children's behavior in early childhood programs was a function of their interaction with three environmental factors. These factors were (1) the extent to which the staff had considered the importance of the physical environment and how it was arranged, (2) the use of materials, and (3) the amount and kind of teacher–child interaction. From these findings, Day designed an evaluation approach using observations of children's natural behavior during their day in the program. Thirty-four behaviors subsumed under seven generic categories of child behavior are used to record children's behavior in activity centers at a number of times during the program day. The seven categories are: task involvement, cooperation, autonomy, verbal interaction, materials, maintenance, and consideration.

Besides naturalistic observational data, Day's process includes a developmental profile of each child and a description of the program by activity or learning center. This information is collected and organized onto summary sheets, so that staff can evaluate the program's effect on children and plan modifications if necessary. Using the same process, these modifications can be monitored and fine-tuned as required.

The strength of both the Prescott and Day approaches is that they see behavior as a function of the interaction of the child and the environment. They do not focus on a few individual characteristics of the child in isolation but adopt a comprehensive approach to determine how the program activities influence child behavior.

Both of the above approaches are primarily child-centered. They do not consider what roles the caregivers or parents have in the program, how the program affects these adults, and how this may in turn affect their behavior in the program. As Bronfenbrenner (1977) has argued, the understanding of development goes beyond the traditional observational approaches of examining the unidirectional effects of the program and the staff on the child. To understand the child's behavior and how it is affected by the environment, reciprocal processes need to be examined. That is, not only should the effects of the caregiver on the child be examined, but the effects of the child on the caregiver should be included in the study. In addition to including a reciprocal process in an evaluation study, the influences of the children's parents should not be neglected.

Bronfenbrenner notes that theoretically the idea of reciprocity is widely accepted—that is, that what one person does influences another person present, and vice versa. However, this notion is seldom followed up in psychological research. I might extend this observation to the area of evaluation, and particularly to evaluation efforts in early childhood programs such as day care. Typically, in most day care evaluation projects, children and how they are affected by the adults and events within the setting are the focus of the investigation. The child is viewed as a passive agent who contributes little if anything to his or her own development, nor is the child seen as influencing others, particularly adults, or the events that occur within the setting. This approach to evaluation assumes a unidirectional rather than reciprocal notion of causality (Reese and Overton 1973). Takanishi (1979) has argued that "evaluation of early childhood programs could benefit from a reciprocal causation perspective in which both children and their environments are viewed as changing over time" (p. 152). In taking such a perspective, Bronfenbrenner suggests that an examination of the relationship between caregivers and children can be clarified by examining the complexity of the interactions, the emotional relationships between the individuals, and how power is shared within the relationships.

By concentrating so heavily on the child in the past, we have failed to realize the impact of day care on other individuals within the setting. Stress experienced by adults indirectly affects the kind of care children receive. Recently reports have documented the fact that child caregivers experience personal stress as a result of working closely and intensively with children over an extended period of time (cf. Clark, Fuqua, and Hegland 1982; Couture 1983; Maslach and Pines 1977; Mattingly 1977; Pines and Maslach 1980; M. J. Reed 1977; see also chaps. 4–5, this volume).

Bronfenbrenner has hypothesized that the impact of the quality of the relationship between the caregiver and child "increases as a direct function of the level of reciprocity, mutuality of positive feelings, and a gradual shift of balance of power in favor of the developing person" (p. 59). Extending this hypothesis to day care and the stressful situation, projects that consider these kinds of interpersonal structures and

Photograph by Michael Wetteland

their consequences have most meaning for the improvement of day care programs. When a wider ecological developmental view of day care evaluation is accepted, we will be less likely to repeat our mistakes and will contribute more to meaningful positive change in day care.

APPROACHES INVOLVING PARENTS

McSpadden (n.d.) described a "formative" or ongoing evaluation approach that involved parents and teachers working together to determine program priorities, monitor their implementation, and assess their effectiveness. This evaluation procedure, as implemented by the Central City Day Care Center of Salt Lake City, Utah, was not designed simply to enhance communication between parents and teachers. Rather it was designed so that the ideas and concerns expressed by the parents would result in alterations in the program.

The evaluation consisted of three components that examined various functional levels of the day care program. One component assessed individual children's needs and strengths; one assessed individual classroom functioning; and the third component looked at center-wide concerns. Within the component concerned with individual children, data were gathered through formal and informal screening and individual testing. All aspects of the children's development were examined co-operatively with parents throughout the year, as was ongoing individual educational planning.

Classroom evaluation and planning were carried out through monthly meetings between parents and teacher. This process developed curricula that would meet the individual needs of children and take into account each child's family situation. It also enhanced communication and understanding between parents and teachers and provided a means for an ongoing assessment of each classroom's activities. Three volunteer parents from each classroom were trained and paid for their participation in this phase of the "formative" process. During each meeting, parents reported on what had occurred during the month, how their child responded to the activities, and whether any progress had been made. Teachers also reported on progress and what alterations in classroom activities needed to be considered. By focusing on one area of the curriculum each month, all areas were involved in these specific planning and evaluation processes.

The center-wide component of this evaluation process involved interviewing parents over a period of five months. Parents were hired to administer to other parents a different questionnaire each month on one of five topic areas: (1) parent involvement, (2) child behavior and discipline, (3) multiethnic awareness, (4) health and nutrition, and (5) school readiness. Parents were intentionally used to collect the data to maximize rapport between parents and the interviewers and thereby improve the validity of the information gathered through the questionnaire process. It was thought that parents of children in the program would feel more comfortable and open in expressing their views to another program parent than to a member of the program staff or a stranger.

As a result of this evaluation process, McSpadden reported that productive growth took place when "everyone" was involved in the process; where this did not happen, the process was not as effective. The key to the success of this approach was a communication process that was quick, direct, and constant. The use of this formative evaluation process convinced the staff of the program that parents and staff can work together on an equal, cooperative basis, each contributing different skills for the improvement of the program. As McSpadden stated, "Flexibility can be operationalized into the program so that educational responsibility can mean being responsive to needs — needs of the children, the parents and family, and the staff" (n.d., p. 35).

Recently, Winget, Winget, and Popplewell (1982) reported research in which parents were included in the formal evaluation of family day care homes. Questionnaires were sent to parents who were currently or who had in the past twelve months used the services of a family day care home that was applying for renewal of its license. The questionnaires asked parents to rate "the provider and facility, such as safety of the outside play area; . . . a provider's skills relative to specific developmental age ranges, such as language development; and enumeration of strong and/or weak points of the day care home" (p. 197). In addition, general information was gathered on such matters as how long a family had used the services of the day care provider.

The information received from the questionnaires was used to produce "provider profiles" that helped the licensing agent to provide feedback to the providers and formed the basis of a discussion about improving the quality of child care in the home. Besides the use of this information for the evaluation of individual child care settings, a county summary, including a "general overview of parents' perceptions of licensed family day care, was distributed to county, provider, and planning groups" (p. 197). The comprehensive, possible impact of this evaluation approach reflects an ecological view of day care. Furthermore, the process extends the power of parents to assure good care for their child, not only by letting them give their opinions but also by educating them about some of the aspects of day care that need to be considered in selecting a facility. Our society has not done a very good job of educating parents as consumers of child care. Other creative efforts at involving parents in similar processes need to be explored.

Informal Methods

Many simple evaluation measures that can be devised by program staff or parents do not require a great deal of technical skill and can be useful in providing information about many aspects of any child care program. These methods can be used by themselves or in conjunction with more formal approaches. While they do not by themselves provide a comprehensive ecological perspective, they can help provide such a perspective.

For example, one can decide what it is that one wants to know about (e.g., program equipment, parent involvement) and construct a checklist or a short-answer questionnaire. The checklist simply records whether enough of various kinds of equipment are available for the children's use, or whether a person is highly satisfied or not with some aspect of the program. The short-answer questionnaire may be given to staff or parents so they can voice their views regarding certain program policies and procedures.

Open-ended questions that require more than a yes or no response usually provide more meaningful information. For example, a question about what the staff thinks about the program's in-service policy would elicit more understandable information if it were stated directly — "We would like to know your views about the center's in-service policy. Please use the space below to state your opinions" — rather than indirectly — "Do you agree with the center's policy regarding in-service training?" A "no" response to the later question does not indicate where attention needs to be directed to improve the in-service training.

Interviews with parents, staff, and even children can provide useful information when planning change. All that is needed are a few questions to guide the discussion, a paper and pencil to record notes, or better yet a cassette tape recorder. These interviews can be held individually or conducted as part of a staff or parent meeting.

Neugebaurer (1981) asked readers of the *Child Care Information Exchange* to share some of their evaluation ideas with other readers. He reported how Dr. Nancy Reddy, executive director of Episcopal Child Care Center, Inc., in Jacksonville, Florida, developed an instrument for evaluating teacher performance. This instrument, called the Reddy Focus in Time (FIT), focuses on objective events rather than subjective opinions in such a way that caregivers are much less defensive in discussing children's behavior in their classrooms. Other subscribers to *CCIE* offered "field-tested" ways to evaluate director–staff relations. More encouragement should be given to the sharing of informal approaches that caregivers have devised themselves.

Dick Rowe (1978) has provided three good suggestions for ways to collect evaluation information informally. His "critical incident technique," an observation by one unbiased party, and a "program audit" are easy but useful ways to gain insight about a program's operations. The *critical incident technique* is designed to get a relatively detailed description of someone's experiences in the program. These incident descriptions could be about either a negative or a positive experience. By gathering several of these responses, practitioners can begin to see a pattern of responses that they would not usually see by simply asking someone if he or she was satisfied with the way the program was operating. Rowe suggests that staff or parents could be asked to tell about some incident in the last six months that they felt particularly good about and one incident they did not feel particularly good about. This approach could use either the short-answer questionnaire or the interview formats mentioned above.

It is important to note that the question directs the person's response to a particular concrete situation rather than asking the person to abstractly identify what it is that he or she likes about the program. Rowe provided the following example to demonstrate this point.

For example, if a director asks a parent what she doesn't like about the program, she might state — "The teacher never listens." On the other hand, if she is asked to relate a time when she felt upset, she might describe how one morning she told the teacher not to feed Johnny the regular meal but to have him drink milk and take the special medicine she was leaving; and when she returned she found Johnny had eaten a regular meal and had not been given his medicine. From asking the same question to other parents and probing this parent in more detail, the director may find this has never happened to other parents and only once to this parent. Furthermore, it is revealed that on that morning the parent was rushed and didn't have time to give a detailed explanation and instructions.

If only the first story is collected, the director might conclude improperly that the teacher is a poor listener and needs to attend a training session on improving listening ability. On the other hand, if the incident information was available, the conclusion might more properly be that a formalized procedure is needed whereby parents can leave written instructions for the teacher on special diet or medication instruction. The critical incident enabled a real problem to be identified, but the real problem was quite different from the initial generalized statement (p. 9).

The *observational approach* asks someone knowledgeable about child care (such as a director from another center) to visit the program for the day and provide a brief written or oral report of his or her impressions. Rowe suggests that this procedure can be especially useful in evaluating the center director's performance, which is particularly difficult for directors to do themselves. By discussing the director's performance with the staff and the parents, the outside observer can feed back information to the director without jeopardizing relationships.

The *program audit* that Rowe describes is very similar to what I have called an ongoing evaluation process. Through the use of checklists or the other techniques mentioned above, the program would be periodically provided with information about various aspects of its functioning. Through this feedback system, problems can be identified early and corrective action can be taken, instead of waiting for a crisis to occur. One example suggested by Rowe is a one-page monthly parent feedback form that might ask parents how satisfied they are with the way the center has been treating their child this month, or, if they could make any changes, what would they be. With a little creative effort and some planning, program staff and directors can easily get a more informed awareness of how the program is functioning.

SUMMARY

In conclusion, let me reiterate that meaningful program change is most likely to occur only when evaluation information is collected through a cooperative effort involving program staff, parents, and evaluators. To facilitate this procedure and reduce resistance on the part of program staff, an ongoing evaluation process that is an integral part of the program should be established. From this approach a cumulative understanding of the life of the setting and the meaning it has for all its participants can be gained. Evaluators should seek to extend the power of the evaluation process to all concerned by adopting an ecological perspective, focusing on reciprocal processes involving children, staff, and parents, and avoiding the traditional unidirectional view of events.

Finally, in implementing this evaluation approach, both formal and informal methods can be used. It will take considerable effort and some courage on the parts of individuals in day care to institute the kinds of processes recommended here. However, the outcomes can be quite beneficial.

PART III

Changing Day Care

Chapter 9

CHANGE THROUGH REGULATION

Gwen Morgan

The period of the eighties is a critical one for day care. There will be growth in all forms of day care, placing strain on the states' regulatory systems. Several alternative scenarios could unfold. In one scenario, an old-fashioned and poorly staffed regulatory system would become a barrier to the needed growth, unable to respond to the new volume of work and unresponsive to changes in the expectations of the public. Impatient to meet needs, the general public and the legislatures would blame all day care problems on the regulators and would remove or severely limit their power to protect children. In the other scenario, the regulatory system would be improved to meet the challenge, to assure that growing day care programs have a basic level of quality with access to information for ongoing improvement from the start.

In some states the first scenario is already unfolding. By deciding against updating its 1972 Guides for Day Care Licensing, the federal government, hostile to regulation, abandoned plans to provide leadership to states. States report political efforts to reduce staff, weaken standards, exempt church-run programs, and deregulate family day care. There appears to be a trend to exempt more people from licensing (Adams 1982).

Children do not appear to be any safer in day care in the eighties than they have been in the past. In San Francisco (1 December 1981) a banner front page headline reading "Horror in Day Care Center" described a death from abuse in an unregulated family day care home. Complaints of harmful care in unregulated situations are increasing, and include reports of sexual exploitation of children (cf., Texas Department of Human Resources 1980). Legislators and the general

163

public tend to forget the potential harm that could be inflicted on children without the preventive safeguarding offered by regulation. It takes a tragic fire, a death, or other horror story to remind the public of the importance of heading off disasters through regulation.

The second scenario, reform and improvement of our regulatory systems, is especially important at this time. New policy will not happen without effective advocacy. Key to any such effort is the caregivers who work with children, parents, and the specialists in the field. These are the groups with the most knowledge about children's needs and the most responsibility for bringing that knowledge to bear on public policy. If they do not speak out for children and their families, it is not likely that better policy can be made.

Child specialists, however, have very little knowledge of regulation. Unaware of the complexity of the topic, we tend to act on a set of unexamined assumptions, most of which are not accurate (G. Morgan 1979). When regulation is taught, it tends to be presented in the context of these unexamined assumptions. As a result, the field of practice is poorly prepared to develop and persuade policymakers to implement a sound regulatory strategy for the eighties. We may even be a force of resistance to reform.

Some of the unexamined assumptions about regulation that are common in our field include the following:

- Regulation refers to one system, called *licensing*.
- Regulation is the same thing as *standards*.
- The value of a regulatory system is judged by how high the standards are set.
- Licensing standards cover the physical aspects of day care but not the program. They should cover the program.
- Consultation is the most important function of licensors.
- Regulatory standards are professional specifications of quality.
- Regulatory standards should be written by child care experts.
- Flexibility is always good. Using police powers is always bad.

None of these assumptions is completely valid (G. Morgan 1979).

This chapter will summarize some of the information that is needed for examining these assumptions. It will describe many forms of regulation and the need for a strategy that combines regulatory and nonregulatory avenues to quality day care programs. It will identify issues and suggest needed reforms.

THE MANY FORMS OF REGULATION

Regulation, as the term will be used in this chapter, *refers to any uniformly applied system of quality control across programs.* It consists of three parts:

- Establishment of standards
- Application of standards to programs
- Use of sanctions to assure that programs meet the standards

Regulation is one major function of government. Government may provide, purchase, and regulate services. In the case of day care, it does all three. Its regulatory responsibility extends to all day care, not just to care that it purchases. Day care has been determined to be in the public interest, even when offered by private providers.

Regulation is not synonymous with *licensing.* In the case of day care, licensing is only one of at least four major baseline permissions that a private day care provider must seek and receive before lawfully providing the service:

- Day care license and registration
- Zoning
- Building and fire safety
- Health and sanitation

All these baseline permissions are granted by very different government bureaucracies, each under its own statutory mandate, each supported by its own constituencies, each established for a different public purpose, and each having its own requirements. New providers trying to navigate this regulatory maze for the first time may view it as a time-consuming and inefficient system. In reality, in most places it is not a system at all but four different systems operating independently and not fitting together. Improving the regulatory maze will entail giving attention to all the systems, not just the day care licensing system (G. Morgan 1974).

These four baseline systems set a floor of quality below which no private provider may care for children. Above that floor, other forms of regulation may in some cases specify higher levels of quality (Class 1969). High levels could be specified by: approval of government-run services, which should at least be equal in quality to those provided by the private sector; certification for government-purchased day care services; credentialing systems for caregivers; and accrediting systems for model programs. These last two forms are sometimes regulated in the private sector; the basic protection of children is always a government responsibility.

Table 9.1 shows the forms of regulation and the standards used between the basic floor of quality and the ceiling (G. Morgan 1982; Class 1969). Of course, regulation is only one of many methods through which quality is approached; the others have been discussed throughout this book. The nonregulatory approaches include:

- Training
- Consultation
- Evaluation
- Parent education
- Community education
- Newsletters
- Information and resource

Table 9.1. Regulatory Means of Achieving Quality

CEILING OF QUALITY	
TYPES OF STANDARD	REGULATORY METHOD
Standards for model programs	Accreditation of recommended programs
Qualifications required of staff	Credentialing
Funding specifications	Certification for funding
Administrative regulations for public programs	Approval
Basic preventive requirements	Licensing Safety Sanitation
FLOOR OF QUALITY	

Operating a program below an acceptable standard or without a license is a civil wrong.

Child abuse and neglect by a day care operator is a crime.

Adapted from Morgan (1982).

Table 9.2. Levels of Quality

Type of Standard	To Whom Applied	By Whom Established
Licensing	All	Licensing agency
Purchase Standard	All using funds from the agency contracting or vouchering for service	Funding agency
Accreditation	All who voluntarily seek it	Peer group, local 4-C, resource center, or public agency
Goal Standards	Educational for the field	Experts

It can be seen from table 9.1 that different levels of quality could be achieved by these various forms of regulation. Basic quality necessary for any child in day care is established through a state's baseline system of licensing and other permissions. A higher tier of quality could be certified for funding. A third tier could be those programs seeking voluntary accreditation that could be offered either by government agencies or by a private organization. Even higher than all three tiers are the goal standards in the field, enlightening and inspiring the field of practice so that the state of the art improves over the years. These tiers do not exist in a systematic way across the country. They may be conceptualized as is shown in table 9.2.

Day Care Licensing and Registration

The cornerstone of regulatory administration for day care is the state licensing law. Licensing is the "administrative lifting of a legislative prohibition" (Freund 1935). First the legislature, in response to public concern about potential harm that could come to children in day care, essentially abolishes the service. In most states, the law reads that "no person may provide care for children. . . . " The state then restores the right to provide the service, only to providers who meet the standards established by a designated agency of the state government and who apply for and receive an official permission by the agency. This official permission is the license, or permit. If the agency fails to establish standards or if standards cannot be met, then providers of care cannot legally operate.

The standards established by the agency are usually written through a democratic process by a task force representing many interests and by public hearings on the draft. When finally officially promulgated by the agency, standards become lawlike statements establishing the rights of children and their parents to receive a specified level of care. Those providers not meeting these standards are not permitted to care for children. The word *standards* may be confusing because it has two different meanings: a uniform measure, and a banner waved on high. *Requirements* is a more understandable term.

Licensing requirements are called *minimum* requirements: care provided must *at least* meet these requirements. It is important to remember that minimum does not mean *low*. A minimum floor of quality could be set very high. Over time, as providers reach higher levels of quality and as knowledge about the needs of children increases, requirements can be raised. Requirements can also be made less stringent. In most states, the democratic standard-setting process takes place approximately every five years.

Because they have the force of law, requirements must be enforced uniformly and fairly. Children must have equal protection. Licensors cannot impose their own ideas or exhibit favoritism for friends. Today requirements must be written in clear and reasonable terms. They must emphasize the concrete and measurable, rather than vague and unenforceable concepts such as "warmth" or "adequate provision for."

The emphasis on the measurable may be partially responsible for the myth that licensing deals only with physical arrangements. That myth also stems from confusion of licensing requirements with building safety and sanitation requirements. When an aspect of day care is felt to be important to regulate but intangible, those writing the requirements do their best to make the language as clear and concrete as possible, using measurable things as proxies for the intangibles whenever possible. Over the years, however, it may be that what was previously thought unmeasurable may become measurable. For example, Prescott and David (1976) describe seventeen different measures for "softness." The future may hold increasing emphasis on elements once thought too unmeasurable to regulate.

States regulate the physical amount of space, equipment, staffing patterns, health of staff and participating children, qualifications and character of staff, discipline, parental involvement, and the program of activities. In 1975 (Hopkins 1975), thirty-three states described requirements for educational programs, and an additional five states had requirements for educational materials. Six more states described supervisor qualifications and duties in such a way as to clearly indicate that program quality was intended. A total of forty-four states addressed program in some or all of these ways.

There is great variation in requirements among the states. Studies done in 1972 (Conserco Consulting Services Corp.), 1975 (Hopkins), and 1980 (L. Johnson) suggested that change was occurring in the direction of general improvement during the seventies. More recent indications showing weakening of the system have appeared.

It is by no means clear that it is desirable for states to write detailed program requirements. Rather than greater standardization and bureaucratic oversight, quality might better be achieved through a policy of increased autonomy for classroom staff and parents as they pursue their own goals of quality.

The question to ask is not "How high are the standards?" but rather "What aspects of day care are important to regulate by government, and what aspects are important to maintain program autonomy over?" A more appropriate strategy detailing program requirements might include a greater emphasis on director training and qualifications.

Consultation is another approach to quality. It was once generally thought highly desirable for the licensing agency to offer consulting services. In practice, the regulatory authority of the agency inhibits good consultation. Consultation works best when the consultee chooses the consultant and can terminate the relationship at will.

On the face of it, licensing is a powerful legal protection for children. Yet there are major limitations to its power. There are no simple and pure rights anywhere in society. Every right clashes with someone else's rights, and all regulation requires trade-offs. Children's rights often lose priority to adult rights because children are a powerless group. The specialists who work with children usually equate needs with rights, in a human rights context, with little understanding of the complex trade-offs in legal rights in the regulatory field. At present, providers' rights to fair treatment sometimes supersede children's rights to have the requirements enforced in a timely way. Providers should have due process but not at the expense of children. To strengthen children's rights in day care, some states need to improve the enforceability of their laws, and almost all states need better training in law enforcement for their licensing staff.

A second limitation on the power of licensing involves the will of the public. Government is carried on with the consent of the people. Requirements cannot be made unless providers are able and willing to meet them, parents are willing to pay for them, and the general public is willing to support their enforcement. The standard-setting process itself is, therefore, important as a way of achieving a consensus about where to set the baseline of requirements at a given time among all interests.

The history, values, and culture in a state influence what can be accomplished in regulatory policy. One interesting clue to the general support for quality, state by state, is the percentage of full-day centers that have early childhood specialists on their staffs for three- to five-year-olds. The range is from 12.8 percent in Louisiana to 68.7 percent in Vermont. The wide variation probably reflects differences not only in what the state requires but also in what requirement the public supports.

Family day care (see chap. 2) presents a major challenge to regulatory policy. The past two decades have seen an enormous growth in employment among mothers, many of whom use family day care. Regulation will not and cannot control this volume, because a large number of parents are already using family day care regardless of its regulatory status.

Alternatives suggested for regulating this form of care have many variations but generally fall into three categories: deregulate it, develop some feasible way of covering it through a regulatory method, or license it in the same way in which centers are licensed (G. Morgan 1974, 1980).

Deregulation is very attractive to policymakers, and it may have support from middle class parents. Deregulation means removing some or all of family day care from the licensing definition. Voluntary licensing and voluntary registration, practiced is some states, are actually forms of deregulation, since they do not offer baseline protection to all children, even though they may affect the quality of better providers.

Registration has arisen as a needed regulatory reform that could reach the large volume of family day care homes with a feasible commitment of state staff and maintain enforcement authority to back up parents. In most states, registration is either a form of licensing or it is directing regulation, but it does not guarantee inspection prior to operation. The family day care homes are already providing care, and providers are simply required to register the fact that they are caring for children and to certify that they meet requirements. Inspections are made when parents complain, when a question is raised by the application or by a reference, and when a home is randomly selected for spot checking. Parents are given a copy of the requirements and are encouraged to report any lack of compliance. As a further development of the idea of parental responsibility in partnership with the state, some states give parents a checklist to send back. This system appears better able to cover the volume of home providers without becoming a bottleneck than one in which providers cannot lawfully care for children without prior inspection. It may also be an improved regulatory method because of its emphasis on the role of parents. Although registration appears to be working (Adams 1982; Texas Department of Human Resources 1980), it could get bogged down unless a computer capability is built into it. Some states are finding that the turnover in family day care makes the lists of registered homes obsolete when done manually.

The licensing of family day care *systems* would be another improvement in state policy. Though there is interest in this improvement among states (Adams 1982), few have actually implemented it. Some states are licensing family day care systems under their definitions for licensing child placement agencies. A family day care system, however, is more like a day care center in its rights and relationship with the state regulatory agency than it is like a child placement agency, where the state has enormous powers because the children placed are wards of the state. This reform needs its own statutory language for day care. In contrast to independent homes, traditional licensing is feasible for family day care systems, since a large number of children can be protected with one license, as in the case of centers. Requirements would spell out the required role of the central administering agency and its visits to its homes. If a home did not meet requirements, the system would have to either improve it, drop it, or risk losing the system license. This reform would improve the coverage of some homes. However, it is not likely that a state could force all homes to become part of systems. It is therefore not a complete answer to the issue of regulating family day care.

Licensing is also needed for *group homes,* which usually care for between six and twelve children in a residential setting, with staffing to meet ratio requirements. If such a license is not legally defined, homes have to seek a day care license — even when they have adequate staff — if they take in one child beyond the definition of family day care. This is one factor that is keeping family day care underground.

Group homes are not likely to be very numerous. In those states that license them, there are not many. They are a potential high-quality service that should be encouraged, even though there will be a limited number of residential settings able to meet requirements.

To be effective, licensing needs not only an enforceable law and reasonable requirements supported by providers and the general public; it also needs a base in an agency that will support a vigorous consumer protection effort, back up efforts to eliminate harmful programs, and seek out unregulated ones. Such an agency would have to seek an adequate budget for adequate staff.

It is important to know whether the standards are implemented, whether there is public support and consensus among providers for them, whether there is enough staff to implement them, and whether the licensing law is enforceable. A state with high standards that are not upheld does not have an effective regulatory program.

Adding a layer of complexity to the maze, a few major cities have both state and city licensing. Further, licensing is only one aspect of regulation affecting day care; it will be important to improve other systems as well. These other systems are zoning, building and fire safety, and health.

Zoning

Zoning is a method of local land use control accomplished through dividing a city or town into differentiated zones and writing rules for what can take place in each type of zone. The rules are called zoning by-laws or ordinances and are the responsibility of local planning officials.

Zoning can become an obstacle, either deliberately or inadvertently, to day care. Sometimes citizens use zoning to keep out needed services. More often, day care may be prohibited because it is not listed among uses that can take place in a zone. Day care may be considered by local officials to be a commercial use, rather than a community service. In reality, day care, whether for profit or not for profit, has a public purpose. Still, it may on occasion be banned as unsafe in commercial zones and as commercial in residential zones.

When day care is not clearly permitted in a zone, day care providers must seek a zoning variance, which requires a public hearing. Here providers may encounter arbitrary opposition based on lack of information about the effect of day care on a community. The fact is that family day care homes have no more impact on a community than families with children of their own (Oakland City Planning Department 1974).

Local zoning officials, if not informed that day care is already well regulated through licensing, may add additional requirements that are not consistent with licensing requirements. Such planners are generally responsive to new community needs; they simply lack information.

Even though zoning is not connected to licensing, a licensing agency can make the connection by requiring zoning approval as a precondition for seeking a license. Since there are good arguments for exempting day care from zoning, the licensing requirements should not require zoning approval, thus giving local zoning the force of state law in the wording of the licensing code. Some states, aware of this problem, have stopped referring to zoning in their licensing codes.

Zoning is enforced by building inspectors in local governments who are more likely than planning officials to view day care as a commercial use. It is likely that the local community will enforce its own zoning without the help of the state licensing requirements.

Building and Fire Safety Codes

Depending on the community, there may be one building inspector enforcing both building safety and fire safety, or there may be inspections by both a building safety and a fire department inspector. The inspection is done by a local official based in the city or town hall. There has been a trend in the seventies for states to adopt a uniform building code for the whole state, rather than permitting each city to develop its own. However, many cities still have their own local codes.

These technical codes for construction add to the cost and start-up time of day care. The money and time spent may be invaluable in the protection offered to children, or it may be unnecessarily rigid. Given the number of family day care homes, the requirement of an inspection prior to operation for every home would present a major obstacle to family day care. State building officials tend to view family day care as a small institution simulating a home, rather than as an actual home sharing part of the day with a very few children. Further, the building inspection will trigger the application of zoning rules. For these reasons, there are many communities where family day care providers cannot apply for a license or registration because the prior requirement of a building safety approval brings with it requirements that few homes could meet.

The Life Safety Code of the National Fire Protection Association, national guidance material for the state building codes, divides day care into three categories and tries to offer appropriate codes for each: centers, family day care, and group homes. These materials provide some guidance to states for realistic building requirements.

Even though the licensing agencies do not control the building safety system, it will be important to them in the eighties to be sure that building codes are appropriate for day care, rather than for large schools, residential institutions, and hospitals. The use classification is also important. Day care is not an institutional use and should be regulated as a less formal community service; as a small school in the case of centers; or as a simple residential use in the case of family day care. Further, it will be important to develop some system that cuts across the types of regulation so that all the necessary inspections can be made in a reasonable time.

Health and Sanitation Codes

The fourth and last set of baseline regulators who must approve day care before it can operate is the health system. To protect against the spread of epidemic disease, food poisoning, and other environmental hazards, a great number of codes are developed. States where the health department is also the licensing agency tend to blur the distinction between health codes and the licensing code, but even though inspections are under control of the licensing division, the provisions of the health code are not.

Only one state, Vermont, has reviewed all its health codes and developed a day care sanitary code so that providers know what requirements they have to meet. In other states, it is impossible to find out how many codes apply and what their applications are for day care. Codes that were developed for hospitals and restaurants tend to be applied, sometimes inappropriately for a small service like day care.

Photograph by Jean Berlfein, courtesy of Child Care Employee Project

For family day care, as in the case of building safety, it is preferable to write any additional day care health requirements into the licensing requirements, rather than adding specific day care health requirements to the already complex health codes.

Approval of Public Programs

A license is a permission to operate and applies to the private sector. When a public agency runs programs, it should meet the same requirements, or better ones. But the public agency's mandate to operate is contained in its statute from the legislative body. It is difficult to conceive of how the licensing agency could legally withdraw that mandate or permission. Both legal problems and serious political problems would result. Even though some states do say they license public agencies, states have not removed licenses from public agencies or stopped them from providing services. It seems more sensible to develop a different regulatory method for public agencies, with different sanctions for failing to meet requirements. This aspect of quality control has not been well developed in the states.

Credentialing

A credential required for a member of a day care staff is itself a form of regulation. It can be made voluntary, or it can be added to other regulations as a condition for funding or for licensing. Training and credentialing of staff are dealt with in chapters 1, 5, and 10.

If the quality of the staff is assured, the need for detailed directions for running the program is lessened. If in the future more emphasis is placed on credentialing staff or directors in either preservice or in-service capacities, this could affect how many and what kind of requirements would be desirable to apply through licensing.

Fiscal Regulation

When government buys or creates a service through grant or contract, it can establish specifications for the quality it wishes to support. Head Start's performance standards, the now defunct federal day care requirements, and state standards for certification for funding are all examples of purchase or grant specifications. Since the federal requirements for day care were abolished in 1981, it is now up to the states to determine standards for purchase.

Funding requirements differ from licensing ones in several important ways. The relationship of the state to the provider is that of purchaser or grantor rather than licensor and is based on contract law, not on the police powers that governments use in the public interest. In many ways it is a less powerful tool for enforcing policy than is licensing, since it affects only those day care children who are eligible for public subsidy. The government can withdraw its funding support if standards are not met, but in theory the provider can continue to operate as long as someone else will pay for the service. In licensing, however, the state can close down programs that do not meet its requirements.

The state can spell out a higher level of requirement as a purchase specification, as many states were already doing by using the federal standards. The state of the art in the field serving the general public may be different from the quality of funded care. Higher funding standards tend to price out the general public, resulting in a subsidized system that serves only the poor and another system that serves the general public. Over time it would be hard to avoid a social class stigma in the subsidized system. This stigma could have a more adverse effect on quality than the positive effect of the higher standards.

Solving this set of problems is a challenge. Solutions differ from state to state because the problem varies with the past history of both federal standards and licensing. The three-tiered system of standards suggested earlier in this paper would work in some states if the state does not set the second level so much higher than the base level that parents could not buy the same service the government buys.

Fiscal regulation is not limited to an input-standard-measurement technique; it can also develop techniques for evaluation based on both inputs and effects.

Accreditation of Model Programs

Neither baseline licensing nor funding requirements can assure high quality. As we have seen, nonregulatory means are as important as regulatory tools. However, the existence of a voluntary system for accrediting programs that are offering a high-quality program for children and parents could stimulate the field as a whole. If there were such a system, the presence of this third tier of quality would clarify that government licensing requirements are not standards of high quality but simply the baseline for permission to operate.

An accreditation system is difficult to implement, except perhaps in very wealthy communities. It is difficult to reach agreement on what standards should be used when the accreditation should be denied.

Accreditation could be granted by either a government agency or by a private group. A few communities have instituted such a system, and at least one state has attempted, although not successfully, to establish a statewide accrediting system. The National Association for the Education of Young Children is studying whether a system of program endorsement could be offered as part of its services to the field.

The kind of accreditation we are discussing here does not mean a complex, formal system such as is used in the case of public education. The system would probably need a peer review method to reach consensus among experts about what standards should be used, some means of visiting programs to help them meet the high standards, and some methods of reaccrediting them to assure continued high performance.

THEORIES OF DEREGULATION

There is agreement among both liberal and conservative lawmakers that some types of regulation should be abolished and that others should be reformed. The rhetoric of deregulation is obscuring the need for greater precision in distinguishing between what regulation is desirable to keep and what regulation is on its way out. For example, we deregulated the control of airline routes and prices but not the qualifications of airplane pilots or safety measures controlling the equipment.

As this example demonstrates, regulation by government is not all of the same type. Four categories reflecting different purposes for regulation provide some useful distinctions:

- Regulation of prices and entry into a field
- Regulation of the quality of services, the environment, or products for protection of the public
- Regulation to account for the public dollar
- Regulation of the states by the federal government, or of local governments by the states

The first type, control of prices and entry into the field, are attempts to remedy economic instabilities. Large federal commissions regulating entire industries, such as the Federal Communications Commission, are in this category. It also includes occupational licensing, when the major concern is to limit competition and control the market. This type of regulation is seriously questioned by scholars and policymakers who challenge whether such control of competition is really in the public interest when it leads to higher costs to the public.

Both licensing and credentialing of day care should be seen as belonging in this first category. If the emphasis of the credential is on the needs of children and their parents for quality care, its value is less in question than if the emphasis is on the needs of caregivers and is an attempt to limit growth of forms of care. Of course, the needs of caregivers deserve attention and strong policy support through labor regulation rather than children's regulation.

The second category includes various social regulatory agencies involved in consumer protection and citizen rights. Unlike the agencies in the first category, these agencies are seldom popular with the industries they regulate because they take the position that the public interest takes precedence over economic gain. These types of regulation can have clearly recognized value (as, for example, in the case of the regulations that prevented the use of the drug thalidomide in this country), particularly in any situation where individual members of the public cannot make an informed choice. Critics of regulation of this type claim that it does not always take into account the costs of the benefit or the clashing demands of different social goals. In this category, strong public support for regulation will probably continue, particularly in response to disasters and perceived threats, with cost-and-effect analysis becoming routine. Continuation of regulation will depend on the public perception of the dangers averted.

Day care licensing has a long history of offering genuine consumer protection, and its rhetoric should more clearly identify it as this type of social concern. Public health agencies have been among the oldest and first agencies to protect the public against hazards; they offer various forms of regulation of this type, including their day care health codes. Building safety codes can be seen in the same way, and they have shifted in emphasis from the protection of property to the protection of life. The federal day care requirements were also motivated by social concern for children and their families, even though their legal basis was in the funding relationship, the third category.

The third category of regulation, intended to establish accountability for public funds, produces a great deal of frustration with red tape. Despite the presence in Washington of a Commission on Red Tape, there are no signals that the ever-increasing paperwork connected with accountability is abating. This type of regulation appears to be exempt from official reform, even though public opinion is strongly anti–red tape. Day care providers struggling with contract procedures and paperwork could get public support if they have feasible reforms to suggest.

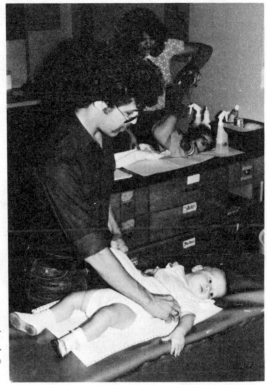

Photograph by Michael Wetteland

The fourth category, regulation of governments by other governments, is one in which the Reagan administration has made a determined effort through block grants to reduce federal control over state policy. At the local level, there is also strong resistance to state mandates and controls, which will inhibit efforts to deal with zoning issues from the state level.

It is obvious that these categories of regulation are very different. Despite the tendency of current rhetoric, broad generalizations about the nature and value of regulation are not valid. Most of the criticism of the regulatory agencies stems from study of the first type. With the exception of regulations affecting hospitals, regulation in social services has received little study.

Behind the criticism of regulatory policy has been a theory that the regulators are inevitably captured by the regulated industry (Stigler 1971). The theory includes the belief that a regulatory agency has a life cycle (Bernstein 1955), beginning with a youthful commitment to its mission of protecting the public. As it encounters the checks and balances on its powers, it learns to adapt to these realities and to become friendly with the regulated, with whom it has much in common. In its organizational old age, it maintains the status quo and at worst becomes the captive of the industry it regulates.

These theories are a generation old and have reached the public consciousness and the Congress. They may never have been completely valid for all types of regulation and may not be totally applicable to day care regulation, which has not been studied from this perspective. Furthermore, there is evidence that inventive regulatory reforms have already been instituted to avoid the anticipated dangers of agency senility or capture. More recent theorists, observing these successful efforts, suggest a new concept of "recycling" that implies that a deliberate revitalization can take place, in contrast to the bleak determinism of the life cycle theory, on the one hand, or a naive optimism on the other (J. E. Moore 1972).

When applying these ideas to day care, any effective strategy will ally itself with regulatory reform and will build in devices for renewal of commitment to consumer protection goals.

Child development specialists, in their advocacy of licensing for day care, may give the appearance of wishing to erect a protective wall around a favored group of practitioners. It is important to make a conscious effort to avoid giving the appearance that licensing represents the interests of the field of practice at the expense of children and their families or that licensing is to be used as a device to restrict the amount or type of care available to parents.

REFORMING THE REGULATORY SYSTEM

Licensing needs a new image as a vigorous consumer protection program that involves parents in original and creative ways and safeguards children from harm that would occur without the regulatory protection.

Each state is different, and each will have its own specific plans for improving its regulatory system in the eighties. All will need to be sure that there is adequate staffing to do the needed tasks and be equally sure that the needed tasks are feasible, given the limited amount of available tax support, since plans for sizable expansion of staff would probably lead to deregulation instead.

Following is a list of reforms that have been mentioned earlier in this paper and other actions that might be considered for improving the regulatory system.

More Effective Licensing

• Encourage a modest increase in licensing staff for centers and group homes; realistic work loads based on number of licensed units and expected growth.

• Institute civil service requirements for licensors that guarantee knowledge of law enforcement, rights of licensees, and basic concepts of regulatory administration, as well as day care programming and management. Consider requiring licensors to have been day care directors.

• Centralize licensing, rather than diffusing quality controls into regional operations. Assure local interest in some way, possibly by advisory groups at the local level to the licensor.

• Develop licensing requirements for group homes, and license them.

• Register family day care homes; develop computer capability; provide an adequate number of registrars.

Improved Standards

• The federal government or a national organization should maintain an ongoing record of current state requirements for licensing, building code requirements for day care, and specific day care sanitation codes for use by other states at the time of revising requirements. The same organization should keep information about relevant research findings in connection with the requirements to justify adding, keeping, or dropping requirements when knowledge changes.

• Consider adding the standards development process to the licensing statutes to assure that licensing agencies follow sound practices of interest representation and consensus building.

• Develop orientation materials for task force standard-setting participants to assure good communication and full understanding of the nature of licensing requirements.

A Stronger Role for Consumers

• Encourage development of a greater role for parents in routine inspection and reporting on compliance; establish more routine channels for consumer feedback.

• Enhance the complaint mechanisms and educate the public and parents to use it when noncompliance is observed.

Removing Barriers to Day Care Development

• Build a separate start-up and technical assistance office to help new applicants get their license, and to assist employers and other groups interested in starting day care. Separate this assistance from the licensor, but assure that they work together.
• Amend state zoning enabling legislation to permit centers and group homes in any zone as an educational community service that enhances the community; permit family day care as a customary home occupation. Require local zoning ordinances to use definitions that reference state licensing definitions.
• For independent family day care homes, write one licensing code that incorporates requirements for building safety, sanitation, and licensing, with only one inspecting agency for any requirement not applied to residential occupancy.
• For new centers and group homes, develop a local-level coordinated system for inspections that responds to the applicant in reasonable time.
• Develop a day care sanitation code at the state level, in the Public Health Department, for centers and group homes.
• Be sure the classification of centers, and group homes, as to type of use is appropriate in building codes. Family day care should be a residential use, without additional requirements beyond what are applied to dwellings where families live. Be sure the requirements themselves in building codes are reasonable for centers and group homes.
• Reduce red tape and paper requirements as much as possible. For centers, consider abolishing renewal, substituting an annual updating of all records kept at center, available for inspection.

Fiscal Regulation

• Train the same staff to inspect both for licensing and funding requirements, and to understand the rights and relationships under these very different forms of regulation.
• Overhaul the rate-setting process. Be sure that the relation between rates of reimbursement and the cost of providing care that meets requirements is clear. If the state is not paying the full monetized cost of care, it should clearly know what proportion of the cost it is paying, so that providers can seek local or other funds.
• Experiment with evaluation systems, and rating systems, in the funded system. Competition for higher ratings might be encouraged.

Output measures might be used in addition to the input measures now used.

LICENSING ENFORCEMENT AND IMPROVED COMPLIANCE

• Examine statutes and make changes needed to assure a range of tools for implementation: powers to inspect, injunctive powers, fines in cases where revocation is too harsh a penalty.

• Use public awareness more by publishing lists of providers that have high compliance, by posting notices of violations at programs. Develop rewards for high compliance and timely cooperation.

• Involve providers in the appeals procedures. A peer panel will be fair to providers, but is less likely to overprotect them inappropriately than a less informed hearing official.

• Develop routine procedures and working relationships with resource and referral centers so that they are informed about pending actions and violations of requirements.

• Develop policy and possibly statutory change to clarify state responsibility when children in day care are abused and neglected, specifying the respective roles of licensing and child protection.

IMPROVING DAY CARE QUALITY

• Credential a child care specialist above the classroom caregiver level by the licensing agency; permit clear mobility and career paths upward from entry roles, both through college training and required in-service competency based training

• Require day care directors to have been classroom staff, or to employ child care specialists in supervisory and training roles. Require directors to have skills and knowledge for managing an organization.

• Develop training and technical assistance at the local level with an emphasis on sharing resources in the day care system and the community, with a strong voice for participants in the training and in identifying training needs. Require ongoing training in licensing requirements; credit conferences and workshops at professional meetings toward the training.

• The funding agency for day care should buy training from Head Start training programs; Head Start training should purchase training from organized day care training efforts.

• The licensing agency should develop a consultant list for needs beyond consultation relating to requirements; try to set up a fund to help pay for consultation if programs cannot pay themselves.

• Offer a voluntary credential for family day care providers; pay a higher state reimbursement rate for credentialed family day care.

• Develop a relationship between licensing and funding requirements and staff and any organization accrediting model programs.

Although government regulation is not the only approach or even the best approach to achieving high quality, it is a necessary part of the overall day care system. The law is a blunt instrument in achieving the fragile values sought in our quest for quality.

Those who want to make day care better need to ask not "What should the standards be?" but the more important questions, "What aspects of day care are best regulated by government, and what aspects are best left in the hands of parents and staff?" "What mix of regulatory and nonregulatory actions will best protect children from harm and result in improved quality?" In doing so, we should always be clear about the power and the limitations on the power of each of these actions to bring about change.

Chapter 10

TRAINING INDIVIDUALS: IN THE CLASSROOM AND OUT

Elizabeth Jones

Day care is not school. Day care is a space and time where adults and children live together. It should be comfortable, interesting, and growth-producing for both.

The competent day care giver is a person of any age and either sex who likes children, is willing and able to nurture their physical and emotional needs, has good ideas for things to do, is good at being with children in an unobtrusive way, and has personal integrity — a set of values and attitudes toward being in the world that serve as the basis for his or her interactions with children.

One does not necessarily find all of these qualities in the same person. My twenty-three-year old son, who has no prior experience in child care but is a skilled outdoorsman and an alert observer of the things around him, has been working in day care recently, in a center in the barrio. His ease in "hanging out" with the children has led his director, who is a professionally trained Anglo, to say, "He's such a good model for my teachers." Those teachers are mostly middle-aged Latino women with experience in parenting. They do not "hang out" with children. They fuss over them and nurture them and feed them and scold them and keep them clean and safe and well fed. A balance of styles is one of the criteria for a good staff in a day care center — that, and opportunities to learn from each other and challenge each other's assumptions.

Competence in child care is learned through education, or through experience (including parenting), or through being in touch with the child in oneself. The basis for good care giving may be either professional or experiential. Professional education teaches attitudes and behaviors and the rationale for them. The competent professional not only acts appropriately but can articulate the reasons for his or her actions in child development terms. Experience also generates attitudes and behaviors. The intuitively competent caregiver makes decisions on the affective rather than the rational level, drawing on "mother wit" rather than on textbooks.

The two most familiar models for competent child care are teaching and parenting. Each has limitations as a role model for the behavior of child caregivers. The nursery school teacher, who engages in many though not all of the behaviors appropriate for caregivers and who has developed a rather complex definition of his or her responsibility for the development of the whole child, is not a familiar model for many of the people working in day care; many of them never went to nursery school. They were all parented, however, and they went to elementary school; they know how those people behave.

Elementary teachers, who work with older children, have traditionally defined their role in relatively narrow terms: to effect the direct transmission of academic skills and social expectations. Teachers are people who give directions, correct errors, and manage the behavior of children in large groups. Relatively few teachers spend much time giving hugs, wiping noses, changing clothes, or helping children get to sleep—all important activities of caregivers. Parents, who do all these things, are usually with children only individually or in small groups; they do not have to acquire group management skills. Nor are all parents actively aware of their importance as guides for children's learning.

Both teacher education and parent education offer possible approaches to the education of day care givers. Teacher education often begins with technique and curriculum, to be transmitted by the trainer and gradually mastered by the teacher. This direct training seems efficient, just as schools assume that direct training of children can be made efficient. But our schools are full of children who have been "taught" but have not learned. Similarly, it is common knowledge that teachers rarely teach as they were taught to teach; that is ivory tower thinking. They are more likely to teach as they themselves were taught and as the old hands in the classrooms next to theirs teach.

Some parent education, likewise, relies on direct transmission of information by experts: this is how to be a good parent. For parents ready for that particular information, it may be helpful; it makes others just feel more inadequate. And so there is another strong tradition in parent education that begins with respect for parents' own experiences and motivation, building programs on their interests and questions and helping them recognize their own competence (Greenberg 1976; Sale 1972).

I believe strongly that any training aimed at increasing quality in day care needs to build on caregivers' best instincts, their own values, and their sense of what is right for children and for themselves as adults with children. Quality is a function of relationships, and these grow out of personal integrity and caring, which cannot be taught. Caregiving is indeed an art that can be practiced and questioned and analyzed and made better, but it cannot be taught directly.

This chapter, then, is written from a clear point of view about the nature of training for learners of any age. Learners are not empty vessels, waiting to be filled by experts. They are persons with a wealth of meaningful experiences. Their learning is necessarily sequential; that is, they will learn only what they are ready to learn, in response to questions they are asking for themselves.

Early childhood education, unlike other levels of education, has a long tradition of beginning with the child and the teacher rather than with curriculum and methods. Relationships are seen as central to teaching and learning: my task as parent or preschool teacher or caregiver is *to get to know this child* and *to get to know myself* in the context of the environment in which we find ourselves. Our mutual learning grows out of our shared relationship.

Training also implies relationship. If caregivers are to respect children as individuals, they must experience respect for themselves as individuals. Effective socialization into a role requires laboratory as well as lecture. A beginning caregiver needs as role models not only experienced caregivers, with whom he or she can observe and work, but also trainers and supervisors *who treat the caregiver the way they would like him or her to treat children,* who take this individual seriously as a person and are respectful of his or her needs, interests, and desires.

Training in this mode begins with the caregiver him- or herself. Who are you? What do you care about? Why are you here? What interests you about children? What gives you pleasure in being with them? What are your goals for them? How can we help you to be more effective in meeting your goals?

Competence in child care, as I stated above, is learned through education, or through experience including parenting, or through being in touch with the child in oneself. In the barrio center I mentioned, my son's competence comes from his being in touch with the child in himself. He has not lost his delight in snakes and walks in the mountains, ball games and polliwogs and capture-the-flag; and he is willing to share those things with kids. The older women teachers have gained their competence through parenting; they enjoy being responsible for children and taking good care of them. Neither he nor they have had any prior training; in this, they are typical of the majority of child care givers. Nor have they a long-term commitment to the field. He will be quitting to build trails this summer and go back to college in the fall. If the women stay, it is probably because they are unskilled; they have no training for anything else.

Day care is, and will doubtless remain, in large part an entry-level job. Most proprietary care, some nonprofit care, and family care all rely on minimum wages to remain cost-effective. In entry-level hiring, one looks mostly for intuitive competence: Does this person like children? Is he or she responsible? Given this fact, professionalization as the only model for child care training is unrealistic.

The strong push within the field for professionalization comes out of concern for status, salaries, and quality of program in day care. Quality care of young children, we professionals believe, requires skills and knowledge. We reject the popular view that *anyone* can take care of little children. Historically, of course, it is true: older sisters, teenagers, elderly grandmothers, and uneducated mothers have all made their contributions to child rearing, more or less successfully. Their work has been seen as necessary but not of economic importance or requiring any specific skills. As we recognize that work traditionally done by women has been arbitrarily devalued in male-dominated societies, we grasp for the perquisites of professionalism: How else will we ever move beyond a "babysitter" image?

Further, as children are increasingly being cared for outside their own families, and often in large groups, the skills of caregivers become a matter of wider community concern. The frustrations inherent in child care — a nonstop, emotionally and physically demanding task in which adults have a great deal of power over children — are such that safeguards against child abuse of all sorts are needed. Children raised in their own families are protected, by no means infallibly, by family members' love for and pride in them. Children cared for by persons with no long-term commitment to them need other safeguards that training can help to provide.

To sustain quality in care-giving, an adult has to feel both important and competent. Feelings of importance result from feeling affection for and receiving affection from the children in one's care and from belief in the significance of one's work. Feelings of competence come from frequent successes in one's work and from skills developed through experience and training.

In the discussion of types of training that follows, I am making the assumptions that (1) professional skill is a matter of degee, not of kind. The professional is skilled at analyzing his or her behavior. *All* caregivers can be helped to analyze their behavior at some level. (2)

Photograph by Michael Wetteland

Training at every level needs to begin with respect for the person being trained as someone who already knows a lot and whose training will build on that knowledge. We have all been children; that, if nothing else, gives us an experience base for understanding the children we care for. (3) Although the majority of caregivers do not stay in the field for long, we will be better off if we take the long view of their training. Such a view is concerned with the development of the person, not simply with the rapid acquisition of technical skills. It is justified, I think, for three reasons: (1) Unlike most other entry-level jobs, caregiving focuses not on inanimate objects but on children. It requires relationship building, not just technical skills. (2) Caregivers who are treated as valued persons are more likely to value themselves in the setting, thus staying longer on the job. Young children need all the stability of relationship they can get. (3) Most entry-level jobs in our economic system are dehumanizing, a fact that has impeded the development of the people — the under-educated, nonwhites, and women — who work at them, and thus the development of society as a whole. The field of early childhood has a long commitment to humanizing environments for children. This commitment needs to extend to the adults who care for children.

Training of child care givers takes place both in-service and pre-service. In-service training may be conducted on the job by colleagues and supervisors, or it may be provided by an external source such as a college or a field training program. In the latter case, the caregiver is employed and uses his or her job experience to meet the requirements of the training program. In-service training may be required by an employer or by licensing standards or may be voluntary. Employers may or may not choose to support voluntary training opportunities such as conferences, workshops, and classes through subsidy and released time and through increases in salary or status.

Preservice training is provided by high school, vocational, and college programs at lower-division, upper-division, and graduate levels. Some college training is aimed primarily at technical, other training at professional competence. Short-term preservice training may be offered by employers and is generally specific and practical, providing an orientation to the demands of the job. The short-term resources of conferences and workshops may help preservice students get a sense of the field and the people in it.

Training for family day care givers is usually in-service but is sometimes preservice, when new caregivers are being recruited in a community. It is significantly different from training for center care because it deals not with adaptation to a new environment but with effective care-giving in one's own home and the responsible exercise of autonomy. Each type of training is discussed below.

IN-SERVICE TRAINING

In-service training may be provided through staff meetings, through workshops and conferences, through field-based consultation, and through college classes.

Staff Meetings/Staff Relationships

Most administrators and supervisors in day care have previously been caregivers, accustomed to putting children's needs first. In their new role, they need to change this focus to the needs of the adults who work directly with children, to enable *them* to put children's needs first. Christina Morgan (1980) has described her experience as the new director of a day care center for school-aged children in which she inherited a staff about whose competence and motivation she had serious questions:

> I sincerely believe that only when individuals feel that they are important and cared about, and only when their needs are being met,

are they capable of doing the same for others. My role as an administrator to a great extent has been to try to get to know what the needs of my staff are. I have spent a great deal of time listening and encouraging and defending each and every staff member. I have tried very hard to let each person know that I think s/he is important and that I feel her/his needs deserve to be met. I have struggled with biting my tongue (sometimes not very successfully), saying nothing so that individuals could find out for themselves. Because we are all fallible, we are still struggling together. I think I can honestly say that we are all trying to be more humane with one another and that perhaps some day our program will be one in which there is room for everyone to grow (pp. 46–47).

A year and a half later, she wrote:

We really have become a community of people caring about each other. There is space for people to be themselves and yet there is also room for real emotions and honest conflicts.

For people to grow I think you have to create a climate of trust. Each of us can change only when we open ourselves up to possibilities, and we can do that only when we feel safe and accepted. I was able to gain trust by focusing on people's strengths instead of their weaknesses, and by giving adult needs priority.

Because people had the freedom to create their own environments, they established places that reflected and met their needs. Over time they came to trust each other's space as well.

Because they had the time to get to know one another in a context other than with children (workshops, rap sessions, staff meetings, coffee-klatching, etc.), and because they did not need to compete to prove their worth, they were able to relax and find out that they had more in common than they thought. Since we stressed communication skills and honesty, they had opportunities to confront in a positive way, and they learned alternative ways to resolve interpersonal conflicts. We have come to see each other as real people with faults and virtues (pp. 103–104).

Beginning with the premise that "learning is effective only when it is an active decision on the part of the learner," Morgan began by enabling staff to make decisions about their room environments, asking them for lists of things they needed and providing shelves to free adults from continually doling out supplies. Environmental changes do change behavior, and it is easier to change physical space than it is to change behavior directly (see Prescott, chap. 3 of this book). Knowing that they had power over their own space, staff were then freed to be generous with it — and generous in relationships as well.

Good training is individualized. In-service meetings required of everyone on a center staff may be useful *if* they provide lots of opportunity for peer interaction, for staff to ask relevant questions of each other. In-service meetings that are primarily lectures by visiting experts will inevitably address themselves to the questions of only a few staff members.

Resource people for staff meetings need to be carefully chosen:

> We carefully screened those we invited to participate as consultants in the Center Meetings against our criteria for a "non-expert" expert:
> Human warmth as well as professional competence.
> Ability to share learning experiences rather than play the role of didactic "teacher."
> Humility, pragmatism, and a sense of humor.
> Being able to sense "where the group is at" in terms of psychological and practical needs (Sale et al. 1972, 149).

Workshops and Conferences

Conferences for adults are like open classrooms for children; they offer a wide variety of choices. Participants can decide which sessions will meet their individual needs and thus take responsibility for their own learning, as well as enjoy the stimulation of new people and places and the sense of being part of a larger enterprise. Programs that subsidize staff members' participation in workshops and conferences are acknowledging the staffs worth and their capacity for growth.

Field-based Consultation

Field-based consultation and training provide opportunities for the caregiver to be observed in action. When observations are used skillfully by a consultant as the basis for helping caregivers think analytically about their work — in effect, to generate theory out of practice — they may serve as a particularly effective form of training.

Riley (1980), who believes that "the most critical of all teaching skills is observing and interpreting child behavior" (p. 10), modeled and shared this skill with the caregivers with whom he worked as a consultant. In order to teach, "tools of thought" — both concepts and related experiences that serve to illustrate the concepts — are needed.

The concepts are the easy part. At the drop of a reflex, I will cite chapter and verse of various theories, ideas, concepts, and their supporting data and applications. If I did just this the teachers would be amazed and impressed, but probably learn very little which they could use the next day when a four-year-old throws his spinach across the table.

Connecting a meaningful experience to each concept is a more difficult task. If I were conducting a workshop, it would be much easier: I could plan ahead exactly which ideas I wished to teach, and prepare a workshop experience for each. But consulting at the preschool site allows no such preparation. I never know ahead of time what the day's curriculum will be.

For my supply of connecting experiences, therefore, I depend upon written observations of the pre-school day, and storytelling (p. 3).

After observing in the program and writing his observations, Riley met with the staff at the end of the day.

I usually begin the after-school meeting by reading all of my observations. This always prompts lots of discussion of what was happening, why, what could have happened instead, and so forth. I try to keep my observations objective (rather than interpretive) so that these discussions can be open, brainstorming, fun exchanges, rather than congratulating/accusing/defending interactions.

In the course of these discussion I, the consultant, have ample opportunity to interpret the observations through the perspective of various concepts and theories of human development and early education. It is my chance to teach. It is my chance to take hold of an experience which some of the staff shared just hours before (and which all of us can identify with since we know all the people in it), and to connect a concept or theory to it. I grab the specific experience, and squeeze the general pattern out of it.

Under these circumstances if the theory has any truth to it, and if I have applied it to the right experience, then it will make enormous sense to the staff. Their faces will light up with "ah-ha!" The theory will come alive, and the staff will sense they have really learned something. They have learned a new and useful way of looking at experiences they actually have. Since they have a personal experience to connect the theory to, and since they see that they can *use* the theory, therefore they are more likely to remember it and make use of it.

Under these circumstances if the staff look blankly at me or ask "So?," then I must infer that either: (1) I don't understand this theory well enough to apply it correctly; or (2) I haven't the words to make it understandable to these people; or (3) this theory is bunk (pp. 4–5).

That is teaching from observing. Where does the storytelling come in?

Inevitably, there are many useful concepts for which I can find no examples in my notes of the day. What then? How do I connect a meaningful experience to the concept when no experience is available?

Easy: I cheat. I make up an experience. I weave a picture of words in the air. Usually it's an experience from another preschool or from my own preschool teaching. Sometimes it's a story I've heard. Sometimes I just make it up. All of these options go under one title: story telling (p. 79).

Field-based consultation is sometimes offered by college instructors, particularly in community colleges that offer credit for work experience. More often, it is made available through the CDA program. The Child Development Associate credential is awarded to experienced caregivers who demonstrate their competence in working with young children. With the help of his or her adviser, an early childhood professional, the CDA candidate prepares a portfolio documenting his or her work with children and is observed on the job by the adviser, by a parent representative, and by a national CDA representative.

The CDA process may be undertaken as part of the in-service training of the agency that employs the candidate. The majority of Head Start training nationwide, and much of that for day care staff, is CDA training (Child Development Association National Credentialing Program 1981, p. 8).

Some CDA training is offered through local colleges. In some instances, the offering is a single portfolio course. In others, a series of courses related to CDA competences is offered with credit acceptable toward an associate or bachelor's degree.

CDA credentialing differs from traditional college-based training in several ways:

- Assessment of competence is based on job performance rather than performance in college courses. The credential is awarded solely on the basis of demonstrated competence, rather than on the accumulation of class hours.

- Formal training is not a requirement. A candidate who is already competent may take the initiative in demonstrating that fact.
- In the assessment process the candidate her- or himself and a parent serve as equal members with the professionals on the assessment team. CDA credentialing is consciously antielitist; it values experience-based competence equally with academic-based competence.

College Classes

Where state licensing requirements include college classes for all day care staff, in-service training becomes an important function of the colleges, especially the community colleges. (Caregivers must *take* classes; they need not have completed all the classes in order to be employed.) Such colleges may serve two quite distinct populations in their early childhood programs: day students, typically young women just out of high school who may have little or no experience working with children; and evening students, employed in day care programs and winding up their long day with a three-hour class. In-service classes need to be more than lecture. They need to provide new experiences and draw on those that their students bring to the group — to keep students awake, to respect the validity of what they already know, and to make theory practical.

PRESERVICE TRAINING

A friend of mine teaches community college classes in music for young chidren. She enjoys her evening classes, full of people who work daily with children and are eager for ideas for activities to get them through the day, as well as ready to discuss some of the reasons for the things they do with children. But she has been frustrated by her day students, who are not yet involved in child care. I suggested that with them perhaps her approach should be quite different — that it needs to begin with the students themselves, and with their own feelings about their experiences with music as children and as adults. "Oh, I don't think I'd want to teach *that* course," was her first response. "I want to teach people about children's music." A couple of weeks later, "Maybe I would," she said. "But it would be different."

Preservice training for people without much experience with children does need to be different. It needs to focus on child development, to help prospective caregivers get in touch with children and with the child in themselves. When we teach child development and the other courses in the early childhood curriculum, what we are really trying to do is to enable students to understand what it is like to be a child. An adult who wants to provide meaningful experiences for a young child must be able to put her- or himself in that child's shoes, to understand what the world looks and feels like at three years old. Because learning is sequential for each individual, training needs to begin with what learners already know. They have all been children; they have access to that experience. They can look at their own experience and that of their fellow students; there is a wealth of it in any group.

What do they already know about childhood? What are their questions and concerns? Where can they find some more children to learn about? Just as in in-service training, the understanding of theory grows out of experience. The academic tradition has tried to reverse this tradition, teaching theory before permitting any doing. The outcome has been a lot of graduates who know the words but do not know how to relate them to the real thing.

Storytelling is another source of understanding. Good college teachers tell lots of stories out of their own experiences with children. And they recommend books: first-hand accounts of other teachers' experiences, stories for children that convey something of the quality of children's thought and feeling, and stories — fiction and autobiography — written for adults about children.

Direct experience with children, both observation and participation, is crucial. In the best programs it happens from the very beginning. Students need to learn to observe child behavior in detail, and they need to learn to build relationships with children. They need access to good caregivers who can serve them as models for working with children as responsible adults. They need a great deal of opportunity to try it for themselves and to talk about it with peers.

Preservice training has three main advantages over in-service training:

- It offers, at many colleges, experience with chidlren in an "ideal" setting — a preschool laboratory with plenty of adults, plenty of material, skilled teachers to serve as models, and time to talk about it all.
- It offers students opportunities to observe in a variety of settings, to get an idea of the wide range of possibilities and practices in programs for young children and to do some sorting out of their own values.
- It offers leisure for thought, the chance to try new things, the chance to focus on one child or one activity without needing to be responsible for the whole group. Being responsible is certainly a learning experience, but sometimes it makes it hard to see the forest for the trees. Being a learner, a student in a preschool is freeing; it justifies time out to think. Some in-service training also has this quality. The experienced caregiver who takes a summer off to earn credit in a college laboratory school, for example, may well enjoy the best of both worlds.

Preservice, like in-service training, needs to capitalize on the diversity among its students, encouraging them to learn from each others' differences and to challenge each others' assumption.

TRAINING FOR FAMILY DAY CARE GIVERS

Quality family day care provides chidren a good home away from home. All day care should be "as good as a good home" (Prescott 1978). Family care is in a better position than center care to rely on the homemaking/parenting model as its basis for quality.

Family day care begins with the environment of the home. What is there to be learned by children in this home and community? Homes offer a variety of spaces, events, and activities. The family day care giver is a homemaker as well as a child watcher; children can observe and help him or her at work in kitchen, garden, house, and market. Family day care homes often include a wide range of chidren; there are littler ones to help care for, bigger ones to imitate.

Training for family day care givers should not aim toward making homes "more like nursery school," using planned curriculum and activity ideas offered by preschool experts. Homes do not, and should not, have a curriculum in any formal sense; learning activities emerge out of the business of living together, a spontaneous process. Training should provide a mutual support system, a chance for caregivers to share their experiences and to draw on resources of their choice.

In the Community Family Day Care Project in Pasadena (Sale et al. 1972), project staff invited caregivers to participate as resource people. For example, caregivers were asked to demonstrate their methods and techniques to Pacific Oaks college students and to attend monthly Project Center Meetings with the staff.

The project concentrated first on building trust, second on providing challenge — a necessary sequence for any effective training. Staff functioned primarily as listeners during the first year, "encouraging information and opinion exchange, building self esteem and raising status, reflecting and interpreting feelings" (p. 186). Later, staff emphasized more "goal-oriented behavior" on the part of the caregivers and helped them recognize their own power and competency as caregivers.

Project staff relied on the diversity among group members to provide questions and challenges. Diversity makes an environment more educational. It can also make it less safe, so group leaders need skills in facilitation, and openness to differences and disagreements. "We strove to maintain a balance between insuring that FDCMs [family day care mothers] feel good about themselves and working in the best interest of the FDC [family day care] children," and they saw the best interests of children as requiring them to challenge some of the practices of the caregivers (p. 148). In the second year,

> We — the staff — should move from our position of accepting all information with equal approval to providing input that indicates where we stand on critical issues such as discipline. We knew that in many cases the quality of care provided by FDCMs was astonishingly high, given the constraints under which they frequently operate, but we felt a responsibility to provide new ideas, resource people, and things that would help to improve what exists without damaging the unique qualities of each FDC home (p. 8).

People risk such new growth only when they are already safe — when their survival and security needs have been met. The task of the first year was to provide this base of trust.

A developmental sequence was predicted in group discussions in which caregivers in the earliest sessions focused on getting to know each other, building trust, then moved to talking about their individual problems, and finally moved into making "generative" statements, conceptualized in terms of Erikson's stage of growth "in which the teaching and learning function expresses itself through a caring commitment to others' needs, particularly those of the next generation." To encourage and support in family day caregivers the quality of generativity, the project itself had to be generative, abandoning "the traditional concept of the professional as recipe-dispenser" and viewing the project "as a developmental process requiring time, patience, and conflict to achieve results" (pp. 10–11).

Progress was analyzed by observations of Center Meetings, looking for statements made by the caregivers that gave evidence "of awareness and concern for FDC problems and solutions" (p. 181).

STAGES OF BECOMING A CAREGIVER: CHANGES IN TRAINING NEEDS

In "Teachers' Developmental Stages," Katz (1977) has described teaching/caregiving as a developmental process that generates different growth needs at each stage. The new teacher's concern is for survival; he or she needs "support, understanding, encouragement, reassurance, comfort and guidance," (p. 8) as well as help with specific skills and with understanding the complex causes of behavior. His or her need is for constantly and readily available in-service training. In the successive stages — consolidation, renewal, and maturity — his or her training needs to change; increasingly, the caregiver is ready for interactions with diverse colleagues and for exploration of more abstract questions. Survival-stage training needs to be on site; later training can take place in other settings, including colleges. Katz (1977) states:

> The timing of training should be shifted so that more training is available to the teacher *on* the job than *before* it. Many teachers say that their pre-service education has had only a minor influence on what they do day-to-day in their classrooms, which suggests that strategies acquired before employment will often not be retrieved under pressure of concurrent forces and factors in the actual job situation (p. 12).

In-service training, then, needs to be individualized. While members of a center staff have common concerns that can be addressed in a group (What shall we plan for next week? How could we change our physical environment? How can we get to know each other better?), they also have very different training needs depending on their levels of experience, and training opportunities ought to address these differences.

Any training should empower. It should build on the real capabilities, needs, and interests of the person, and it should challenge the person to grow from the point where he or she now is. Adults who work with children need to be active learners themselves in order to be alert to children as learners.

The training programs that have been described above each represent a commitment to a group of caregivers *over time*. Turnover of staff is a major problem in day care, and hard work and low pay may well be the primary reasons for it. But there are day care centers characterized by unusual staff stability that pay no better than centers with higher turnover and that expect their staffs to work at least as hard. What they have achieved is high morale, an outcome of self-respect and respect by colleagues, and the sense of being an important part of a shared task that is worth doing. Training that begins by taking the individual seriously as a person offers hope of building morale. Crash training, in which one tells people what to do and tries to make them do it, simply will not work in the long run; people so trained are not likely to stay long. It is a better risk to try to modify the job to fit the persons in it, so that the nonmaterial rewards will keep them there long enough for real growth.

Franchise day care, among the various types of sponsorship, is probably least likely to risk this sort of commitment to staff. Franchise care, like franchise food service, attempts to satisfy its customers through predictable uniformity of product and to invest most heavily in those aspects of the program that are most predictable: plant and equipment. Crash training on the job may well meet the needs of these services best. Franchise care appears to be growing most rapidly in those states that do not have training requirements for day care personnel — requirements that expose staff to influence from trainers outside the center.

The Issue of Professionalism

In some states, including California, a major strategy toward increasing quality in early childhood programs, including day care, has been the requirement that all caregivers take college courses. As the academic preparation of some caregivers has approached that of elementary teachers, a base has been established for advocacy of comparable salaries, especially in day care centers sponsored by school districts. However, the insistence that day care givers are teachers, and the acceptance of an elementary credential as appropriate preparation, have had negative as well as positive effects. One is the tendency to use school as a model for day care, overemphasizing cognitive curriculum and direct teaching of skills and concepts. A second is the tendency to increase the communications gap between caregivers and parents, especially low-income parents. As the level of formal education and professional experience of caregivers increases, parent–caregiver communication and parent–caregiver agreement on child-rearing values decrease (Powell 1978).

Day care needs professionals — people whose training and experience have given them not only a firm base of "theory in their bones" but also the ability to articulate it, to think analytically about what they do intuitively. Such people may serve children in a wide variety of roles. I know several who are choosing to be family day care givers, valuing the task autonomy and intimacy of relationships possible in this setting. Many serve as trainers and as advocates for children, families, and caregivers.

Day care will also continue to need many caregivers who are nonprofessionals, whose competence with children is experiential and intuitive. Training should build on their existing competence, enabling them to broaden their repertoire, increase their confidence, and stimulate them to think critically about their values, their goals for children, and children's developmental needs.

At all levels of training, adults, like children, need the opportunity to learn through play, through the exploration of choices in a rich environment (Jones 1980). Adults, like children, need the experience of being asked what they would like to do, not told what they have to do, in the process of becoming more competent caregivers for young children. People whose competence is respected are more likely to keep growing in competence than those who are told or shown that they do not know much. It is hard to do any job well if one does not like what one is doing; it is particularly hard to care for children under these circumstances. Training opportunities need to be resources to explore; caregivers need the chance to be decision makers, to say "This is what *I* want to do next." That is playful, in the very best sense. Children become active learners through play. So do adults.

Chapter 11

PROGRAM DEVELOPMENT AND MODELS OF CONSULTATION

James T. Greenman

PROGRAM DEVELOPMENT

The development of programs, like the development of people, is a complicated subject for discussion. Consider the following case histories.

WOODBURN COMMUNITY DAY CARE

Woodburn Community Day Care was organized by a group of parents and community members and opened in a church basement with thirty-five preschoolers. Ten years later, Woodburn was one of the finest infant/toddler day care programs in the region, serving forty-five infants and toddlers and thirty pre-schoolers. In the intervening ten years, the program experienced two moves to new sites, three major space reorganizations, a staff strike/director firing, major staff-parent-board conflict, severe funding crises, and major curriculum overhauls. The pattern was steady improvement of quality care, a sharp decline, and finally a slow, steady climb back up.

GARDEN DAY CARE

Garden Day Care was founded by a teacher as an all-day pre-school for thirty children. With the exception of some new furnishings, modest curriculum changes, and some new faces, the center has remained essentially the same reasonable-quality program throughout its twelve-year existence.

All programs develop and change. Some, like that at Woodburn, undergo sharp upheavals and transformations. Others, like that at Oakdale, appear to emerge, settle, and live peacefully ever after. Some deteriorate and collapse, others perpetually wobble along.

A program is a web of purposes and expectations reflecting the influence of past and present actors. It is a product of its history and context. Organizational necessity and tradition have led to a culture: particular ways of life, beliefs, values, and attitudes. A program has a particular sociointellectual ambience (Katz 1977) that stimulates or dampens staff or program development. Programs, like people, can be ambitious, unassuming, erratic, healthy, or sick. The growth and development of child care programs (or other organizations) has not been well studied. Analysis of the rise and fall of programs, metamorphosis achieved or aborted, small hard-won victories, and opportunities missed, would have made the writing of this chapter much easier.

In 500 B.C., Heraclitus surveyed the world around him and decided that everything was in a perpetual state of flux; everything changes. Fifty years later another Greek philosopher, Parmenides, viewed the same world and proclaimed that nothing ever changes. In day care, on the one hand change is constant. Staff come and go, as do children and their parents. Children are daily developing into different beings, while young parents beside them are growing into their new roles. Simultaneously, staff are developing new skills and adopting new perspectives, or burning out and losing early enthusiasms.

Yet it often seems as though nothing changes in day care — day after day the same routines, the same problems and issues. The faces may change, but it feels the same. The continual change that is going on underneath, paradoxically, reinforces the power of routines and set policies, since they serve as barriers holding back chaos, and this in turn produces the sense of day-to-day sameness.

This chapter has two primary goals: first, to analyze program development in a manner helpful to potential change agents (program development refers to planned efforts to improve the program); second, to consider various consulting models that are directed toward changing programs or program components.

The following themes will surface in the discussion. First, one should never underestimate the complexity and power of the status quo. *Whatever is occurring is happening for a reason.* It may not be consistent with program goals. It may appear to be self-defeating. Neither the rationale nor the result may have been closely considered for some time. In any program, "History and tradition have given rise to roles and relationships, to interlocking ideas, practices, values, and expectations that are 'givens' not requiring thought or deliberation" (Sarason 1971, p. 228).

For example, it is not uncommon in day care centers to have a policy requiring children to be at the center by 9:00 A.M. to ensure that the morning's activities proceed without interruption and that children do not miss scheduled events. In one program this practice was a "given" and, as a matter or course, was applied when infants and toddlers were added to the center. After five years of operation, a parent of an infant (with early mornings free) questioned the practice, noting that it was not necessary in terms of infant routines, which were individualized. Further, an implicit premise underlying the practice seemed to be that the time the child spent in the program was more valuable to the child than the time a parent might free up to have with his or her child. After some controversy, the center decided that the parent was right and that the center should be encouraging parents to spend time with their child and shorten the length of the child's day at day care. They established late-morning entry times for toddlers and preschoolers and allowed infants open entry. As a side effect, the center began to consider other "givens," many of which were holdovers from a half-day nursery school model.

People do what they know how to do. They also for the most part do what is most enjoyable (or least obnoxious). Most of the time, they believe in what they do. In an institution, the individual's actions are meshed with the actions of others, and consequently there is continual pressure to continue present behavior. There is a strong tendency to view outcomes as the result of the psychology and behavior of individuals, to see both problems and solutions as residing in people. Most problems, however, are embedded in the culture and systems of the institution, and changing the individuals may not in itself produce change.

The status quo has a logic, however peculiar. Like the deranged but compelling (to some) logic of the nuclear arms race, the logic can often withstand the simple presentation of sensible alternatives.

Genuine and lasting progress tends to be hard won. Most improvement exists only on paper, or is of short duration, or results in side effects that cause problems in other areas. Problems in child transitions between activities, better intergroup coordination, discipline, and parent communication tend to be "solved" many times.

Successful planned improvements, at least those that proceed smoothly, seem to be the product of both seized opportunities and a realistic approach — realistic in terms of the time and human material resources necessary relative to the complexity of the changes sought. Programs that have a solid sense of purpose and goals — thoughtful programs — are able to discover and make good use of opportunities that occasionally arise: a new funding source, a skilled volunteer, the right idea at the right time. These programs are better able to avoid the turmoil and instability that result from being too opportunistic or ambitious.

If realism is an important variable in efforts to improve programs, then some conceptual framework that gauges the complexity of the change required should be useful to change agents. Misreading the depth of change required sharply reduces the likelihood of success. Figure 11.1 illustrates a continuum of change efforts ranging from relatively simple quantitative changes that enrich programs (for example, an influx of new materials), to major transformations that restructure the program's organization, resources, or mission.

The following are some of the factors that determine the complexity of the change being sought.

Changes in Behavior and Attitudes

Two important questions to ask about change are: How much behavioral or attitudinal change is necessary? How much unlearning or new learning is involved? Adding half a dozen songs to a group's repertoire involves very little change. However, asking an unmusical teacher to begin having music time is change of a different order. And asking a teacher who conducts a music group in a rigid and controlling manner to try a different approach might be even more difficult because he or she has some unlearning to do as well as learning a new way of behaving.

Successfully making the transition from teaching preschoolers to becoming a toddler teacher requires considerable rethinking, discarding ingrained behavior, and learning how to put together a very different sort of classroom. The difficulty of that particular transition is

Figure 11.1. A Continuum of Program Growth

ENRICHMENT	DEVELOPMENT		RESTRUCTURING
More books	Fewer transitions	Reorganize	Add infants
New songs	New learning area	classroom	New organizational
Pillows		More parent	chart
		influence	New curriculum

widely demonstrated by the large number of toddler classrooms that simply treat toddlers like smaller, ersatz preschoolers. *We do what we know how to do.*

Number of People Involved

How many people will have to change their behavior? Outcomes in a day care center are the result of a group process. The more people (including children) who are required to change in order for the improvements to take effect, the more difficult the change is to make. Democratizing the decision-making structure in a center requires both staff and administration to unlearn old patterns and learn new behavior and attitudes. A simple change in a classroom's routine may reverberate throughout the program and affect field trip or meal schedules, staff break times, or the use of common space.

In one program, an assistant teacher returned from a workshop eager to try some of the ideas she heard on developing free choice times. She was blocked by the lack of interest or understanding shown by the other staff. After some of the other staff received similar training, some changes were instituted.

Time Frame

How much time will be needed for the change to be initiated and take hold? Time — adult time to plan, meet, and work away from children — is by far the most precious resource that day care programs possess. To effect major change in all but the most authoritarian programs requires some time to analyze and consider alternatives in order to achieve some understanding and reasonable consensus and to subsequently maintain changes and work out difficulties. This is a huge and fundamental (and unfortunately, rarely recognized) distinction between day care and half-day nursery programs, lab schools, and kindergartens. It is not uncommon for the three to six people who work together in the same classroon *never* to have the opportunity to meet together during working hours. An effort in one center to individualize aspects of toddler schedules by changing certain routines and redoing the room arrangement fell short because the effort required too much time to achieve. From the time the program decided that individualized schedules were desirable and achievable to the institution of the changes and the working out of kinks (four months), some staff turnover had occurred, the director's attention was pulled elsewhere, and the consultant who had helped to promote and initiate the change was no

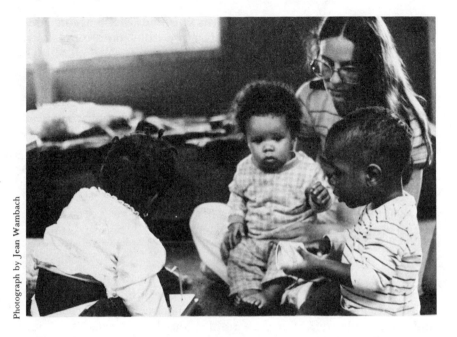

longer available. Eight months later, the schedules were no more individualized than before.

Changes in Resources or Allocation of Resources

What changes in resources or in the allocation of resources are necessary? In one center, a newly hired director was determined to change one class from a highly authoritarian, teacher-directed structure to one allowing for more self-selection and relaxed learning. Before proceeding very far, she realized that her attempt would go nowhere without an increase in open shelving, teacher storage, and certain learning materials. The director decided that materials could be reallocated from the other classrooms in the center. Unfortunately, she underestimated the negative reaction of other staff to her redistribution of the wealth, and she soon found herself awash in side effects. It is tempting here to lay blame righteously on the teachers as being typically possessive and territorial, as the director at the time did. Yet in universities, corporations, the halls of government, and even convents, rugs, desks, and window size become the object of vicious bureaucratic battles. The teachers involved were by no means atypical human beings and were legitimately concerned about their own scarce resources.

As one takes into account all of the above factors, one can assess the complexity of the change and place it on the continuum shown in figure 11.1. There is no intrinsic value in labeling a change "enrichment" or "restructuring"; the utility lies in fully thinking through everything that must in fact happen in order for the better outcomes to be realized and calculating the real magnitude of the effort required. It is critical to stress the outcomes desired, because the outward appearances are much easier to change than the results. In countless programs, new curriculums have been instituted on paper and changes mandated in teacher behavior. But in actuality, neither the way the teachers taught nor the children's experience changed very much (Goodlad and Klein 1974).

Effecting Program Development

BUILDING CHANGE INTO THE PROGRAM

Ideally, program development is built into the organizational processes. For any particular way a program does things to accomplish its goals, there is always a universe of alternatives, various means that may more or less effectively accomplish the desired ends. The more capable an organization is of routinely generating and considering alternatives, the more program development there will be. Figure 11.2 describes a rational planning and evaluation process that ensures continual organizational renewal.

The program goals are tied to the mission of the organization. The program is organized in such a way that day-to-day plans are implemented to achieve the goals. Outcomes are closely watched and evaluated to ensure consonance with program goals. Goals are also evaluated to assess their continuing relevance. Unfortunately, as Neugebauer (1975) discovered, few day care organizations (or organizations of any kind) have reached this point.

While day-to-day survival usually requires nearly all of a day care program's attention, elements of the above process occur in all programs with varying degrees of consciousness and effectiveness.

SITUATIONS THAT GENERATE CHANGE

If program development is not built into the process, where does the impetus for change usually come from? It is critical that change agents be able to recognize those conditions most likely to stimulate change and potential growth. Four kinds of situations can lead to change: (1) an external threat or command; (2) an externally generated opportunity; (3) an internal opportunity or vision; and (4) an inter-

Figure 11.2. Planning and Evaluation Process for Child Care Programs

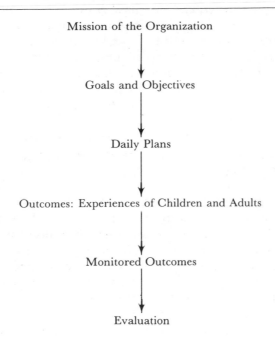

Mission of the Organization

↓

Goals and Objectives

↓

Daily Plans

↓

Outcomes: Experiences of Children and Adults

↓

Monitored Outcomes

↓

Evaluation

nal problem or need. Change in a day care program can occur in response to any of these situations.

EXTERNAL THREAT OR COMMAND. Changes in funding or regulatory standards, or in the enforcement of standards or changes in the day care market, probably stimulate more change in day care programs than anything else. Since 1981, the lowering of regulatory standards has resulted in programs reluctantly or otherwise lowering their standards to keep their costs competitive. At the same time, public funding support has largely declined. Many programs have had to change dramatically to survive. For example, previously under Federal Interagency Day Care Regulations (FIDCR), programs serving federally subsidized children had to meet one-to-seven staff-child ratios for preschoolers. When FIDCR was phased out, one center had no choice but to revert to one-to-ten ratios (the state minimum) because to do otherwise would price it out of the market, and they would also no longer be considered as an eligible program to serve subsidized low-income children. Changing the ratios had a major impact on the structure of the program.

Instead of having two groups of fourteen children, the center now had to think in terms of ten children in a group: one or two groups of twenty children, one group of thirty, etc. Thus, a change in ratios meant rethinking total enrollment, distribution of enrollment by age, allocation of space, and even curriculum. The program eventually decided that the best alternative was teaming a multiage (ages 3 to 5) group of thirty children to two teachers, and a shift from a teacher-directed structure to a structured environment learning center approach.

Competition for enrollment is an impetus for some programs to change. If parents chose other homes or centers, programs have little choice but to change or close.

EXTERNALLY GENERATED OPPORTUNITY. The availability of new or increased funding obviously stimulates change. State funding designed to help homes or centers start up, meet licensing standards, or increase services have had a major impact on upgrading day care. Public or private grants to provide health or social services, build playgrounds, and serve new clients have altered the development of many programs. The opportunity for training, the services of an intern or consultant, or the connection to a support network also can spark program growth. One energetic college intern working with family day care homes for one semester was able to set in motion relationships among a half dozen homes that led to joint field trips, a mutual support network, and regular equipment exchanges.

INTERNAL OPPORTUNITY OR VISION. New staff can bring a new perspective, new ideas, and new energy. Programs with active parental and community support (see chap. 6) can draw strength from these groups. Networking, even simply within the center staff, and training can revitalize and inspire staff to rethink existing practices. For example, in a program of moderate size that had experienced almost no turnover for five years, the turnover of two teaching positions occasioned major program growth and a revitalized curriculum. Two newly hired staff members proved highly compatible and together brought to bear such enthusiasm and new vision that any lethargy and resistance of the director and other staff were swept aside.

INTERNAL PROBLEM OR NEED. Change is often a coping response to problems. When things are not working, we are forced to rethink our assumptions. Day care programs are serving three populations: workers, parents, and children. The need for change may become clear through expressions of dissatisfaction from any of these groups. Staff or parents may complain or leave the center. Children of course can express their need for a change by making our lives, and their own, miserable.

Key Roles

None of the conditions described above necessarily lead to program growth. Improvement, or maintaining quality in spite of adversity, is dependent on the attitude and behavior of those in key roles: the director, teachers, parents, and in some programs, board members and community people. (The latter three roles have been addressed in previous chapters.)

THE DIRECTOR

The director is usually the central figure in a day care program. Prescott and Jones (1972), among other observers, have noticed that the director's leadership style and attitudes are often predictive of important center characteristics.

However, the director's role varies considerably from center to center. The theater provides a convenient analogy to the day care center. In a small owner-operated center, the director may play all the major roles and thus be equivalent to the playwright, leading actor, and janitor. In a center that is part of a large chain or a social service bureaucracy, a day care director may be given a script (curriculum and policies), a stage setting (the environment), the role of actor (teacher), and the job of seeing that the script is followed in a manner that satisfies the audience (parents).

A director is usually in a position to serve as a catalyst for, or impenetrable obstacle to, change. He or she is usually in a position to shape the course of the change and to reinforce (or subvert) the planned direction. It is a mistake, however, in most programs to overestimate a director's power. Directors, like presidents, coaches, and others who have authority, are almost immediately confronted with the reality of the limits of their power.

My own experience is instructive. After five years as a college teacher of child development and early education and a consultant, and some years as a day care teacher before that, I became director of a large day care program. In my consultant work, a good deal of my time had been devoted to programs establishing infant/toddler programs. As a director, I therefore had a clear sense of what the program outcomes should be for babies and parents, and I was fairly sure of the means—that is, how the program should be organized and the expectations of adults. Shedding my consultant role with its limited powers, and cloaked in my director's mantle, I was ready to quickly transform my new program. Instead, it was a two-year process to change the existing practices and expectations. Directives are effective only when staff fully understand both the whys and hows of what is being required—rarely the case when speedy change is sought. Teaching the staff, finding compatible, talented teachers who could take sound concepts and apply them to their day-to-day realities, and my reinforcement of the small but increasingly sure steps in the end produced real program growth.

A director's job is to create and sustain the climate in which staff flourish and work together to realize program goals. The director sets the tone; he or she, if effective, creates a climate of respect, trust, and care, where adults and chidren are recognized and valued as individuals. The emotional climate—the presence or absence of warmth, security, and humor—is heavily influenced by the way the director relates to children, parents, and staff. Given the need for a sensitive, caring person who is able to respect and trust others, how does a director create an atmosphere conducive to program development?

NOTICING. Noticing what teachers are doing sustains efforts to change: reinforcing the minor achievements and small miracles generates a relationship that allows the director to work with staff in solving problems. Recognizing a teacher's new room arrangement, a caregivers's frustration in handling a difficult child, a creative field trip, and communicating that recognition to the staff member results in a teacher's feeling valued as a professional and less isolated.

ROLE MODELING. A director models the way in which the program expects adults to relate to each other, to children, and to materials. A climate of acceptance and of excitement at learning and achievement is generated if staff see the director embodying these qualities in his or her behavior.

A director is a role model whose behavior shows others how one should respond to situations. Two day care centers, both experiencing funding cuts, plumbing failure, staff turnover, or the like situations common to day care, may have very different atmospheres. One director's crisis mentality may instill a perpetual sense of chaos, panic, or cynicism, but a director's calm recognition that such problems are ever-present may encourage the staff to go cheerfully about their business, making the best of things while working toward achieving higher ground.

CONSCIOUSNESS RAISING. An important responsibility of the director is simply bringing things that are happening on the floor to a conscious level of awareness, above the haze of the daily, weekly, and monthly routine. A difficult transition that forces children to wait and adults to act as overseers, or results in energy-sapping chaos may have long been accepted. A director can point out what children and adults are actually experiencing and the context in which it occurs.

AWARENESS OF TEACHER PERSPECTIVE. Directors aware of certain tendencies that seem to be ever-present in day care can often overcome them with effective supervision.

> *Desensitization*: Caregivers can become desensitized to some of the real pains (and joys) of childhood. For example, an infant caregiver who witnesses the separation pain of a dozen children and parents day after day may become less sensitive to the real pain the child or parent is feeling that happens to them only once a day.
>
> *Noncommunication*: A common tendency is for the staff to develop a routine that works and follow it, and, rather than jointly plan

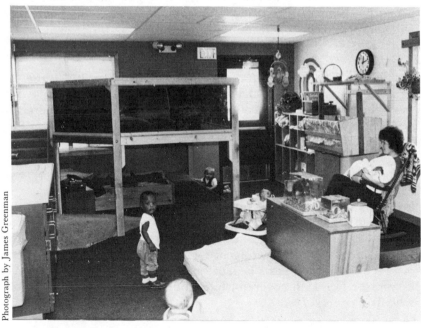

Photograph by James Greenman

activities and curriculum and evaluate, only discuss what is
necessary to maintain the routine (see chap. 5).

Territorialism and possessiveness: Teaching, like all human endeavors,
involves the use of territory. The closed-door, self-contained
classroom is rarely present in child care, but the tendency for
teachers to become territorial about space, and possessive about
materials — and children — is certainly present and can impede
intergroup coordination and maximum use of resources.

Burnout: Any of the above tendencies may be related to burnout,
which is, most simply, the point where a staff member is emotionally and sometimes physically unable to do the job (and very
well may not be aware of it).

STATING EXPECTATIONS CLEARLY. Clear statement of expectations
to both staff and parents is a critical element in effecting and maintaining change. Given the scarcity of meeting time, an effective director
usually combines written statements — memoranda, program manuals,
classroom and parent handbooks, or wall posters — with verbal communication to make expectations clear and coherent.

PERSISTENCE AND FOLLOW-THROUGH. Most efforts at program
growth fail because they are not sustained. The director's ability to
persist in pushing for particular changes and tracking the progression
of changes may be a determining factor in program growth.

TEACHERS

Few meaningful changes in day care do not in some fashion require changes in teacher behavior, and much program growth occurs
as teachers increase their knowledge and skills. Teachers' interest in
new ideas is a major catalyst for classroom change. It is, however, difficult for individual teachers to spark overall program growth, given
the general lack of time devoted to collegial interaction. However, as
in the case we saw when two new teachers revitalized a program,
teachers acting together can be a potent force for program change (or
for maintaining the status quo).

When planned changes do not take effect, it is always tempting
(particularly for directors, consultants, and trainers) to see the failure
as stemming from the intransigence, laziness, or ignorance of teachers,
or to see the problem as a lack of sensitivity to children's needs. Yet
as Sarason (1971) discovered while studying efforts to change public
schools,

First, those who attempt to introduce a change rarely, if ever, begin the process by being clear as to where the teachers *are*, that is, how and why they think as they do. . . . As a result, teachers react in much the same way that many children do and that is with the feeling [that] they are both wrong and stupid. Second, those who attempt to introduce a change seem unaware that they are asking teachers to unlearn and learn. Third, if there is any one principle common to efforts at change, it is that one effects change by telling people what is the "right" way to act and think (p. 193).

It is true that many teachers or caregivers resist change and have only a limited vision of the possibilities of improvement. This is perhaps not surprising, considering how little value is assigned to their roles in terms of money and status, the fact that time for planning, thinking, and professional development is rarely compensated, and the number of changes they must cope with day in and day out. Perhaps under the circumstances it is surprising how many day care staff do push for program development.

Strategies for Change

Sarason's observation about the way in which decisions are made in schools applies to many day care programs as well:

Decisions frequently are made at the top of the administrative hierarchy, without regard for two likely consequences: the reactions of individuals and groups to the *manner* and *means* by which decisions are made, announced, and implemented, and equally as important, their reaction to the *contents* of the decision in light of prevailing attitudes, relationships, and ongoing activities. Decisions are made as if there are no means–ends problems and as if one was not dealing with a social system in which the introduction of change is no small matter (Sarason 1971, p. 16).

A change agent confronts the two sets of paradoxes. First, in order to "sell" a change, one is often tempted to minimize the extent to which individuals will have to change their thinking or behavior, and at the same time to maximize the potential benefits. The unfortunate consequence of minimizing is that because changes in thinking and behavior will be minimal, real change will also be minimal; the potential benefits will not be realized, and disappointment and loss of credibility will be maximized, which will likely hinder future change efforts.

The second paradox is that while it is important to have a realistic sense of proper timing and of how long it will take to effect the change, a realistic view might discourage any attempt to change. Rarely does there appear a good time, or an adequate time, for major change. The way out of this paradox is a blend of boldness and calculation. Boldness is necessary, in the sense of proceeding with a confidence that change can be introduced and sustained. But boldness will not help if key individuals are on vacation or tied up with other matters, or if the time to hold meetings or the resources are simply not there. Calculation of the necessary steps in the process of introducing and implementing the changes increases the chances of successful innovation.

Program growth is possible when staff come to believe that all is not fine and that the possibilities for better outcomes exists. Weber (1973, p. 477) notes that for teachers, often "only this conviction of the necessity for change can give them the energy and courage to sustain the anxiety of public change, to risk actualizations that are inevitably inadequate and fumbling. . . . Their attempt to change will be partial and will be adapted as they are reflected on. But they will not return to the old." Failure to convince teachers of the necessity or desirability of the change invites failure.

Programs where the necessity for change is embedded in the culture of the program experience the most growth. The more rational the process of planning and decision making, the more opportunities to improve seem to be recognized, seized and sustained.

CONSULTATION AND PROGRAM GROWTH

Consultation Models

Future sociologists may consider the second half of the twentieth century as the "age of consultants." It is increasingly common in all sorts of organizations to find consultants there, practicing their trade — experts for hire tending to organizational difficulties. What purposes can they serve in day care settings, and how might they accomplish their purposes?

Until relatively recently, consultation in day care was largely limited to consultants employed by state agencies. Today consultation is not limited to the services of public agencies. In many parts of the country, resource and referral centers, training programs, university extension divisions, and other organizations make consulting services available to day care programs. Graduate student practicums or internships in some departments involve a consultation experience. In day care and early education, no less than in business and other human services, consultants are readily available. Throughout this chapter and book, the complexity of day care programs and the difficulty of achieving real improvement have been stressed. Consultation models have considerable potential to effect change because they can apply a variety of means to change the organizational processes to produce improved outcomes for children, parents, and staff. Clarifying goals, raising expectations, training individuals, reinforcement of morale, and other means can be a part of a consultant's repertoire.

A TRADITIONAL MODEL

Keister (1969) outlines a traditional consultation model. When an organization has a problem that it is unable to handle internally, consultation is sought. Keister posits certain generic principles of consulting (pp. 6–7):

- Consultation is a voluntary relationship solicited by the person needing help. Unsolicited consultative "help," however wise it may be, seldom achieves the mutuality of purpose that is vital to effective consultation.
- The consultant relationship is temporary, and either party to it is free to terminate the relationship at any time.
- The consultant's first obligation is to clarify problems and causes, thereby setting the focus for the consultation.
- Having helped the client clarify the nature and cause of the problem for which consultation is sought, the consultant then helps him or her to find and evaluate alternative solutions.
- It is the client's prerogative to accept and act upon or to reject any of these courses of action.

Keister views the consultant's authority as stemming from three sources: community sanction (the authority accorded to the consultation agency), superior knowledge, and skill.

The consultant's responsibilities do not end with serving the client. Consultants in day care have to uphold the standards of the agency that employs them and also consider the children and families served and the community at large. Keister's consultants fill three primary functions. First, they are experts in day care, bringing a knowledge of child development, parents, curriculum, management, and legal requirements to the operators. A consultant is secondly a "master at relationships." His or her skill in this area determines whether the client is able or willing to use the knowledge and skill of the consultant. The third function of the consultant is helping the operator to make maximum use of community resources. Other roles the consultant may be called upon to play include those of "motivator, human relations mediator, teacher demonstrator, and teacher educator."

While Keister's consultants were early childhood program generalists employed by a state agency, her guidelines as to the nature of the consulting relationship also apply to consultants with a more focused expertise, such as health, food and nutrition, or finance.

THE ENABLER MODEL

The enabler model was developed as a consultation model in the Head Start Planned Variation Project (Holt 1977; Katz 1977). A consultant, called an "enabler," was matched with a community that was "ready to work hard for change in its programs" (Holt 1977, p. 2). Enablers have to have the same range of knowledge and expertise described by Keister, only more so.

Enablers work with communities. Part of their responsibility is to uncover and utilize the community's strengths and resources. Assuming that people in local programs will benefit most when they discover their own strengths and talents, an enabler functions so that these discoveries are part of the outcome (Holt 1977, p. 4).

The enabler model is based on the premise that the relations among people are powerful determinants of both what and how they learn from each other. The model assumes that the most meaningful learning takes place when people need it, feel they need it, and define the need.

The enabler model is predicated on both a qualified enabler and a qualified community that recognizes the need for change, one where those considering using the enabler model are "willing to involve the total program: the children, the parents, the administration, the staff of all component areas, and other concerned groups or individuals within the community. Change in any one phase of programming necessitates and causes corresponding or accommodating changes in other areas" (p. 5).

The model assumes that participants will have a sense of commitment great enough so that they will be prepared to be actively involved for a long span of time, often for up to two years. The model does not meet the needs of a community desiring a crash program, and "since the model presumes sustained commitment and change, it is not appropriate in agencies unable to accept altered basic attitudes, role definitions or duties of individuals or groups" (p. 6).

The enabling process has four stages:
1. *Establishment and assessment*: Relationships are established as the enabler comes to know the programs, people, and community. Through skilled questioning, the enabler facilitates the identification of problems and goals. Preliminary planning and the setting of priorities occurs.
2. *Technical assistance*: In this stage, the enabler will serve as an active resource — training, leading discussions, providing problem-solving techniques (not solving problems), and providing resources. He or she will observe in classrooms, work alongside teaching staff, and may demonstrate techniques. Clarifying goals and priorities and stimulating and supporting self-evaluation are important elements of this stage.
3. *Consultation*: The enabler steps back now, and "after the peak of training services, the advisory or true consulting functions of the enabler become more central in the work. The consultant will do less answering and more to facilitate people finding their own answers. It is important that programs understand this shift, for instead of 'Yes, I'll do it,' the enabler begins to respond 'You do it. I'll help'" (p. 11). The enabler helps the programs network with other community resources and establishes relationships with other agencies. He or she continues to give feedback on participants' performance and reinforces ongoing evaluation and clarification of goals. Modeling "how to enable growth" continues as the enabler supports and reinforces increasing personal competencies and program improvements.
4. *Termination of service*. The previous phase was a transition to autonomy. The final stage wraps up the consultation by ensuring that the means exist to sustain the achievements of the enabling process.

The enabler model is not limited to those situations for which it was designed, community planning for Head Start programs. It can be applied to any setting where there is adequate commitment of all the relevant participants over time.

THE YALE PSYCHO-EDUCATIONAL CLINIC APPROACH

Not all consulting takes place in settings where everyone is ready to work hard for change or in the clearly defined relationships described by Keister. A support agency, training program, or college may seek out programs and offer consultation. The approach of the Yale Psycho-Educational Clinic (PEC), reported by Seymour Sarason and his colleagues (Sarason et al. 1966; Kaplan and Sarason 1969; Sarason 1971) provides some insight into unsolicited consultation experiences, which Keister believes rarely are successful.

One of the central beliefs that guided the clinic efforts was the need to avoid the traditional consultant role, which rarely provides extended opportunities to experience first-hand the social context in which problems are manifested. It was the social context that would be the object of change. "We had to be part of, and intimately know, the setting in which our services would be rendered. . . . Over the years, we had learned that although the consultant role could be a valuable one, it was frequently limited by the fact that the consultant's knowledge of the problem was based on verbal reports that were incomplete or partly in error" (Sarason et al., p. 43).

PEC consultants and school officials used to the traditional consultation process often had quite different perceptions of the consultation process:

> From his (the superintendent's) point of view my functioning, like everyone else's, should be characterized by clear-cut purposes and procedures, possess definite beginning points and end points, and produce readily observable results. He felt that since the initial "familiarization" phase (Phase I) of my involvement had come to an end, it was time for me to report my results and to launch myself into Phase II, or, in effect, to get down to serious business . . . a forceful fast-acting, dramatic program of lecture meetings with teachers in which I could begin telling them what they needed to know and what they needed to do (McIntyre 1969, p. 41).

One can visualize the reaction of the superintendent listening to the consultant report after a month involvement:

> I explained the progress I had made, that I was beginning less to feel like a total stranger in the schools, that I had not yet run across a single teacher who was uncooperative, that things seem to be going

rather well, but that I had simply not yet finished observing in all the classrooms. This was met with a kind of shocked silence (McIntyre 1969, p. 41).

A second basic tenet was to go beyond dealing with the problems presented to the consultant and actively look for other problems. Staff of the Psycho-Educational Clinic studied schools from the vantage point of intervener and changer. "The process of us offering and giving help allowed P.E.C. staff to see aspects of the setting that they never would have seen if not in the helping role" (p. 47).

More than the provision of services to children or improving the performance of individual teachers, the consultant hoped to understand and improve the organizational processes that would maximize the talents and resources available and create conditions under which future remedial work was unnecessary. Conditions that affected morale, performance, and communication were to be uncovered and made evident. The assumption was that the psychologist would bring to bear his or her clinical training in observing and understanding human behavior in the school setting. What precisely the consultant would do at the schools was not preordained. His or her role would take shape in the process of coming to know the school: its culture, people, and organization. Similar to the enabler model, the match between the setting and consultant also shaped the consultant participation. How much time the consultant would spend in the classrooms, with children, at meetings, and the kinds of interaction the consultant would have with teachers and administrators would vary from school to school. If successful, the consultant's relationship to the school ultimately was not that of invited guest or periodic visitor but that of someone perceived as integral to the organization.

Establishing the relationship envisioned above is by no means easy, under any circumstances. To develop mutual trust, consultants from the PEC were open in sharing their feelings and took care to suspend their judgments, viewing teachers and principals on their own terms. Principals and teachers found that consultants could talk the same language and would listen and be supportive without judging them. The initial wariness and distance-producing deference to "the expert" was dispelled (when the approach was successful) following a breakthrough — some opportunity arising where the consultants proved themselves and gained the acceptance of teachers as people who "know" the reality, how to handle children, or how to really help, and the individual consultant is seen as "someone as available to share her anxiety and doubt, her concern and involvement about a situation in which she experiences herself as acting in ways and in settings for which she has not been professionally trained" (Sarason et al. 1966, p. 170).

I employed basic elements of the PEC approach while serving as an unsolicited consultant whose services were made available to three day care centers. In my initial written and face-to-face communication with staff parents and board members from the centers, I made explicit the assumptions underlying my approach:

1. All programs want to improve whatever they are doing.
2. Most of the energy and resources available are tied up with day-to-day survival.
3. Most programs are to some degree suspicious of "consultants," "experts," or other resources outside the center because of
   a. The above-mentioned people's inability to demonstrate awareness of the reality of the center's situation;
   b. A natural, built-in defensiveness that comes with poor pay and little recognition and status for doing a difficult job with inadequate resources.
4. If a mutual realtionship of trust, cooperation, and recognition of joint talents and limitations can be achieved and effective communication established, programs are willing to work with others who may be able to help.
5. The role of a consultant is to help centers to do what they want to do better and to assist in creating ways to make the process of planning, implementation, and evaluation work more effectively.
6. A consultant can fulfill this role by
   a. Committing the necessary time and energy to help;
   b. Bringing an outside perspective to bear;
   c. Applying knowledge and/or skills and/or resources not available to the center.

I suggested that for me to become knowledgeable about the values, goals, and program of each center and the ways in which I could be useful, and for them to come to know and trust me, I needed to talk regularly with the director, board, and staff and spend time at the center observing and participating in the classrooms. I'd like to attend staff meetings, board meetings, and other meetings that they thought might be important. Initially, I'd commit one six-hour day a week to your program on site. As we became knowledgeable about the goals and expertise of each other, the ways that we could together effect positive change would become clear.

As in the PEC approach, I, as consultant, went beyond problems presented to me and uncovered goal-defeating conditions and conditions leading to organizational craziness:

> All those interpersonal and intergroup maneuvers, alliances, and conflicts which absorb the participants in such a way and to such a degree as to produce two related results: the lives of individuals or subgroups in the organization center around issues of power and influence; and the purposes of the organization are transformed and distorted to conform to the needs of individuals and subgroups (Sarason 1971, p. 41).

My purpose was to help the organization (or individuals) to recognize and confront a negative condition in ways that kept it below the point where program goals or individual growth were stymied.

As with the enabler model, my activities grew out of the match between myself as consultant and the center. In one program, support and validation of the director, assistance in reorganizing administrative practices and communicative process, and relatively formal staff training predominated. In another extensive classroom observation, dialogue with teachers and informal participation at staff meetings occupied the most time. As with the PEC experience, once trust was established, authoritative support for staff was an extremely important function.

Issues in Consultation

ALLEGIANCE

Who is the client to whom the consultant is answerable? Whose goals and priorities are placed in the forefront and whose ignored? The "center" or "community" are abstractions representing the interests of different groups.

A major and difficult task for a consultant is to develop close, trusting relationships with individuals at the setting while still being perceived as standing outside the center's politics. Issues of power and status, income, beliefs and ideology, job security, and personal ambition permeate all organizations. An outsider who gets "inside" any setting soon comes to see the often Byzantine complexity shadowing simple issues, particularly if things are not going well. Organizational improvement may result in changes in the balance of power, redistribution of benefits, altered responsibilities, or jobs lost. A consultant who is an effective change agent may be realistically seen as a threat to some individuals.

Consultants may well be in a position to know what is really going on, to see beneath the public front of the director or teachers. They may uncover problems and mistakes, ignorance and incompetence, or the disparity between ideals and outcomes. If the consultant is perceived as a political ally, a source of information, or an evaluator of staff, then his or her effectiveness will be diminished.

In Keister's model, or when a consultant is utilized for a specific function, most often the director defines the "reality" of the situation in the center, the problems to be solved, and the parameters of the answer. In the enabler model, one of the enabler's functions is to help the communities establish a process that will direct their effort to change. In the PEC approach, the "client" emerges out of the interactions between the consultant and the setting. In each model, there is a recognition that the consultant is more than a hired mechanic. A consultant brings to the setting standards and principles, part of which is a recognition that his or her responsibilities extend beyond the individuals who call the consultant in or sign the checks.

Another important set of questions to ask is, Whose hands get held? Who gets listened to? Who gets validated? Simply being available as a willing and understanding listener is a valuable role to play in a day care program. In the enabler and PEC approaches, it is made clear in the beginning that the consultant's perspective is broadened by the reality of staff and parents and children. It is not surprising that a director may feel somewhat threatened by this approach. In an organization struggling to survive or grow, defensiveness and paranoia are not strangers. And it is important to recognize that consultants are not only in a position to threaten a director's status quo and are privy to information the director might like to possess, but they are often able to do precisely what a director would like to do, given the time: develop a relaxed, trusting relationship with staff. Directors bound by the tyranny of paperwork and daily crises may view consultants playing a supportive, validating, teaching role with staff with envy and longing. That is exactly what they envisioned themselves doing when taking on the job of director.

When the consulting role is primarily limited to advising the director, consultants are largely limited to the director's view of reality (Patterson 1978). This may impair the efficiency of the change effort. Consultants who define their clients in a wider sense will develop a wider perspective. However, there is the danger that confronted with a more complex reality, consultants will achieve clarity by molding the reality to conform to their own biases and preconceptions and to justify their own familiar ways of behaving. Like teachers, consultants do what they know how to do.

ETHICS

Consultants are in a position to do damage to an organization. An unskilled or overambitious consultant can wreak havoc in organizational morale, reduce productivity, and do real harm to individuals. The consultation models that present the most potential to effect real program growth — the enabler model and the PEC approach — can also do the most damage. Consultants have to be honest about their own beliefs and biases and have an absolute respect for confidentiality.

A consultant needs to view people and institutions on their own terms, not on the basis of preconceived assumptions. Consultants come with varied backgrounds and are likely to identify more fully with some participants than with others — directors, teachers, or even children. The ability to go beyond the identification is important.

Perhaps more damage has come from a consultant's hubris (or the arrogance of the agency or training program employing the consultant) than anything else. A knowledge of one's own limitations is the core of a consultant's ethical sense. It is precisely because anyone can call him- or herself a consultant that is so important. One does not have to look hard to find training programs employing inexperienced graduate students as trainers and consultants on the implicit theory that it is not hard to stay one step ahead of practitioners in the field. Nor is it uncommon to find former practitioners "consulting" about problems they have had relatively slight or narrow experience with.

COST

Consulting models, particularly models such as the enabler or PEC approach, appear costly to use compared with training models. Time spent "becoming less of a stranger, " generating trust, and wading through a democratic participatory process appears far less productive than time spent conducting workshops, writing manuals, or issuing reports. The latter provide concrete measures to weigh against costs. Yet if costs were calculated against real changes in outcomes experienced by children, parents, or staff, consultation might turn out to be a very cost-effective change effort.

Consultation is not cost-effective if a program is unable to use a consultant effectively. A program in constant turmoil or resistant to change is less likely to benefit from using consultants.

CONCLUSIONS

Consultation in its varied forms hold promise as a vehicle for improving day care. An individual working with a program has the potential to facilitate individual and program growth. Advice and training can be focused around the program's real concerns. Changes that will cause improvement can be encouraged and reinforced. The outside perspective that consultants carry with them, more removed from everyday life at the center, can help a program to achieve real insight into its functioning and increase the program's universe of alternatives.

Realizing the potential of consultation depends on the skills of both the consultant and the program. If a consultant is lodged in a support agency — a resource center, informational and referral service, or an agency like the Yale Psycho-Educational Clinic — the consultant has supports to facilitate his or her skill and understanding of the consultant role. At the same time, programs have a service they can use over time.

Perhaps, in the long run, the value of consultation lies in the understanding the consultants achieve about the real world of day care. Consultation experiences can add both breadth and depth to those who teach and write and administer programs. The gulf between theory and practice, laboratory and real world, may be lessened and more real improvement achieved.

Chapter 12

INFORMATION, REFERRAL, AND RESOURCE CENTERS

Patricia Siegel
Merle Lawrence

Within the past decade, America's need for child care has risen steadily. We are experiencing profound changes in family structure, work patterns, and child-rearing practices that are not to be perceived as short-range phenomena.

The supply of child care services has not developed within any rational framework of regulations, policy, or legislation. States vary greatly in their commitment to developing, funding, and regulating child care services, and this variation is repeated and confounded at the local level. The resulting child care system is like a patchwork quilt made up of public and private programs provided by individuals and groups in a variety of settings, including homes and centers, licensed and nonregulated services. The pattern and style of these services vary greatly from community to community, depending on needs, parents' preferences, and available resources. Policy analyst Gwen Morgan (1981) accurately describes the child care supply as a nonsystem, an amalgam of services and programs operating in a "purchase-of-service" environment, lacking visibility or a clear point of access. She notes that, "Its parts are not well linked and the individual programs do not perceive themselves as interrelated and do not commit themselves to a common set of goals."

Despite drawbacks, the "purchase of service" child care delivery system has some advantages over a uniform, federally managed child care program. Most important, it promotes parental choice, and in

The research for this chapter was supported by a grant from the Ford Foundation.

so doing upholds the general public's opinion that the government should not become overly involved in something that is still perceived as an intrinsically private matter. Parents have very individualized notions about what kinds of caregivers and settings are best for their children, notions that are grounded in their perceptions of family, child rearing, and culture. Unfortunately their attempt to match these preferences with existing services is often full of painful difficulty and anxiety. Informal family and neighborhood information networks are no longer adequate as a sole source for child care news. Some recent research efforts that have examined child care searches and neighborhood information networks confirm that, especially in urban neighborhoods that are experiencing rapid social changes and increasing isolation among residents, parents have no simple or comprehensive source of child care information (Powell 1980). Powell's study of parents' search processes in Detroit concludes that an effective, informal referral system of neighbors did not exist.

In the absence of a good source of information about child care services in their community, many parents are forced to wander through the child care world collecting what bits and pieces of information they can find about available services from the yellow pages, bulletin boards, newspapers, friends, and family. This is particularly true for family day care and other in-home arrangements that are usually the least visible in the network of child care services. Child care choices made in a hurry, or without a full view of the range of available services, can cause painful disruption to an entire family.

Child care providers often fare no better than parents in this disorganized search process. Providers have a full-time job caring for young children. They are not always able to spend time on the phone describing their program or responding generously and graciously to parents who drop in without an appointment to find out about their services. Without the time or money for publicity and outreach, some providers are invisible to parents, parents who may be desperate to find the very type of program these providers have to offer.

Community leaders, employers, and elected officials are beginning to realize that securing child care arrangements is not necessarily easy for their constituents. They are recognizing that child care is an important, needed service in their communities. However, their efforts to more fully understand and plan for child care needs and services are often frustrated by the lack of clear understanding of what child care is, what services are available, and what parents want.

In response to the needs of parents, providers, and communities for a good source of updated information about local child care services and unmet needs of the community, a new type of child care assistance program has evolved over the past ten years, known as *child care information and referral* (CCI&R). The cogent policy issue of the 1980s has moved beyond the arguments of the previous decade concerning whether day care is inherently harmful to children and child–parent relationships. The focus of child care policy in this decade is to understand what kinds of child care systems are already functioning in various communities, to identify what kinds of services parents feel would best meet their varying needs for child care, and to respond to these patterns of services and needs by stabilizing and improving the existing child care market.

CCI&R has been suggested as one economical and viable solution to the current child care dilemma by a diverse array of child care experts and analysts, as well as by providers and consumers of care. It almost seems as if CCI&R is the only program that everyone can agree has great potential for fixing the leaks in a very troubled ship. In a recent article on the policy issues surrounding CCI&R, Levine (1982) sums up the reasons why these programs are viewed in such glowing terms:

> From a policy perspective, CCI&R is important because it may improve the functioning of the child care market in a number of ways: matching supply and demand; maximizing consumer choice; and providing data about patterns of supply and demand that can be used for planning at the community level and aggregated for state or national purposes (p. 380).

However, there are cautions inherent in designating one relatively new program as the key to such profound problems in today's child care market. While the potential of CCI&R is great, it must not be viewed as a kind of "Barbie Doll" program, capable of some chameleon-like ability to become all things to all people as outfits and accessories are added to the basic model. There are many problems ahead for any program that attempts to satisfy both components of a delivery system, consumers and providers. The needs of each separate group — as well as separate segments of each group — are often in conflict. This chapter will describe how different CCI&Rs are attempting to deal with these issues in communities that manifest such widely varying constellations of these problems.

EVOLUTIONARY TRENDS IN CHILD CARE
INFORMATION AND REFERRAL

The pioneers of CCI&R services came from a variety of service and philosophical perspectives. Despite the diversity of their origins, their motivations for organizing CCI&R services were surprisingly similar. Basically, they wanted to make the day care system in their communities work better. Across the country, CCI&R services developed out of two different perspectives, that of parents and that of child care providers or community planning groups. It is the embracing of one or a combination of these perspectives that has had the most profound effect on how CCI&R programs have identified and tackled the problems occurring in their local child care community.

Parent-initiated Programs

Programs such as the Childcare Switchboard in San Francisco, Bananas in Oakland, and the Child Care Resource Center in Boston grew out of the difficulties and frustrations the staffs of the CCI&Rs had experienced in finding child care for their own children. The impetus for the formation of these organizations came from parents already involved in cooperative playgroups. They realized the need for a service that would help parents with children of similar ages who were seeking a cooperative child care arrangement to meet. In the course of providing referrals for cooperative arrangements, it became clear that parents needed information on the total spectrum of child care services available in the community.

Coupled with their realization of the need to expand their referral services to parents, these early information and referral (I&R) services quickly became frustrated with the shortage and imbalance of the supply of child care programs and services in their communities. Their frustration prompted the development of support services, such as technical assistance in licensing and start-up, provider training, toy and equipment resources, and provider forums for sharing common problems and concerns.

Already frustrated by the unmet needs of the parents they counseled and the confusion of providers facing the morass of local and state regulations, these fledgling organizations took the next logical step in the evolution of their services. They jumped with both feet into the advocacy arena. Partly out of the enthusiasm of being the new outfit on the block and partly out of naiveté, these pioneering CCI&Rs took on such complex issues as battling discriminatory licensing practices

LOOKING FOR CHILDCARE IN SAN FRANCISCO?

CHILDCARE SWITCHBOARD 282 7858

SINGLE PARENT RESOURCE CENTER	**821-7058**
TOY CENTER	**285-7223**
FAMILY DAY CARE PROJECT	**826-1130**
CHILDCARE ISSUES	**826-1130**
PROGRAM ASSISTANCE	**826-1130**
CHILDREN'S COUNCIL	**647-0778**

PLEASE POST

and restrictive eligibility rules for subsidized care and seeking greater use of community development dollars for child care. Their unique consumer/provider perspective gave them a fresh approach to long-standing policy dilemmas in the child care field. Parent-initiated referral services had arrived.

Provider- and Community Planning-Based Groups

The impetus for CCI&R services in other communities came from a quite different perspective, that of child care providers and local child care planning efforts. It was mostly the latter environment that gave birth to groups like the Olmsted County Council for Coordinated Child Care (4-C's) in Rochester, Minnesota, and the Pre-School Association of the West Side (PAWS) in New York City. The Olmsted 4-C's was established through the efforts of the local United Way Child Care Committee. The committee was formed in 1969 to identify, define, and describe the existing facilities, public and private, for care of preschool children in Olmsted County. However, they also became interested in knowing how else children were being cared for. A small fact-finding study of 100 families and 10 employers to assess child care needs convinced the United Way Committee that they needed to broaden their scope and representation to include all types of child care facilities, as well as parent consumers. The Preschool Committee was renamed the Child Care Committee, which subsequently served as the catalyst for the formation of Olmsted 4-C's. CCI&R services were an integral part of Olmsted 4-C's from its inception.

The broad mission of the Olmsted 4-C's was to establish a center "to coordinate local child development services, to promote increased and improved day care facilities, . . . and to help parents make wise choices for the care and development of their children" (Sherlock 1973). It is worthwhile to note that Olmsted 4-C's has recently adopted a new name, " Child Care Resource and Referral, Inc." Despite the fact that I&R services represent a relatively small portion of the agency's total budget, the director observed "that the information and referral piece is the most stable part of our whole operation" (Sherlock, personal communication, 1980).

At the same time that the United Way in Olmsted County was addressing child care problems on a county level, community groups in other parts of the country were examining child care on a neighborhood level. PAWS is a good example of the community planning/provider origin of child care I&R services. In 1969, local child care programs, Head Start, co-ops, nursery school, and regulatory agencies in New York City organized a conference to share their common needs and problems. PAWS evolved as a communication link among the programs whose representatives attended the conference. One of PAWS' first-established activities was a referral service for parents who were unable to obtain child care from members of the PAWS organization.

While PAWS developed an I&R service, a companion agency, the Day Care Consultation Service, also emerged in New York City to meet the technical assistance and advocacy needs of community-based child care programs in Manhattan. Both PAWS and the Day Care Consultation Service had office space at Bank Street College and worked together in a close and collaborative fashion. As a result, PAWS did not develop the training and technical assistance services frequently provided by other CCI&R agencies.

CORE AND ANCILLARY SERVICES: MAKING THE SYSTEM WORK BETTER

Despite the diversity of origins, CCI&R agencies throughout the country have emerged with a remarkably similar orientation to the communities they serve. This common service orientation entails

Matchmaking: a commitment to parental choice in child care and respect for all parents' ability to choose the child care setting most appropriate for their own child.

Universality of services: a willingness and capacity to address the CCI&R needs of all parents regardless of income and family circumstance.

Inclusive referral system: a capacity to work nonjudgmentally with all sectors of the provider community, including home and center-based, public and private, profit and not-for-profit groups.

Community-level networking: a cooperative relationship with community agencies and institutions that serve children and families.

Knowledge of child care policy and programs: a thorough familiarity with child care regulations and public policy issues.

It is within this philosophical framework that CCI&R agencies have developed a set of core services designed to reach the three separate — and at times overlapping — constituencies: (1) parent/consumers; (2) providers of child care services; and (3) community agencies/planners/elected officials and others who benefit from or are affected by I&R services. Not surprisingly, these recipients of services are the very same groups that, alone or in concert with one another, initiated and nurtured CCI&R programs. Ongoing contact with each of these diverse groups has prompted the development of three basic types of CCI&R services:

- Information and referral
- Technical assistance: training
- Advocacy: community education

The mix and match, and subsequent fit, of these core services with local community characteristics has given rise to diverse populations of CCI&R providers. While local child care regulations, supply characteristics, and client demographics are important factors, the origin and subsequent evolution of a CCI&R agency has the greatest impact on how its constellation of core and ancillary services unfolds.

It is important to understand how child care I&R differs from generic I&R (information and referral addressing a range of needs and issues), as well as from other types of nonspecific I&R services. In an unpublished paper prepared as part of *Project Connections* (Ohara et al. 1979), Marvin Cline, while noting that the two kinds of agencies did many of the same things, pointed out that their work also reflected different professional and organizational goals. Generic I&R serves a wide range of client needs and must therefore maintain very comprehensive and often complex data on the widest possible range of community services. Generic I&R services are staffed primarily by two types of professionals: social workers and information specialists. Handling a large volume of I&R requests for an overwhelming array of programs and services requires a large staff, often volunteer, and places severe limitations on the level of involvement that I&R counselors can have with both their clients requesting referrals and the programs or agencies to which they refer.

Child Care Information and Referral

CCI&Rs, on the other hand, have emerged from a completely different set of professional, consumer, and service identities. The *Project Connections* study revealed that CCI&Rs tend to draw staff from the professional ranks of the providers to whom they refer clients, including child care and child development specialists as well as family counseling and parent education experts. Our review of the history of CCI&Rs reveals another identity from which these agencies evolved: parents as consumers of care.

The importance of these professional and nonprofessional orientations to delivering effective CCI&R services can best be understood by acknowledging the uniqueness of the child care provider market and the complex needs of its consumers. The I&R function is a CCI&R's raison d'être. In its simplest form, I&R is a process of assessment, matching, and linkage. The virtual maze of child care services that can meet needs necessitates I&R counselors who are experts in child care, either through having been consumers themselves or as being child care professionals. Parents contacting such services want and need to understand the wide range of options available to them. They must be able to compare alternatives and make choices that best suit their situation. They require very specific and often quite detailed information about caregivers and programs, including meals, fees, low-cost options or subsidies, program philosophy, and availability of transportation.

Yet it is more than simple information transfer that makes I&R useful to parents in their child care search. Perhaps the most important aspect of the referral process is the counseling, discussing with parents what to look for when considering each of the various child care options: informing the parent about matters such as the licensing requirements for each type of care, discussing what specific aspects of each type of setting to look for, and explaining how to do a thorough site visit and interview with each provider. Surprisingly, many parents are quite timid about asking to see a provider's home or facility, or talking about fee policies, toilet training philosophies, or discipline approaches. Today many parents feel insecure about their parenting skills, including their ability to make good child care choices. Our increasing reliance on professionals to teach us many kinds of skills, which in the past were imparted within our family units, carries over into child care decisions. CCI&R is an attempt to empower parents with these skills by offering consumer education tips and guidelines in choosing child care. The commitment to maximizing parental choice is the foundation of most CCI&R referral policy and philosophy.

While their actual referral practices vary, all CCI&R agencies work within certain boundaries when making referrals. Parents frequently ask referral counselors questions such as, "Could you tell me which home *you* think is best?", but the CCI&R agency must be careful not to give parents a sense that their referrals are in any way equivalent to a "Good Housekeeping stamp of approval." If a parent perceives the CCI&R as making judgments about any program, then conceivably that parent (and a court of law) could impose liability on the CCI&R agency when and if the health and safety of the child were endangered in the program recommended by the CCI&R. Responsibility for selecting and employing a child care provider has to rest with the parent.

The amount and type of detail contained in a CCI&R child care resource file, and the types of child care programs included in the child care resource file, affect the referral process and often reflect the philosophical and organizational style of the individual CCI&R agency. For example, when CCI&R services are provided under an umbrella organization with public sponsorship and liability (such as that of a school district or local municipality), concern for potential liability and objectivity may mean that the CCI&R agency under that umbrella can only refer to child care centers and family day care homes that are licensed or inspected by someone else. School districts in California have refused to allow CCI&R agencies to refer clients to in-home caregivers because no one licenses them, and hence there is a fear of increased liability. On the other hand, private nonprofit CCI&R agencies with parent roots, like the Child Care Resource Center in Boston and the Childcare Switchboard in San Francisco, have developed expansive child care resource files that include playgroups, in-home caregivers, shared care, and babysitting exchanges. Their parent perspective has given added visibility and access to these types of care.

Enabling parents to become wiser child care consumers can have a direct impact on parents' satisfaction with and commitment to a specific child care arrangement. But it may also have a more far-reaching impact on improving the overall quality of child care services. Educated consumers demand better services, services that do more than meet minimal regulatory standards or provide a cost-competitive program. CCI&R agencies' role in educating parent consumers may actually provide a piece long missing in the puzzle of establishing quality child care services. Regulatory officials, training programs, and professional child care associations continue to debate how they can most effectively affect the quality of available child care services. However, the parent/consumer may be the crucial key to improving services in today's child care marketplace. This is particularly true in the current climate of deregulation and cuts in funding for training programs. As parents are educated to make knowledgeable child care decisions, programs that do not meet parents' quality standards will simply fail to maintain an adequate enrollment and will fall by the wayside. CCI&R programs are the most logical link in the consumer education process, and as such they may hold the most promise for affecting quality care issues.

The CCI&R service performs another function that improves the child care market on the community level by contributing to the stability of existing child care providers through the referral function. Many private day care homes and centers operate in a state of financial insecurity, a condition exacerbated by fluctuating or chronic underenrollment. G. Morgan (1981) underscores this problem by noting that both the existence and magnitude of supply depend on its full utilization. Unfilled child care spaces lead to provider failure and a loss of supply. Thus everything a CCI&R agency does, including the most simple information service, contributes to the magnitude of supply. By resolving the dilemma of visibility for new child care services, I&R services enhance their ability to develop a successful, long-term child care program. Existing programs that are having enrollment problems can be identified and assisted.

In addition to this primary connecting role, many CCI&R programs also provide a wide range of ancillary parent support, referral and education services, including parent peer support groups, employment and housing referrals, toy-making workshops, publications on choosing child care, and parent education classes. Some CCI&R services even engage in client brokering, a social casework service wherein parents are given personal assistance in locating, choosing, or entering specific child care programs or social services that they could not have accomplished through a straightforward referral or information transfer. These ancillary services are particularly evident in CCI&Rs that were parent-initiated.

Training and Technical Assistance

It was in response to parents' needs for more child care options and providers' needs for stabilizing and improving their services that CCI&R agencies developed the second group of core services — training and technical assistance (T/TA) to existing and potential providers of child care. Even in communities where licensing agencies offered an introductory workshop or community colleges developed child care training programs, many providers lacked the time, knowledge, and resources to get their services off the ground and, once licensed, to keep them functioning efficiently. Family day care providers, in particular, were without resources to guide and encourage them through the tangle of licensing forms and procedures or to offer them the sound business and planning expertise that so often means the difference between success and failure. To meet these provider training needs, CCI&Rs developed basic technical assistance functions, including providing regulatory information and start-up assistance, help with site, facility, and program development, advice about fiscal and administrative management, and funding and planning consultation.

Today, technical assistance services are being delivered by CCI&Rs in a variety of formats, ranging from simple telephone consultation by one staff member to separately staffed and funded components responsible for planning and delivering technical assistance services through workshops, site visits, and private consultation.

Some CCI&Rs have filled the long-standing gaps in family day care training by helping to organize local family day care associations or informal networks of providers. These groups mobilize for mutual support, legislative advocacy, and to provide substitute caregivers and other types of assistance that have been unavailable for home-based caregivers in many traditional training settings. Special family day care projects within some CCI&R agencies provide training and technical assistance on an ongoing basis, including not only formal training workshops but also more intangible but no less important kinds of informal assistance and problem solving in parent–provider disputes and day-to-day operations.

In the heyday of Title XX training grants, many CCI&R agencies secured contracts to develop and implement training programs for day care home providers and centers that offered fairly elaborate types of assistance, from help with food and nutritional and curriculum planning to information about business techniques, home safety, and parent–provider contracts. Many CCI&R groups have maintained these services despite federal funding cutbacks.

In addition to these core technical assistance and training services, CCI&R agencies have developed a set of ancillary provider support services designed to give centers and homes more direct types of assistance in program management and day-to-day operation. Provider support services can include toy and equipment lending libraries, bulk purchasing of food and supplies, sponsorship of the federal Child Care Food Program, nutrition education and training workshops, CDA credentialing courses, and job files and caregiver substitute lists.

The underlying purpose in offering these services to providers is both to augment and stabilize the supply and to improve the quality of child care within a community — that is, to make the local day care system work better by working with the provider sector. Each CCI&R agency's particular orientation to technical assistance services for providers, however, is guided by the attitudes, perceptions, and professional orientation of the agency's founding groups.

In the *Project Connections* study, CCI&R groups with provider roots — therefore, with well-established child care credentials — were generally perceived by child care providers as a resource for technical assistance and support services. Examples include Orlando 4-C's and the Child Day Care Association of St. Louis, both of which offered more direct provider training and technical assistance than I&Rs that developed from a consumer perspective. Their technical assistance activities focus primarily on child care centers, due to both their agency's professional orientation and their role as administrators of Title XX block grant funds for subsidized voucher services.

It is more difficult for the organizations with a consumer orientation to effectively gain recognition within the child care center provider community, unless they also have staff with solid professional training in the child care field. Parent-oriented I&R services, such as those in Oakland and San Francisco, have geared their provider technical assistance services to focus more heavily on family day care homes and alternative, informal child care, instead of centers. These groups have developed start-up support services for parent-initiated child care options, such as playgroups, babysitting exchanges, in-home babysitters, and share-care situations. These child care options are rarely found in I&R services with provider origins.

COMMUNITY EDUCATION AND CHILD CARE ADVOCACY

The constant contact of CCI&R agencies with parents needing child care and with providers struggling to develop and maintain services stimulated the development of the third core service — community education and child care advocacy. Many CCI&R services report that they could not comfortably accept hearing the frustrations of parents and providers without attempting to do something to work toward improving the child care situation in their communities. An I&R counselor from the Childcare Switchboard once commented, "By the end of my phone shift I feel like I'm sitting on a time bomb of unmet needs." The responses and projects that individual CCI&R groups have developed in this area vary greatly, but all serve to give a public voice to the unmet needs of the parent and provider community.

Communication is the most basic form of community education. Publication of a monthly or bimonthly newsletter, and developing and maintaining good contact with local media that can help cover and explore local child care issues, are standard practices of CCI&R agencies.

Many CCI&R agencies have developed more expansive community education or advocacy projects, such as ongoing needs assessments, intensive local child care education projects, and aggressive advocacy in the child care and child service arenas. CCI&R groups have become acutely aware of their unique impact on the funding, regulatory, and legislative processes that affect the child care programs they serve. They have recognized that the crucial links between basic research, needs assessment surveys, and the development of appropriate child care policies and programs were missing in their communities or were so isolated that they were virtually useless. A well-researched report has little impact on policy if it is locked in a file drawer at an institution of higher learning.

CCI&R agencies are in a singular position, because they have the potential to combine research (child care needs assessment), public policy, and the advocacy and dissemination mechanisms so often divorced from one another. CCI&R agencies can accomplish the four crucial steps in effective advocacy and policy formulation:

1. Identifying "policy-relevant" data bases: knowing what are the relevant research questions in the community, targeting them, and collecting the data;
2. Gaining familiarity with data relevant to the problem;
3. Knowing how to most effectively use the data; and
4. Disseminating the data to specific audiences that develop and implement child care policy.

Because CCI&R agencies are active members of the child care advocacy community, they are in the best position to establish their data needs by determining what the current policy issues are and what information will best illuminate and explain these issues. CCI&R agencies are also directly in touch with the group most affected by child care policy — parents and children as consumers of child care.

> To be most realistic, a needs assessment must include some indication of what people really want now and will want in the future in child development services. It is not sufficient to analyze the statistical data from a needs assessment survey without also surveying the attitudes of the potential recipients of the services [and determining] what kinds of programs families wanted and what they would be willing to spend for them (Education Commission of the States 1976).

Too often I&R agencies, in their beginning stages, choose to overlook the development of even simple intake data systems that would document baseline child care needs data, such as the age of the child, hours of care needed, type of care requested, residence, and referrals.

Some agencies, particularly the more service-oriented ones, have viewed data collection and dissemination as activities that intrude upon and perhaps impede their ability to offer services to parents and providers. When funding is limited, staff time and energy has been funneled into direct I&R and technical assistance services, often to the detriment of an agency's ability to provide adequate documentation and public education about unmet child care needs in the community.

Although "unmet needs" research and public education may not be a primary goal, agencies must not overlook their pivotal role in collecting, documenting, analyzing, and reporting survey data on child care needs and services on a local level on the basis of their parent intake/follow-up systems. The development and implementation of continuous unmet child need surveys, which is essentially what a good intake/follow-up system entails, provides both an immediate and an ongoing mechanism for identifying short- and long-term trends in the child care needs of a specific target community.

The child care needs data collected at intake are an important source of documentation for public hearings and for making funding or budget decisions for child care on the local and — if a network of CCI&R agencies collects similar data — state levels. Also, when the need arises for information about particular policy and program issues, special follow-up telephone surveys can be conducted, and new items can be added to the intake form. The potential to measure the existing supply of child care (by maintaining up-to-date files of child care providers and facilities) and the current demand for particular types of child care services (through continuous child care needs assessment data from a consumer needs perspective) is clearly present in CCI&R agencies with well-developed data collection systems. The statewide child care needs data gathered and compiled by the fifty-five member agencies of the California Child Care Resource and Referral Network have been used extensively by policymakers in California. In 1980, when priorities were being established for a major child care expansion bill (S.B. 863), infant care was designated as a first priority because the CCI&R data clearly demonstrated the need for expanded infant care.

CONCLUSIONS

The history of CCI&R services in the United States is barely ten years long, but some trends and forecasts for the future are already apparent. As a CCI&R agency becomes more visible in a community,

Photograph by Jean Wambach

parents seem to increasingly perceive it as an appropriate conduit for their complaints and concerns about providers and the quality of child care in their community. CCI&R agencies must then face the difficult decision of how to respond to these complaints — that is, how aggressively they should pursue the issues raised by parents with the providers in their files. They must also examine their relationship to regulatory agencies and child protective services vis-à-vis parent complaints. When is it appropriate to become involved in complaints between parents and providers as a third party and report the information to local licensing authorities?

Some experts have suggested that CCI&R groups can and should play a tough role in excluding from their files any program about which they have doubts, further suggesting that child care is a parent's market and that providers will submit to scrutiny because they understand the economic importance of the referrals they receive.

However, this parent/consumer market, not the CCI&R agency, is the ultimate place for controlling quality. If CCI&R groups insert themselves too deliberately in this delicate process, they may find themselves at odds with the provider community, handicapping their ability to successfully help parents select from among the widest range of available options.

CCI&R agencies are coming of age in the child care world and are facing some dilemmas. The image of a "Barbie doll," with an enormous wardrobe and accessories, again comes to mind. Can CCI&R agencies change their costumes every day and attempt to look right and be all things to all people? Can they really give parents what they want, meet providers' needs, respond to community and employer requests, and somehow not look incongruous or contradictory? Does the new employer-supported child care hat go with the old parental-choice dress? Are the provider training boots too worn out to wear to another workshop?

CCI&R agencies must develop their service wardrobes and styles according to local needs. Their greatest strength lies in their ability to be flexible and sensitive to the configuration of child care needs and services in their own communities and to work on these in the realistic context of larger policy issues.

The Contributors
References
Index

THE CONTRIBUTORS

ROBERT FUQUA
    Assistant Professor, Department of Child Development, Iowa
        State University, Ames
JAMES GREENMAN
    Director, Glendale Child Development Center, Minneapolis,
        Minnesota
ELIZABETH JONES
    Professor and Coordinator of Graduate Studies, Pacific Oaks
        College, Pasadena, California
MERLE LAWRENCE
    Staff, California Child Care Resource and Referral Network,
        San Francisco, California
GWEN MORGAN
    Lecturer, Wheelock College, Boston, Massachusetts
ROGER NEUGEBAUER
    Editor, *Child Care Information Exchange,* Redmond, Washington
WILLA BOWMAN PETTYGROVE
    Child Care Planner and Research Consultant, Davis, California
DOROTHY PINSKY
    Associate Professor, Department of Child Development, Iowa State
        University, Ames
ELIZABETH PRESCOTT
    Professor and Director of Research, Pacific Oaks College, Pasa-
        dena, California
JUNE SOLNIT SALE
    Director, Early Childhood Learning Center, University of Cali-
        fornia, Los Angeles
PATTY SIEGEL
    Coordinator, California Child Care Resource and Referral Net-
        work, San Francisco, California
MARCY WHITEBOOK
    Coordinator, Child Care Staff Education Project, Berkeley, Cali-
        fornia

REFERENCES

Abt Associates, Inc. *A study in child care, 1970-1971*. Cambridge, Mass.: Author, 1972.

————. *Family day care in the United States*. Vol. 1 of the National Day Care Home Study. Cambridge, Mass.: Author, 1981.

Adams, D. Family day care regulations: State policies in transition. *Day Care Journal*, 1982, *1*(1), 9-13.

Ade, W. Professionalization and implications for the field of early childhood education. *Young Children*, 1982, *37*(3), 25-32.

Administration for Children, Youth and Families (ACYF). *Title XX day care assessment*. Washington, D.C.: Author, 1981.

Almy, M. *The early childhood educator at work*. New York: McGraw-Hill, 1975.

————. Day care and early childhood education. In E. Zigler & E. Gordon (Eds.), *Day care: Scientific and social policy issues*. Boston: Auburn House, 1982.

Almy, M., & Genishi, C. *Ways of studying children: An observation manual for early childhood teachers*. New York: Teachers College Press, 1979.

Anderson, K. Effects of day care and nursery school settings on teacher attitudes. Unpublished doctoral dissertation, Stanford University, 1980.

Baldwin, A. Speech given at the Third Western Region Family Day Care Conference, reported in *California Federation of Family Day Care Associations, Inc., Newsletter*, 1982, *14*(8), 2.

Bane, M. L., Lein, L., O'Donnell, L., Stueve, C. A., & Wells, B. Childcare arrangements of working parents. *Monthly Labor Review*, 1979, *102*(10), 50-56.

Barker, R. G. *Ecological psychology*. Palo Alto, Calif.: Stanford University Press, 1968.

Beckman, N. Policy analysis in government: Alternative to "muddling through." *Public Administration Review*, 1977, *37*, 221-263.

Belsky, J., & Steinberg, L. D. The effects of day care: A critical review. *Child Development*, 1978, *49*, 929-949.

Bernstein, M. H. *Regulating business by independent commission*. Princeton, N.J.: Princeton University Press, 1955.

Bettleheim, B. *A home for the heart*. New York: Knopf, 1974.

Beyer, E. *Teaching young children*. New York: Pegasus, 1968.

249

Braun, S. J., & Edwards, E. P. *History and theory of early childhood education.* Belmont, Calif.: Wadsworth Publishing Co., 1972.

Bronfenbrenner, U. Toward an experimental ecology of human development. *American Psychologist,* 1977, *32,* 513–531.

———. *The ecology of human development: Experiments by nature and design.* Cambridge, Mass.: Harvard University Press, 1979.

Canfield, J., & Wells, H. C. *100 ways to enhance self-concept in the classroom: A handbook for teachers and parents.* Englewood Cliffs, N.J.: Prentice Hall, 1976.

Cannon, N. Rights of child care workers: A prototype code of rights. *Child Care Information Exchange,* November 1979.

Caplan, N., & Nelson, S. D. On being useful: The nature and consequences of psychological research on social problems. *American Psychologist,* 1973, *28,* 199–211.

Charles R. Drew Postgraduate Medical School, Child Development Division, Pediatrics Department. Unpublished papers from the Infant-Parent Project. Los Angeles: Author, no date.

Child Care Staff Education Project (CCSEP). Improving substitute policies and procedures. *Child Care Information Exchange,* July-August 1981, 23–25.

———. How to develop an effective grievance procedure. *Child Care Information Exchange,* January-February 1982, 37–39.

Child Development Associate National Credentialing Program. *CDA application book.* Washington, D.C.: U.S. Department of Health and Human Services, 1981.

Clark, D. S., & Fuqua, R. W. A comparison of the interconnections between two types of child care programs and homes: Implications for child development. Paper presented at the annual meeting of the Midwest Psychological Association, Minneapolis, 1982.

Clark, D. S., Fuqua, R. W., & Hegland, S. M. Reducing stress in infant care centers. Paper presented at the annual meeting of the Iowa Association for the Education of Young Children, Des Moines, Iowa, 1982.

Clark-Lempers, D. S. The effects of infant day care on the family system. Unpublished masters thesis, Iowa State University, 1983.

Class, N. E. Safeguarding day care through regulatory programs: The need for a multiple approach. Paper presented at the annual meeting of the National Association for the Education of Young Children, Seattle, Washington, 1969.

———. Child care licensing and interstate child placements: An essay on public planning. In John C. Hall, D. M. Hamparian, John M. Pettibone and Joseph D. White (Eds.), *Major issues in juvenile justice information and training: Readings in public policy.* Columbus, Ohio: Academy for Contemporary Problems, 1981.

Class, N., & Orten, R. Day care regulation: The limits of licensing. *Young Children*, 1980, *35*, 12–17.

Coelen, C., Glantz, F., & Calore, F. *Day care centers in the United States: A national profile, 1976–1977.* Cambridge, Mass.: Abt Associates, Inc., 1978.

Collins, A., & Watson, E. *Family day care: A practical guide for parents, caregivers and professionals.* Boston: Beacon Press, 1976.

Conly, S. *Cost implications of the federal interagency day care requirements.* Technical Paper No. 3. Washington, D.C.: U.S. Dept. of Health, Education, and Welfare, January 1980.

Conroy, M. Mothers and preschool teachers: Contrasts in communication, teaching, and discipline. Paper presented at the annual meeting of the National Association for the Education of Young Children, Atlanta, Georgia, 1969.

Conserco Consulting Services Corp. *Day care licensing.* Seattle: Author, 1972.

Couture, K. Burnout and locus of control in daycare staff. Unpublished masters thesis, Iowa State University, 1983.

Cronbach, L. J., Ambron, S. R., Dornbusch, S. M., Hess, R. D., Hoinick, R. C., Phillips, D. C., Walker, D. F., & Weiner, S. S. *Toward reform of program evaluation.* San Francisco: Jossey-Bass, 1980.

Cumming, J., & Cumming, E. *Ego and milieu.* New York: Atherton, 1967.

Day, D. E., Phyfe-Perkins, E., & Weinthaler, J. A. Naturalistic evaluation for program improvement. *Young Children*, 1979, *34*, 12–24.

Day, D. E., & Sheehan, R. Elements of a better school. *Young Children*, 1974, *30*, 15–23.

Divine-Hawkins, P. *Family day care in the U.S.: Final report of the National Day Care Home Study.* Washington, D.C., U.S. Dept. of Health and Human Services, DHHS Publication No. (OHDS) 80-30287, 1981. (ERIC Document No. ED 211-224)

Dreeben, R. The school as a workplace. In R. M. Travers (Ed.), *Second handbook of research on teaching.* Chicago: Rand McNally, 1973.

Education Commission of the States. *The children's needs assessment handbook.* Report No. 56 EC-16. Washington, D.C.: Author, 1976.

Emlen, A. Family day care for children under three. In J. C. Colbert (Ed.), *Home day care: A perspective.* Chicago: Roosevelt University College of Education, 1980.

Erikson, E. *Childhood and society.* New York: W. W. Norton, 1950.

Etzioni, A. *The semi-professions and their organization: Teachers, nurses, social workers.* New York: Free Press, 1969.

Evans. E. *Contemporary influences in early childhood education.* New York: Holt, Rinehart and Winston, 1975.

Fein, G., & Clark-Stewart, A. *Day care in context.* New York: John Wiley & Sons, 1973.

Fitzsimmons, S., & Rowe, M. *A study of childcare, 1970-1971.* Cambridge, Mass.: Abt Associates, 1971.

Flaherty, E. W. The boundaries of government intervention in federally funded services. *Evaluation News,* 1980, *17,* 22–27.

Fosburg, S. *Family day care in the United States: Summary of findings.* Washington, D.C. U.S. Dept. of Health and Human Services, DDHS Publication No. (OHDS) 80-30282, 1981.

Freudenberger, H. J. Burn-out: Occupational hazard of the child care worker. *Child Care Quarterly,* 1977, *6*(2), 90–99.

Freund, E. Licensing. *Encyclopedia of the Social Sciences,* 1935 (9) 451–452.

Fuqua, R. W. The impact of a resource center and training program on family day care: A longitudinal study. Paper presented at the annual meeting of the Midwest Educational Research Association, Des Moines, Iowa, 1981.

Fuqua, R. W., & Greenman, J. T. Training of caregivers and change in day care center environments. *Child Care Quarterly,* 1982, *11*(4), 321–324.

Golan, M. B., Mackintosh, E., Rothenberg, M., Rivlin, L., & Wolfe, M. Children's environments evaluation: Research-built environments. Paper presented at the Environmental Design Research Association Meetings, Vancouver, B.C., May 1976.

Goodlad, J., & Klein, M. F. *Looking behind the classroom door.* Worthington, Ohio: Charles A. Jones, 1974.

Greenberg, P. Seminars in parenting preschoolers. In J. D. Andrews (Ed.), *Early childhood education: It's an art? It's a science?* Washington, D.C.: National Association for the Education of Young Children, 1976.

Greenblatt, B. *Responsibility for childcare: The changing role of the family and the state of child development.* San Francisco: Jossey-Bass, 1977.

Greenman, J. T. Day care in the schools? A response to the position of the A.F.T. *Young Children,* 1978, *33,* 4–15.

Grotberg, E. *Day care: Resources for decision.* Washington, D.C.: Office of Economic Opportunity, 1971.

Gump, P. V., Schoggen, P., & Redl, F. The camp milieu and its immediate effects. *Journal of Social Issues,* 1957, *13,* 40–46.

Gump, P. V., & Sutton-Smith, B. Activity setting and social interaction. *American Journal of Orthopsychiatry,* 1955, *25,* 755–760.

Hall, E. T. *The hidden dimension.* New York: Doubleday, 1966.

Harms, T., & Clifford, R. M. *Early childhood environment rating scale.* New York: Teachers College Press, 1980.

_____. Assessing preschool environments with the *Early Childhood Environment Rating Scale.* Paper presented at the annual meeting of the National

Association for the Education of Young Children, Washington, D.C., 1982.

Hofferth, S. Day care in the next decade: 1980–1990. *Journal of Marriage and the Family*, 1979, *41*(3), 649–658.

————. Day care demand for tomorrow: A look at the trends. *Day Care Journal*, 1982, *1*(2), 8–12.

Holt, B. *The enabler model of early childhood training & program development*. Ames, Iowa: Child Development Training Program, Iowa State University, 1977.

Hopkins, E. State day care licensing regulations and federal interagency day care requirements. *Day Care Centers*, May 1975, *29*.

Hostletler, L., & Klugman, E. The status of the profession. Paper presented at the National Association for the Education of Young Children Conference, Detroit, November 1981.

Howes, C. Caregiver behavior and conditions of caregiving. Unpublished manuscript, University of California at Los Angeles, 1981.

Hymes, J. *Early childhood education: An introduction to the profession*. Washington, D. C.: National Association for the Education of Young Children, 1975.

————. *Living history interviews, book 2: Care of the children of working mothers*. Carmel, Calif.: Hacienda Press, 1978.

Ingison, L. Some realities and necessary antecedents for systematic planning and evaluation. *Evaluation News*, 1979, *10*, 26–28.

Jacobson, D., & Driije, C. *The organization of work in a preschool setting: Work relations between professionals and paraprofessionals in four Head Start centers. Final report*. New York: Bank Street College, 1973. (ERIC Document Number ED 088604)

Joffe, C. *Friendly intruders: Childcare professional and family life*. Berkley, Calif.: University of California Press, 1977.

Johnson, B. L. Marital and family characteristics of the labor force, March 1979. *Monthly Labor Review*, 1979, *103*(4), 48–52.

Johnson, L., & Associates. *Comparative Licensing Study*. Prepared for Administration for Children, Youth and Families. Washington, D.C., U.S. Dept of Health, Education, and Welfare, 1980.

Jones, E. *Dimensions of teaching-learning environments: A handbook for teachers*. Pasadena, Calif: Pacific Oaks College, 1973.

————. Creating environments where teachers, like children, learn through play. *Child Care Information Exchange*, 1980, *13*, 1–5.

Jones, E., & Prescott, E. *Dimensions of teaching-learning environments II: Focus on day care*. Pasadena, Calif: Pacific Oaks College, 1978.

Kamerman, S. B. *Parenting in an unresponsive society: Managing work and family*. New York: Free Press, 1980.

Kaplan, F., & Sarason, S. B. *The Yale Psycho-Educational Clinic: Collected papers and studies*. Monograph series. Boston, Mass.: State Department of Mental Health, 1969.

Katz, L. Teachers' developmental stages. In L. Katz (Ed.), *Talks with teachers: Reflections on early childhood education*. Washington, D.C.: National Association for the Education of Young Children, 1977.

———. Mothering and teaching: Some important distinctions. In L. Katz (Ed.), *Current topics in early childhood education, III*. Norwood, N.J.: Ablex Publishing, 1981.

Keister, D. J. *Consultation in day care*. Chapel Hill: Institute of Government, University of North Carolina, 1969.

Kenniston, K. *All our children: The American family under pressure*. New York: Harcourt Brace Jovanovich, 1977.

Kerr, V. One step forward, two steps back: Child care's long American history. In P. Roby (Ed.), *Child care, who cares?* New York: Basic Books, 1973.

Keyserling, M. D. *Windows on day care*. New York: National Council of Jewish Women, 1972.

Kontos, S., Raikes, H., & Woods, A. Early childhood staff attitudes toward their parent clientele. Paper presented at the annual meeting of the American Educational Research Association, Boston, April 1980.

Kritchevsky, S., & Prescott, E., with L. Walling. *Physical space: Planning environments for young children*. Washington, D.C.: National Association for the Education of Young Children, 1969.

Lasch, C. *Haven in a heartless world: The family beseiged*. New York: Basic Books, 1977.

———. *The culture of narcissism*. New York: W. W. Norton and Co., 1979.

Lazar, I., & Rosenberg, M. Day care in America. In E. Grotberg (Ed.), *Day care: Resources for decisions*. Washington, D.C.: Day Care and Child Development Council of America, 1971.

Levine, J. A. The prospects and dilemmas of child care information and referral. In E. F. Zigler & E. W. Gordon (Eds.), *Day care: Scientific and social policy issues*. Boston, Mass.: Auburn House, 1982.

Levinson, H. *Organizational diagnosis*. Cambridge, Mass.: Harvard University Press, 1972.

Levitan, S. A., & Alderman, K. C. *Child care and the ABC's too*. Baltimore: John Hopkins University Press, 1975.

Lidz, C. S. *Improving assessment of schoolchildren*. San Francisco: Jossey-Bass, 1981.

Lightfoot, S. L. Family-school interactions: The cultural image of mothers and teachers. *Signs*, 1977, *3*, 395–408.

———. *Worlds apart: Relationships between families and schools*. New York: Basic Books, 1978.

Lortie, D. C. Observations of teaching as work. In R. M. Travers (Ed.), *Second handbook on research on teaching.* Chicago: Rand McNally, 1973.

Malone, M. *Child care: The federal role.* Issue brief no. IB77034. Washington, D.C.: The Library of Congress Research Service, 1977.

Maslach, C., & Pines, A. The burnout syndrome in the day care setting. *Child Care Quarterly,* 1977, *6,* 100–113.

Mattingly, M. Introduction to symposium: Stress and burn-out in child care. *Child Care Quarterly,* Summer 1977, *6*(2), 127–137.

Mayor's Advisory Committee (MAC). *Child care: Step by step.* Los Angeles: Author, 1976.

McSpadden, L. A. *Formative evaluation: Parents and staff working together to build a responsive environment.* Salt Lake City: Headstart Day Care Center, no date.

Montes, F., & Risley, T. R. Evaluating traditional day care practices: An empirical approach. *Child Care Quarterly,* 1975, *4,* 208–215.

Moore, J. E. Recycling the Regulatory Agencies. *Public Administration Review,* 1972, *32,* 291–298.

Moore, R. Open space learning place. *New School of Education Journal,* 1973, *2,* 3.

Morgan, C. L. *The journal of a day care administrator.* Unpublished masters project, Pacific Oaks College, 1980.

Morgan, G. *Alternatives for the regulation of family day care homes for children.* Washington, D.C.: Day Care and Child Development Council of America, 1974.

———. Regulation: One approach to quality child care. *Young Children,* 1979, *34*(6), 22–27.

———. Can quality family day care be achieved through regulation. In Sally Kilmer (Ed.), *Advances in early education and day care.* Greenwich, Conn.: JAI Press, 1980.

———. *The day care delivery system.* Boston, Mass.: Wheelock College, 1981.

———. Regulating early childhood programs in the eighties. In B. Spodek (Ed.), *Handbook of research in early childhood education.* New York: Free Press, 1982.

National Safety Council. *Safety education data sheet,* no. 29. Chicago: Author, no date.

Naughton, J. M. Nixon asks overhaul of welfare, with work or training required; urges U.S. aid states and cities. *New York Times,* August 9, 1969, pp. 1, 11.

Neugebauer, R. Organizational analysis of day care. Eric Document Reproduction Service, 1975. (ERIC no. ED 157616)

———. *Child care information exchange. Report #1.* June 1977.

_____. Field-tested evaluation ideas. *Child Care Information Exchange*, Sept.–Oct. 1981, 22–24.

Oakland City Planning Department. *Zoning and child care in Oakland.* Oakland, Calif.: Marcy, 1974.

Ohara, J., Polit, D., Levine, J., Morgan, G., Havens, J., & McKinley, S. *Project connections: A study of childcare information and referral services.* Cambridge, Mass.: American Institute for Research in the Behavioral Sciences, 1979.

Osmon, F. L. *Patterns for designing children's centers.* New York: Educational Facilities Laboratories, 1971.

Patterson, G. *Consultation in high school based education settings: The interfacing of developmental and socio-cultural needs.* Eric Document Reproduction Service, April 1982. (ERIC no. ED 170-623)

Patton, M. The martial arts of evaluation (or how to defend yourself against unscrupulous evaluators). *Evaluation News*, 1980, *17*, 30–31.

Peller, L. E. The children's house. *Man-Environment Systems*, 1972, 2.

Pettygrove, W. B. Competence for children's sake: Summary report of a research project on the Child Development Associate Credential. Ames, Iowa: Iowa State University, 1980.

Pines, A., & Maslach, C. Combatting staff burn-out in a day care center: A case study. *Child Care Quarterly*, 1980, *9*, 5–16.

Powell, D. R. The coordination of preschool socialization: Parent-caregiver relationships in day care settings. Paper presented at the Conference of the Society for Research in Child Development, New Orleans, March 1977.

_____. The interpersonal relationship between parents and caregivers in day care settings. *American Journal of Orthopsychiatry*, 1978, *48*(4), 680–689.

_____. *Finding child care: A study of parents; search processes.* Detroit: Merrill-Palmer Institute, 1980.

Prescott, E. The large day care center as a child-rearing environment. *Voice for Children*, 1970, *2*(4), 7–11.

_____. *The politics of day care. Vol. 1.* Washington, D.C.: National Association for the Education of Young Children, 1972.

_____. *A comparison of three types of day care and nursery school home care.* Paper presented at the biennial meeting of the Society of Research in Child Development, Philadelphia, Penn., 1973.

_____. *Assessment of child-rearing environments: An ecological approach.* Pasadena, Calif.: Pacific Oaks College, 1975.

_____. Is day care as good as a good home? *Young Children*, 1978, *33*, 13–19.

_____. Dimensions of day care environments. Address presented at the Conference on Day Care Environments, Iowa State University, Ames, Iowa, 1979.

Prescott, E., & David, T. The effects of the physical environment on day care. Concept paper for Assistant Secretary of Health, Education and Welfare for Planning and Evaluation, Washington, D.C., 1976.

Prescott, E., & Jones, E. *Day care as a child-rearing environment.* Volume I. Washington, D.C.: National Association for the Education of Young Children, 1972.

Prescott, E., Jones, E., & Kritchevsky, S. *Day care as a child-rearing environment.* Vol. II. Washington, D.C.: National Association for the Education of Young Children, 1972.

Prescott, E., & Jones, E., with S. Kritchevsky. *Group day care as a child-rearing environment.* Final Report to Children's Bureau, U.S. Dept. of Health, Education, and Welfare. Pasadena, Calif.: Pacific Oaks College, 1967.

Prescott, E., Jones, E., Kritchevsky, S., Millich, D., & Haselhorf, E. *Assessment of child-rearing environments: Part I: Who thrives in group day care; Part II: An environmental inventory.* Pasadena, Calif.: Pacific Oaks College, 1975.

Prescott, E., & Milich, D. *School's out.* Pasadena, Calif.: Pacific Oaks College, 1974.

Reddy, N. Day care center size, quality and closing. (Doctoral dissertation, University of Florida, Gainesville, 1980). *Dissertation Abstracts International,* 1980, *41*(6), 2503-A. (Order No. 8029082).

Reed, M. J. Stress in live-in child care. *Child Care Quarterly,* Summer 1977, *6*(2), 114–120.

Reese, H. W., & Overton, W. F. Models of development and theories of development. In L. R. Goulet and P. B. Baltes (Eds.), *Life-span developmental psychology: Research and theory.* New York: Academic Press, 1970.

Riley, D. A method of human development consulting: The teaching of tools rather than answers. Unpublished masters project, Pacific Oaks College, 1980.

Robinson, B. A two year followup study of male and female caregivers. *Child Care Quarterly,* 1979, *8*, 279–294.

Rosenthal, J. President vetoes child care plan as irresponsible. *New York Times,* December 10, 1971, pp. 1, 20.

Rossi, A. S. A biosocial perspective on parenting. *Daedalus,* 1977, *106*(2), 26.

Roupp, R., & Traver, J. Janus faces day care: Perspectives on quality and cost. In E. Zigler and E. Gordon (Eds.), *Day care: Scientific and social policy issues.* Boston: Auburn House, 1982.

Roupp, R., Travers, J., Glantz, F., & Craig, C. Children at the center. Final Report of the National Day Care Study, Abt. Assoc., Cambridge, Mass., 1979.

Rowe, D. Making evaluation work in child care. *Child Care Information Exchange,* November 1978, 5–10.

Rowe, R. Child care in Massachusetts: The public responsibility. Boston: Harvard University, 1972.

Ryan, W. *Blaming the victim.* New York: Random House, 1971.

Sale, J. S. Family day care: The registration controversy. *Day Care and Early Education,* 1980.

————. Position statement on large home-based child care programs. California Governor's Advisory Committee on Child Development Programs, mimeographed, October, 1982.

Sale, J. S., Milich, C. W., Torres, Y. L., Davis, M. P., Nicholic, J. D., & Pepys, M. B. *Open the door — see the people.* Pasadena, Calif.: Pacific Oaks College, 1972.

Sarason, S. B. *The culture of the school and the problem of change.* Boston: Allyn & Bacon, 1971.

Sarason, S. B., Levine, M., Goldenberg, I., Cherlin, D., & Bennet, E. *Psychology in community settings: Clinical, educational, vocational, social aspects.* New York: John Wiley & Sons, 1966.

Seiderman, S. Combatting staff burn-out. *Day Care and Early Education,* Summer 1978, *5,* 6–9.

Sherlock, T. *Rochester and Olmsted County, Minnesota: An example of community organizing in planning for future day care services.* Rochester, Minn.: Olmsted County 4-Cs, 1973.

Simpson, R. L., & Simpson, I. H. Women and bureaucracy in the semi-professions. In A. Etzioni (Ed.), *The semi-professions and their organization.* New York: Free Press, 1969.

South Australian Council of the Childhood Services Commission. *Integrated early childhood services.* Melbourne: author, April 1975.

Steinberg, L., & Green, C. Three types of day care: Choices, concerns, and consequences. Unpublished manuscript, University of California, Irvine, Program in Social Ecology, 1978.

Steiner, G. *The chidren's cause.* Washington, D. C.: Brookings Institution, 1976.

Steinfels, M. O. *Who's minding the children? The history and politics of day care in America.* New York: Simon and Schuster, 1973.

Stigler, G. J. The theory of economic regulation. *Bell Journal of Economics and Management Science,* 1971, *2,* 3–22.

Stonehouse, A. W. *People growing: Issues in day care, no. 3.* Melbourne, Australia: Lady Gowrie Child Centre, no date, p. 7. (ERIC no. ED 219152, 1982)

√ Struer, E. Current legislative proposals and public policy questions for child care. In P. Roby (Ed.), *Child care, who cares.* New York: Basic Books, 1973.

Sutton, B. Consideration of career time in child care work: Observations on child care work experiences. *Child Care Quarterly*, Summer 1977, *6*(2), 121–126.

Takanishi, R. Evaluation in early childhood programs. In L. G. Katz (Ed.), *Current topics in early childhood education*. Vol. II. Norwood, N.J.: Ablex Publishing, 1979.

Taylor, L. *Outcome and process evaluation of a day care center*. Research bulletin ∨ No. 75004, St. John's, Newfoundland: Memorial University, June 1975. (ERIC Document no. ED 157617)

Texas Department of Human Resources, Licensing Branch. *Registration: Evaluation of a regulatory concept*. Austin, Texas: Author, 1980.

Thurow, L. *The zero-sum society: Distribution and the possibility of economic change*. New York: Basic Books, 1980.

Tizard, B., Cooperman, O., Joseph, A., & Tizard, J. Environmental effects on language development: A study of young children in long-stay residential nurseries. *Child Development*, 1972, *43*, 337–358.

Tucker, S. A review of research on home day care. In J. C. Colbert (Ed.), *Home day care: A perspective*. Chicago: Roosevelt University College of Education, 1980.

U.S. Bureau of the Census. *Money incomes and poverty status of families and persons in the United States: 1977*. (Current Population Report Series, No. 116). Washington, D.C.: U.S. Government Printing Office, 1977.

U.S. Department of Labor. *Facts on women workers*. Washington, D.C.: Government Printing Office, No. 893-480, 1980.

U.S. Department of Labor. *Preschools under the fair labor standards act*. Washington: D.C.: Employment Standards Administrations, Wage and Hour Division, U.S. Government Printing Office, 1976.

U.S. Department of Labor. Occupational outlook handbook (1980–81). Washington, D.C.: Bureau of Labor Statistics, U.S. Government Printing Office, 1980.

Waligura, R. *Environmental criteria: Mentally retarded preschool facilities*. College Station, Texas: Texas A & M College of Architecture and Environmental Design, 1971. (ERIC no. ED 058-678)

Weber, L. Dealing with reality: The open corridor approach. In C. E. Silberman (Ed.), The *Open Classroom Reader*. New York: Vintage Books, 1973.

Wessen, P. *Development and implementation of a psychometric instrument to assess job-versus non-job-related strengths among the disadvantaged*. Unpublished doctoral dissertation, Nova University, 1980.

Whitebook, M. *Formation of character: Conservation in the home; A study of day nurseries in the progressive era*. Unpublished masters thesis, University of California, Berkeley, 1976.

_____. Profiles in day care: An interview with Millie Almy. *Day Care and Early Education*, Spring 1981, *8*(3), 29–30.

Whitebook, M., Howes, C., Friedman, J., & Darrah, R. Who's minding the child care workers? A look at staff burn-out. *Children Today*, January-February 1981, *10*, 2–6.

————. Caring for the caregivers: Staff burn-out in child care. In L. Katz (Ed.), *Current topics in early childhood education*, Vol. 3. Norwood, N.J.: Ablex, 1982.

Willner, M. Unsupervised family day care in New York City. In *The changing dimensions of day care*. New York: Child Welfare League of America, 1970.

Winget, M., Winget, W. G., & Poppelwell, J. F. Including parents in evaluating family day care homes. *Child Welfare*, 1982, *6*, 195–205.

Winklestein, E. Day care: Family interactions and parental satisfaction. *Child Care Quarterly*, 1981, *10*(4), 334–340.

Woodward, K., & Glenn, D. Saving the Family. *Newsweek*, 1978, *91*(20), 63–81.

Woolsey, S. Pied Piper politics and the child care debate. *Daedalus*, 1977, *106*(2), 127–145.

Zigler, E., & Hunsinger, S. Bringing up day care. *American Psychological Association Monitor*, March 1977, 8.

Zigler, E. G., & Turner, P. Parents and day care workers: A failed partnership? In E. G. Zigler & W. E. Gordon (Eds.), *Day care: Scientific and social policy issues*. Boston: Auburn House, 1982.

INDEX